MW01001289

THE PRESENCE & THE POWER

THE PRESENCE & THE POWER

Gerald F. Hawthorne

Wipf and Stock Publishers
EUGENE, OREGON

In this volume, the author has regularly quoted from his own translation of the Scriptures and from the Revised Standard Version, copyright © 1946, 1952, 1971 by the Division of Christian Education of the National Council of the Churches of Christ in the USA. Other biblical sources are cited in the text.

The author gratefully acknowledges permission to quote from the following sources:

The Incarnation by B. Hebblethewaite, published in 1987 by Cambridge University Press. Christian Beliefs and Modern Questions by O. C. Quick, published in 1923 by SCM Press.

Wipf and Stock Publishers
199 West 8th Avenue, Suite 3
Eugene, Oregon 97401

The Presence & The Power
By Hawthorne, Gerald F.

ISBN: 1-59244-160-2
Publication date: February, 2003
Previously published by Word Publishing, January, 1991 .

To all my many students,
whom I have had the pleasure of teaching,
who have made life very rich for me
by their eagerness to learn
and the generosity of their friendship,
and to whom I am deeply indebted!
ὁ θεὸς πληροίη ὑμᾶς τοῦ ἁγίου πνεύματος.

Contents

Abbreviations

AB	Anchor Bible
ASV	American Standard Version (1901)
ATR	*Anglican Theological Review*
BAGD	Walter Bauer's, *Greek–English Lexicon of the New Testament*, 5th edition, ed. W. F. Arndt, F. W. Gingrich, and F. W. Danker
3Bar.	3 Baruch
BDF	F. Blass and A. Debrunner, *A Greek Grammar of the New Testament*, rev. R. W. Funk
BNTC	Black's New Testament Commentary
BWANT	Beiträge zur Wissenschaft vom Alten und Neuen Testament
CB	Clarendon Bible
CD	Cairo (Genizah text of the) Damascus
CBQ	*Catholic Biblical Quarterly*
Clem *Str.*	Clement of Alexandria, *Stromata*
1 En.	Ethiopic Enoch
1 Esd., 2 Esd.	1, 2 Esdras
EvQ	Evangelical Quarterly
Epist. ad Serap.	*Epistola ad Serapion*, *Cyril's Letter to Serapion*
ExpT	*Expository Times*
HNTC	Harper New Testament Commentary
HTR	Harvard Theological Review
ICC	International Critical Commentary
In Joh.	Origen's commentary on John
JB	Jerusalem Bible (1966, 1985)
JBL	*Journal of Biblical Literature*

Jdt.	Judith
JTS	*Journal of Theological Studies*
Jub.	Jubilees
KJV	King James Version (1611)
LSJ	H. G. Liddell, H. R. Scott and H. S. Jones, *A Greek–English Lexicon*
LXX	The Septuagint
2, 3 Macc.	2, 3 Maccabees (an apocryphal work)
NAB	New American Bible (1970)
NASB	New American Standard Bible (1971)
NCBC	New Century Bible Commentary
NEB	New English Bible (1970)
NICNT	New International Commentary of the New Testament
NIV	New International Version (1978)
NKJV	New King James Version (1982)
NovT	*Novum Testamentum*
NTC	New Testament Commentary
NTS	*New Testament Studies*
ODCC	F. L. Cross and E. A. Livingstone, *Oxford Dictionary of the Christian Church*^{2},1974
PG	J. Migne, *Patrologia graeca*
Pirqe R. El	a Rabbinic work, Pirqe Rabbi Eleizer
PL	J. Migne, *Patrologia latina*
Pss. Sol.	Psalms of Solomon
RevScRel	*Revue des sciences religieuses*
RSR	*Recherches de science religieuse*
RSV	Revised Standard Version (1952)
SBT	Studies in Biblical Theology
Sir.	Ecclesiasticus (Wisdom of Jesus, son of Sirach)
SJT	*Scottish Journal of Theology*
SNTS	Society of New Testament Studies
StrB	H. Strack and P. Billerbeck, *Kommentar zum Neuen Testament*
TB	Babylonian Talmud
TEV	Today's English Version/Good News Bible (1966, 1976)
TDNT	G. Kittel and G. Friedrich, *Theological Dictionary of the New Testament*
TNTC	Tyndale New Testament Commentary
Tob.	Tobit
TU	Texte und Untersuchungen
TynB	*Tyndale Bulletin*
Vg.	Vulgate
WBC	Word Biblical Commentary
Wis.	Wisdom of Solomon
ZNW	*Zeitschrift für die neutestamentliche Wissenschaft*

Preface

In 1954 I completed the requirements for the degree Master of Arts in Theology at the Wheaton College Graduate School by submitting and defending the required master's thesis. That thesis concerned itself with the subject of this book, namely, the significance of the Holy Spirit in the life of Christ.

My interest in this awe-inspiring topic has not diminished in the intervening years. Quite the contrary. Instead of my interest diminishing, it has grown, and with it has grown the desire to understand more fully why it was that the Spirit of God played such an important role in the life of Jesus of Nazareth, this special person, whom the church has traditionally affirmed to be divine, the Logos, the Son of God, the Second Person of the Trinity. Accompanying this desire to understand has also been the desire to explain, to share with others, with as many people as possible, what I have learned. And so this book.

I did not feel that I was mature enough to publish my thesis in 1954, nor was I certain enough of my conclusions. Even now, more than thirty years later, I still have doubts. Can human persons ever be mature enough to write without presumption (and arrogance) about persons divine? Can people be sufficiently certain about the nature of the Holy Spirit and of Jesus to publish their thinking for others to read? Yet in spite of these doubts and questions, the desire to learn and share has increased within me to such a degree that I feel much like Jeremiah who spoke these words (and I paraphrase): "Although I have said on many an occasion that I will not think about these matters or speak about them again, for they are too great for me, nevertheless they have become in my heart like a burning fire, shut up in my bones. I am weary of holding them in; indeed I cannot any longer" (cf. Jer. 20:9). And so tremblingly I must write, but always with the prayer that these words will help and not hurt, will build up and not tear down, will enlighten the mind and not darken the soul.

Much is owed to too many people to name each one here—people who have written me and phoned me and talked with me face to face, encouraging me to follow through with this project, to finish it and to publish it, if possible. And yet although I cannot personally thank everyone, I must openly thank my college, Wheaton College, and its officers of administration for having confidence in me and for providing me with a sabbatical so that I could bring these ideas together in this more finished fashion. (I want, however, to make this disclaimer—the views expressed in this book are my own; they do not necessarily represent the views of my college.) Thanks also must be given to Word, Inc., for accepting my work, and to its fine editorial staff headed by Mr. David Pigg and Mr. Carey Moore for putting it into such good form. I wish also to express my deep gratitude to Jane, my wife, for doing all the indexing for this volume and for her patience and love, even when the many hours spent at my desk to complete this task have robbed her of the attention she so richly deserves.

Gerald F. Hawthorne
Wheaton College, Illinois
Spring 1991

Introduction

This study has been a long time aborning. It had its beginnings in 1954 as a thesis to complete the requirements for the M.A. degree at the Wheaton College Graduate School. After these many intervening years during which time the embryonic ideas of that thesis have had time to incubate, they come forth now in this more developed form to be made available to a larger audience than that made up of students of Wheaton College, who, having access to the Wheaton College Library, were the ones previously privy to perusing them.

It is necessary to point out at the start that this study is neither a full-blown discussion about the Holy Spirit (pneumatology), nor is it a thoroughly developed, detailed study of the life of Jesus (Christology). Its goal is much more modest than this. Its goal is simply to focus in upon and explore the relationship of the Holy Spirit to Jesus, to raise and attempt to answer the question of why it was that the Holy Spirit played such an important role in the experience of Jesus.

And yet, while this study is a unit in itself and has a rather narrow focus, its peripheral vision must of necessity be wide so as to include what has been written in the available ancient literature about the

Holy Spirit and the person of Jesus. For that which is known and understood and taught about the Spirit in the New Testament is directly related to what was known and understood and written about the Spirit in the Old Testament and intertestamental literature. The abruptness with which the Spirit is introduced in the Gospels in connection with the life of Jesus indicates that for the writers of these Gospels, and for their readers as well, the Holy Spirit was no unknown factor. From reading the ancient texts, they were familiar with stories about the creative presence and power of God's Spirit in the world, even though they themselves might previously never have experienced this creative power firsthand nor even dared believe it possible that they, too, might experience any of this divine *dynamis* in their own lives.

Yet when this new outbreaking of the Spirit's activity took place in the events surrounding the birth of Jesus, those who witnessed it needed no theological explanation to understand, and none is given. They knew what was happening—the past had become present; the old had become new. The seemingly lost power of the Spirit turned out not to have been lost at all. Once again people were conscious that the Spirit was at work in their world, in their history. Once again they knew that this power of God was not solely a phenomenon of the past, something to be read about only, but a power present among them in the here and now to be experienced.

One might possibly infer from the way in which the New Testament begins, with its account of the immediately present action of the Spirit in the life of Jesus (cf. Matt. 1:18), that the very positioning of this event was intended to say that here in this event is *the* connecting link between the Spirit's work in the Old Testament and his work in the New. For the story of the New Testament is not only the story of Jesus; it is also the story of the Holy Spirit in the lives of Jesus' followers.

But to return more directly to the subject of this book, the number of specific references to the Holy Spirit at work in the life of Jesus are admittedly few. They are significant, however, and are augmented by several allusions to the Spirit's effective presence, which, though less obvious, are nonetheless equally authentic and important indications of his creative activity in Jesus' earthly existence. These all cry out for attention and careful investigation. Abrahan Kuyper wrote, almost a century ago, that "the church has never sufficiently confessed the influence of the Holy Spirit exerted upon the work of Christ."[1] To some extent this lament can still be made today in spite of the numerous books that have since been written, both about the Holy Spirit and about Jesus,[2] for to my knowledge no full-blown treatise, no entire book, has been devoted singularly to this subject[3]—this in spite of the fact that the New Testament clearly states that the Holy Spirit attended and affected every phase of Jesus' life, from his birth to his resurrection. It is my desire, therefore, to attempt to rectify this lack with this present modest contribution.

It is not only the number of New Testament texts touching upon the work of the Holy Spirit in the life of Jesus that indicate the importance of this discussion. It is Jesus himself who magnifies its significance. He is held to be unique by the church. He has been, and is today, acclaimed by his many devoted followers as the world's greatest teacher, a worker of miracles, a great prophet, the greatest of prophets, a new departure in life—himself a new way of life, even Life itself, the Savior of the world, the Son of God. His birth was singular, his life unexampled, his death remarkable, and his resurrection unparalleled. Assuming that all this is true about Jesus, and realizing that the writers of the New Testament state that there was a close relationship between the Spirit and Jesus, one cannot avoid asking the question, "To what extent was this extraordinary life the direct result of the Spirit's activity upon it?"

This question leads, then, directly to what this book is about—the significance of the Holy Spirit in the life of Jesus. As has already been noted, the New Testament writers do indeed affirm a close relationship between the Spirit and Jesus. Matthew and Luke, for example, say that the conception of Jesus was brought about by the Holy Spirit. All of the evangelists describe in a more or less uniform way the descent of the Spirit upon Jesus at the time of his baptism. Matthew and Luke especially (but not totally to the exclusion of Mark and John) have considerable to say about the influence of the Spirit upon the ministry of Jesus. The writer to the Hebrews makes a mysteriously intriguing statement about "the eternal spirit/Spirit" by which Jesus was enabled to accomplish "eternal redemption for us" through His death. And other New Testament writers hint at the possibility that the Holy Spirit was *the* power by which God raised Jesus from the dead.

Each of these statements raises its own set of questions. Just what was the nature of the Spirit's work at the conception and birth of Jesus? Was the Spirit the creator of a new humanity? Was he the agent through which the eternal Son joined himself in space and time to the human race? What significance can be attached to the descent of the Spirit upon Jesus? Was its significance that which John the Baptist attached to it—concrete proof that Jesus was the Son of God? What does Luke mean when he writes that Jesus was filled with the Spirit? In what way or ways did this *filling* manifest itself? How did Jesus' performance of miracles differ from that of his disciples? Was his knowledge of what was in people's minds different from that of Peter's when Peter knew, apparently without being told, that Ananias and Sapphira had lied about the sale price of their property? Was the redemption of the human race really brought about not simply by the death of Jesus, but by the death of Jesus made effective through the eternal Spirit? Was the resurrection of Jesus contingent upon the power of the Spirit? These questions are many, and yet they can be resolved into one: What role did the Holy Spirit play in Jesus' birth, life, death, and resurrection; what was the significance of his work in the total earthly experience of Jesus? To try to answer this question, then, is the difficult and delicate task of this book.

Surely one could easily be inclined at this point to say that such a subject is a subject for reverent contemplation, not for critical discussion, and as a consequence draw back from entering into the debate. Surely it is easy, too, to recognize that the way of truth is narrow here, and hence perilous, and thus to assume that the best statement to make concerning these matters is no statement at all. (Some do advise this course of nonaction.) Surely it is easy to feel inadequate before the immensity of such an undertaking, and irreverent in carrying on an academic pursuit about such persons as the Spirit of God and Jesus of Nazareth. And yet one must proceed with firm step, with warm heart, with humility, expecting all the while, in the words of St. Hilary, that God will

> incite the beginnings of this trembling undertaking, confirm them with advancing progress, and call the writer to fellowship with the spirit of prophets and apostles, that he may understand their

> sayings in the sense in which they spoke them, and follow up the right use of words with the same conception of things.[4]

It is necessary now to state what it is I intend to do in this study and how I intend to do this, and at the same time to state what it is I do not intend to do. But first I wish to make a few caveats that will both put my readers on guard and prevent any misunderstanding on their part as they read on:

1. First, I am an incarnationalist. This is to say, it is my studied opinion that the New Testament clearly teaches that the preexistent, eternal Son of God entered into history in the person of Jesus Christ,[5] and that as a consequence this Jesus was, in the ancient words of Melito of Sardis (ca. A.D. 190), "by nature both God and man."[6] Furthermore, I am convinced that this firm Christological position of the New Testament is not the result of some sort of evolutionary process that took place over time in the thinking of its writers, so that at one point Jesus was viewed by them simply as a revered Master and later as divine Lord.[7] On the contrary, I believe that although Jesus is described by these early Christian writers in a variety of ways, this is due *not* to the fact that they, in moving out beyond Palestine into the Gentile world, altered their fundamental understanding of Jesus by adding to this understanding alien factors that were not present from the beginning, but rather it is due to the magnitude of the Person they are describing. If they differ from each other, it is not a matter of "pious imagination's embroidering and enlarging" Jesus, but instead it is a matter of "how to reach any insight that would come near to fathoming him, or any description that was not pitifully inadequate. Successive attempts at word-painting are . . . not evolving away from the original. They are all only incomplete representations of the mighty Figure that has been there all the time."[8] I am an incarnationalist! And I wish my readers not to forget this as they read some of the chapters of this book that may make them wonder.

2. Second, I hold to a high view of Scripture. I start with the assumption that all the New Testament books are the documents of the church, written under the providential guidance of God, written out of faith and commitment—but not for these reasons without any

historical basis[9]—written in all their diversity of emphases to underscore, nevertheless, a fundamental unified interpretation of Jesus.

To put it more clearly still, I affirm that the Holy Bible, of which the New Testament is one part, is God's special revelation to people, that it is the trustworthy, authoritative message of God, essential for a correct understanding of God and his acts, and of ourselves and the meaning of our existences, and that it was inspired by the Spirit of God, given to be obeyed as the voice of the living God (2 Tim. 3:15–17).

And yet, I also affirm that this sacred book was written down by human beings in human language at specific junctures in time and in particular geographical locations, with all the limitations that humanness, language, space and time, and societies and their cultures impose upon such a book.

I affirm, therefore, that the Bible is a joint effort of both God and people in time and space—a product initiated by God and under his direction, so that every part and form of it can be labeled, "God breathed" (*theopneustos*, 2 Tim. 3:16; cf. 2 Pet. 1:21), but also a product of different people, living at different times and in different places, having differing personalities, outlooks, fears, aspirations, and so on, with the result that every part and form of the Bible also bears the stamp of humanness: *omnia ex deo; omnia ex hominibus*.

3. Third, I intend to make no attempt from a critical point of view to determine the historicity of the New Testament texts used as a basis for this study, nor will I endeavor to arrange them in chronological order in order to show a possible progression of Christological thought from the simple to the complex. Other more capable scholars than I have adequately dealt with such topics, and I defer to their works which are ready at hand.[10] Therefore, I will accept these documents for what they are, documents of the Christian church, and treat them accordingly. I will not be asking of them in this study where history ends and interpretation begins. Rather, given these documents in the form that the church now has them, I will be asking what they say about the Spirit and Jesus, and what precisely does what they say mean to anyone who might choose to read them and reflect upon them. What, then, do these texts as they are tell us about who the Holy Spirit is and about who Jesus is?

Having made these caveats, let me now proceed to briefly state what one can expect in the succeeding chapters.

Chapter 1 attempts to raise and answer the questions of who or what was the Spirit of God—essentially a survey of the Old Testament and its description of the Spirit—and who was Jesus?

Chapter 2 concerns itself with the Holy Spirit at the conception and birth of Jesus, and the implications of the Spirit's overshadowing presence at these events.

Chapter 3, a much briefer chapter, deals with the Spirit in the boyhood and youth of Jesus. Here the evidence for the Spirit's presence and effective working in the life of Jesus is slight. And yet after close examination of the texts dealing with this period of Jesus' history, I am convinced that Luke, for he is the only one who mentions this otherwise neglected age-span, intends us to understand that the Spirit was with Jesus as much then as at any other time of his life—God's power present and available to him.

Chapter 4 has to do with the Holy Spirit descending upon Jesus at his baptism, enlightening him, and filling him in preparation for his ministry of service. It also is concerned with showing the role of the Spirit, not only in leading Jesus into the arena of conflict with the devil, but also in enabling him to emerge victorious from that conflict.

Chapter 5, an important chapter, discusses the significant part the Holy Spirit had in seeing to it that the ministry of Jesus was effective.

Chapter 6 is an attempt to show that the Spirit was mightily at work even at the time of Jesus' death, and that the Spirit was the effective power by which Jesus was raised from among the dead.

In these six chapters, with the exception of the first, I have limited myself almost entirely to the documents of the New Testament and have attempted a careful exegesis of all of the pertinent texts. Not every person will agree with my exegesis or with my conclusions; this is to be expected. I ask only that each reader will consider what has been written with an open mind, a tolerant attitude, and a gentle spirit.

One cannot come this far in such a study, however, holding the basic presuppositions that I do, and not be asked still one more very difficult, if not impossible, question: "How is it possible for you to hold that Jesus is both truly human and truly God and both at the same time?" It would be easy to dodge this question altogether by taking refuge in a frank and open admission that it is a mystery beyond comprehension, and that though I believe it, I will make no attempt to understand it or explain it. In fact, one of my dearest friends and colleagues advises me to take this course of action. He wrote:

> Would it not be better exegetically to let the deity and humanity, Spirit and non-Spirit texts stand in tension? It is a mistake, I think, to put on a Procrustean bed of logic the question of how God could be man and yet remain God. A logical synthesis has usually ended up denying one or the other. Indeed, if Jesus was God incarnate, he was a unique being and rules of analogy cannot be applied. Deity manifestations no more impugn his humanity than do human characteristics impugn his deity. It does not satisfy—even logically—to say that Jesus was the God-man and then to reject the grounds offered by the Gospels that he was (and is) Yahweh. His claim to forgive sins in his own name cannot, especially in the light of the rightful observations of the theologians, be softened by an implication (unspoken in the text) that he really only did it in the name or authority of another. . . . I empathize with your struggle.[11]

Perhaps I should take this advice, but there is something within me that compels me not to follow Earle Ellis's genuinely kind counsel. Instead, in light of the overriding thesis of this book, I must try to make one more small, perhaps insignificant, attempt at answering the question of how Jesus can be human and divine, a man and God simultaneously.

Chapter 7, therefore, is just that. It is my small contribution to the ongoing debate, my meager effort to explain the inscrutable, my modest attempt to penetrate into this supreme mystery. It bears the title, "The Spirit as the Key to the Kenosis."

Chapter 8 is the concluding chapter. It attempts to do more than summarize what has been said in all the preceding chapters. Here I try to show that the powerful presence of the Holy Spirit in the life of Jesus in reality becomes a model for contemporary Christians—a model that provides hope for all those who would today be the followers of Jesus in this present world that is equally in need of an authoritative word, a reordering of priorities, a healing touch, and so on, as that of Jesus' day. I paraphrase the words of Professor Moule when I say that I refuse to believe that this book, although it is an academic exercise, has nothing to do with matters of contemporary urgency.[12]

NOTES

1. Abraham Kuyper, *The Work of the Holy Spirit* (New York, 1900), 97.

2. See footnote 30, p. 48.

3. J. D. G. Dunn's extremely valuable book, *Jesus and the Spirit* (London, 1975), comes closest to having done what was my intent thirty-five years ago and is my intent now. And yet, although his book discusses many if not all of the same texts dealt with in this study, the greater part of his book is concerned with the Spirit-experience of the first disciples, the significance of Pentecost, the activity of the Spirit that transformed a Jewish sect into a religion of worldwide significance, and so on. This present book, however, except for the final chapter, focuses solely on the Spirit's work in the life of Jesus.

4. Quoted by A. B. Bruce in *The Humiliation of Christ* (Edinburgh, 1889), 2.

5. See John 1:1 with 1:14; Rom. 1:3–4; 8:3; 2 Cor. 8:9; Gal. 4:4; Phil. 2:6–11; Col. 1:13–19; Titus 2:13–14; Heb. 1:1–3, 8. But see also a different interpretation of these passages by J. D. G. Dunn, *Christology in the Making* (Philadelphia, 1980), 33–46, 114–25.

6. Melito of Sardis, *Peri Pascha*, 8, trans. G. F. Hawthorne, in *Current Issues in Biblical and Patristic Interpretation: Studies in Honor of Merrill C. Tenney*, ed. G. F. Hawthorne (Grand Rapids, 1975), 151.

7. The view of *die religionsgeschichtliche Schule*. See C. Colpe, *Die religionsgeschichtliche Schule: Darstellung und Kritik ihres Bildes vom gnostischen Erlosungsmythes* (Göttingen, 1961), 9.

8. C. F. D. Moule, *The Origin of Christology* (Cambridge, 1977), 7–8, also 2–3.

9. See D. M. Baillie, *God Was in Christ* (London, 1948), chapter 2, especially p. 58; J. D. G. Dunn, *The Evidence for Jesus* (Philadelphia, 1985); R. T. France, "Authenticity of the Sayings of Jesus," *History, Criticism and Faith*, ed. C. Brown (London, 1977); J. A. T. Robinson, *The Human Face of God* (London, 1973), 32.

10. The literature on this subject is vast, but the following bibliography is representative of the differing views: P. Althaus, *The So-Called Kerygma and the Historical Jesus* (Edinburgh, 1959); H. Anderson, *Jesus and Christian Origins* (Oxford, 1964); C. K. Barrett, *Jesus and Gospel Tradition* (London, 1967); O. Betz, *What Do We Know About Jesus?* (London, 1968); F. F. Bruce, *Are the New Testament Documents Reliable?* (London, 1954); R. Bultmann, *The History of the Synoptic Tradition*

(Oxford, 1968); M. Dibelius, *From Tradition to Gospel* (Cambridge, 1971); J. D. G. Dunn, *Christology in the Making* (London, 1980); idem, *Evidence for Jesus* (Philadelphia, 1985); idem, *Unity and Diversity in the New Testament* (London, 1977); R. T. France, "Authenticity of the Sayings of Jesus," *History, Criticism and Faith*, ed. Brown, 101–41; B. Gerhardsson, *Memory and Manuscript* (Uppsala, 1961); E. Käsemann, "The Problem of the Historical Jesus," in *Essays on New Testament Themes, SBT* 41 (London, 1964); G. E. Ladd, *The New Testament and Criticism* (Grand Rapids, 1967); I. H. Marshall, *I Believe in the Historical Jesus* (London, 1977); idem, *The Origins of New Testament Christology* (London, 1977); C. F. D. Moule, *The Phenomenon of the New Testament* (London, 1967); idem, *The Origin of Christology*; G. N. Stanton, *Jesus of Nazareth in New Testament Preaching* (Cambridge, 1974); H. E. W. Turner, *Historicity and the Gospels* (London, 1963); idem, *Jesus: Master and Lord* (London, 1953).

11. E. Earle Ellis, Research Professor of Theology, Southwestern Baptist Theological Seminary, Fort Worth, Tex., in a personal letter to me dated 3/14/90.

12. Moule, *The Origin of Christology*, 1.

1. The Spirit and Jesus

What/Who Is the Spirit?

At the beginning of this study of the significance of the Holy Spirit in the life of Jesus, it is appropriate to pause in order to describe these two principle characters—the Spirit (and it is the Spirit of God, the Spirit of the Lord that is in mind here) and Jesus. By doing this both writer and reader will then have a common understanding of what is intended from the outset. Thus, if disagreement should arise later on, it will not be due to any original misconception.

But how is one to begin? How does one capture in a net of words such a term as *Spirit of God*? How can one adequately grasp the meaning of a word as elusive as *Spirit* so as to express its significance to others? How is it possible for one to explain such an intangible subject? In the questioning words of Professor Berkhof, should we not realize that we are here dealing with things beyond our understanding and, hence, should we not limit ourselves to an act of adoration and gratitude? Can we hope to express the inexpressible? And yet, as Berkhof continues,

> All God's deeds are inexpressible. We can dishonor them all by speaking about them in an irreverent way. But all God's deeds want to be confessed in spite of—no, on account of—their inexpressibility.

> God wants us to love him with all our mind and with all our strength. True theology is an act of love. In this act we cannot be silent about a single one of God's mighty inexpressible deeds.[1]

So a start must be made. Perhaps by beginning with a study of the meaning of the word *spirit* a wedge can be driven in and an attempt be made thereby to split open and lay bare some of the mysteries shut away within its confines.

Etymology

The Hebrew word for "spirit"/"Spirit" (*rûach*) and its Greek counterpart (*pneuma*) both have as their fundamental ideas "breath," "air-in-motion," "wind." Depending on the context in which *rûach* is found, it may refer to a gentle cooling breeze, on the one hand (Gen. 3:8), or to a mighty blast of wind of gale-force proportions on the other (Exod. 14:21; 15:8).

Metaphoricallly *rûach* (and *pneuma*) came to be used of the breath of one's nostrils, and hence, by extension, of the breath of life, of the principle of vitality, of that which demonstrates the existence of all living creatures (Gen. 6:17; 7:15). It is said of animals and of humans that they alike have *rûach*, "breath," "spirit" (Gen. 7:22; Eccles. 3:21), and thus that they live and move and have being. But there are things said of the human spirit not said of the spirit of animals: (1) Only the human spirit is qualified by such descriptive phrases as "the spirit of wisdom" (Deut. 34:9), "the spirit of sorrow" (1 Sam. 1:15), "the spirit of despair" (Job 17:1), "the spirit of lying" (1 Kings 22:21–23), and so on, indicating that humans as distinct from animals are capable of moods, of attitudes toward life, of certain frames of mind, whether these be good or bad. Furthermore, (2) only the human *rûach*, never that of animals, is equated by means of poetic parallelism with the Hebrew word for "heart" (*lēb*), a word frequently used by Old Testament writers to refer to the seat of one's emotions, will, intelligence, and reflective thought. In these instances *spirit* is almost identical with *mind* (cf. Exod. 35:21; Pss. 34:18; 51:10, 17; Ezek. 18:31). Thus there is seen collecting about the word *rûach* (and *pneuma*) the further derived meanings—beyond those of "breath" and "wind"—of "life," "vitality," "attitude," "temperament," "motion," "power," "mind," "intelligence," "emotion," and "will."

Definition of "Spirit of God"/"Spirit of the Lord"

Using this brief survey of *rûach*, one can move on now and think about the Spirit of God or the Spirit of the Lord. The very expression, "the Spirit of God," seems to imply that God, like people, possesses "Spirit," that is, that God, like they, possesses life, vitality, power, intelligence, emotion, will, and so on. But certainly from the viewpoint of the Old Testament this is to say far too little. For the Old Testament writers assert that not only does God possess life, but that he himself is the living, breathing God (Gen. 2:7; Exod. 3:6, 15; Job 27:2). He is the Author of Life and the one who imparts life to all his creatures: "That from [God's] hand is the soul of every living being, and the spirit in all flesh is his gift" (Job 12:10).[2] God sends forth his Spirit and his creatures live; he removes it and they die; all of life thus is viewed as a result of the "breath" of God (Ps. 104:29–30; see 2 Macc. 7:22–23; Zech. 12:1). But in a special sense God breathed his own vital breath into human beings, and they are said to have become uniquely alive (Gen. 2:7), alive with God's own life! Thus when the Old Testament refers to the Spirit of God, *life* is intended—for vitality, livingness, is the essence of spirit, especially of the divine Spirit.

Nor is the Old Testament content only to say that God possesses power. Its writers insist that God *is* power; he is the ultimate in vital energy (Ps. 147:5), and his Spirit is the fullness of creative power universally present (Ps. 139:7). From chaos the Spirit of God created cosmos (Gen. 1:2; Ps. 33:6).[3] "The Spirit, as the source of all energy and life, impregnated, as it were, the deep nothingness or formless void, and out of it came forth at the divine behest the vast realm of the created order."[4] And it is this same power that continues to preserve and sustain and renew this creation (Job 33:4; Pss. 51:10; 104:30). It is the Spirit of God that changes the wilderness into a fruitful field and makes a place for justice to dwell, righteousness to abide, and peace to spring forth (Isa. 32:15–17). It is the same Spirit, the same power, that works to perfect Israel by transforming its heart of stone into a heart of flesh (Ezek. 36:26, 27).[5] The sophisticated forces of human beings are "flesh" (i.e. "utter impotence") in contrast with the *rûach*, the power, of God (Isa. 31:3). Thus the Spirit of God, which can create, sustain, and transform, which can pick up and sweep a person away (cf. 2 Kings 2:16; Ezek. 3:12, 14; 8:3), which can come upon and overpower a person (1 Sam. 19:20–24), which can infuse a person with superhuman strength (Judg. 14:19), which can transform a wayward people into the true people of God (Ezek. 37:7–14), which brings to pass even the ordinary events of life (Ps. 147:18), is preeminently the Spirit of Power, effective power, vitality, activity, life.[6]

Much more could be said, but to sum up this part: to speak of the Spirit of God is in reality to speak of God—even though there is no such precise equation in the Old Testament as "God is Spirit" (cf. John 4:24; but see Isa. 31:3). The Old Testament view of God is that he is creator of all, is over all, is responsible for all, is in all. Hence, whatever he does he does directly. So convinced were the ancients of this fact that they did not even hesitate to say that God incited David to sin by numbering the people of Israel (2 Sam. 24:1, 10), or that an evil spirit from the Lord came to torment Saul (1 Sam. 16:14–16). They understood that all the phenomena of life were due to God. They ascribed all the changes in history and all the ups and down of human existence to God.[7] So when these same writers speak of the Spirit of God, one must not imagine that they had in mind some secondary cause, something wholly separate and distinct from God. The Spirit of God meant to them "that God is a vital God, who grants vitality to his creation, . . . [that the Spirit] is God's inspiring breath by which he grants life in creation and recreation."[8] The Spirit of God, then, is not something totally other than what God is, but is in a sense God exerting his power, God effective, God present and active,[9] God reaching out.

And yet there are hints, too, within the Old Testament that the Spirit is to some extent distinct from God, almost a separate hypostasis (person): "They rebelled and grieved his holy Spirit; therefore he [God] turned to be their enemy" (Isa. 63:10; cf. Isa. 54:6); ". . . And now the Lord God has sent me and his Spirit" (Isa. 48:16); "Teach me to do thy will, for thou art my God! Let thy good spirit lead me on a level path!" (Ps. 143:10); "Thou gavest thy good Spirit to instruct them . . ." (Neh. 9:20), and so on. Or there is the question, "Who has directed the Spirit of the Lord, or as his counselor has instructed him?" in the context of Isaiah 40:13, implying that the divine Spirit acting in creation is a consciously working, intelligent power. True, none of these passages or others like them needs to be interpreted to mean that the Holy Spirit is a hypostasis (a person), but they at least point in that direction. In any case, it is important to discern in these texts an essentially personal character to the Spirit—the Spirit guides, instructs, suffers grief, is impatient, etc. This idea must be preserved if for no other reason than that always the Spirit is so closely related to and associated with God.[10] One can hardly correctly infer from the Old Testament that the Spirit is simply an impersonal force exerted by God from which he intentionally has distanced himself,[11] or that the Spirit is a transcendent being exuding power but demonstrating none of those relations of love and communion that are the essence of personality.[12]

The Spirit of God is rarely called the "Holy Spirit" in the Old Testament (only in Ps. 51:11 and twice in Isa. 63:10–11). This may not be because erratic or irrational behavior among the early prophets was attributed to the Spirit (1 Sam. 19:20–24), nor because it was sometimes said that the Lord sent an evil spirit upon people (1 Sam. 16:14). Rather it was because there was no need yet to find a surrogate for God. There was not yet a strong reluctance to write the name of God as happened later.[13] Thus the common expression of the New Testament, "the Holy Spirit," may not necessarily be an allusion to the ethical nature of the Spirit but rather a way of speaking of the Spirit of God without involving the name of God. Such expressions as "holy hill" (Ps. 2:6), "holy arm" (Isa. 52:10), and so on, that appear with regularity in the Old Testament, indicate that the expression, *Holy Spirit*, whenever used, means little more than "the divine Spirit." Thus *Holy Spirit* was an alternate, though rare, term that the Old Testament writers had at their disposal to refer to the Spirit of God, which, nevertheless, was conceived by them as a good Spirit (cf. Neh. 9:20; Ps. 143:10).

The Activity of the Spirit of God

For the purposes of this study, it is essential now to move on and focus attention on the activity of the Spirit of God. The Spirit is always and everywhere at work, especially in the lives of individuals, and more especially still in the lives of individuals who stand for, or in relation to, the community of God's people.[14] One notices almost immediately that a person's so-called innate faculties—artistic, intellectual, religious, etc.—which the Old Testament writers perceive as gifts from God (Exod. 28:3), are nevertheless quickened or heightened by the Spirit, so that they thereby become still more effective in the service to God and people. Bezalel, for example, is said to have been *filled* with the Spirit of God. Thus he was filled with ability and intelligence and knowledge and all craftsmanship, so that he was especially able to devise artistic designs for the proper fashioning of the designated place for Israel's worship of God (Exod. 31:1–5).

And yet the Old Testament also records instances of the Spirit's activity in human life that seemingly argue against what has just been said here. In these instances it would appear that the Spirit of God is a force from outside that overpowers one's own ability to choose or decide, that sweeps up and catches one away quite apart from that person's free exercise of will (cf. 1 Sam. 19:20–24; 1 Kings 18:12). But this is not the norm and may be but the exception that proves the rule—i.e. that the activity of the Spirit in a human life "does not involve a suspension or supersession of the normal human faculties, but their enhancement and intensification."[15]

But the Spirit of God not only enhances one's native abilities; the Spirit also imparts special abilities. Powers of perception, for example, the capacity to understand, not in any ordinary way, is certainly one of these special gifts. As a consequence, the one so endowed by the Spirit is able to perceive things that are normally hidden from human understanding (Deut. 34:9; Job 32:8; Dan. 5:11; 6:3; Sir. 39:6). Further, the awakening of people to the fact that God is to be found everywhere in creation, and thus in every aspect of human life, is also seen as the work of the Spirit (Pss. 33:6; 147:18).[16] Physical powers beyond the limits of one's own human capabilities (Judg. 13:25; 15:14–15; 16:28–30), prophetic speech (Zech. 7:12), the charisma of leadership (Judg. 3:10), moral stamina (Isa. 28:6), and more, are all understood as gifts, endowments of the Spirit of God to people called by God to undertake some extraordinarily important mission of service to individuals or to a nation.

In continuing the discussion of the Spirit's involvement with people, it is instructive to notice now the expressions used by the writers of the Old Testament to describe this relationship. It is said that the Spirit of God *fills people* (Exod. 31:3; 35:31), *comes upon* them (Num. 24:2; Judg. 3:10), *falls upon* them (Ezek. 11:5), *speaks through* them (2 Sam. 23:2), *rests on* them (2 Kings 2:15; Isa. 11:2),is *poured out upon* them (Prov. 1:23; Isa. 32:15; 44:3; Joel 2:28–29), is *placed upon* them (Isa. 42:1), *enters into* them (Ezek. 2:2; 3:24; 37:14), *catches* them *up* (Ezek. 43:5), and so on.

All of these formulas are but the many attempts at expressing something of the inexpressible—the powerful operation of God upon persons so as to provide them with capacities beyond their own limited capacities, to grant them certain outstanding skills, to equip them with certain supernatural abilities in order that they might perform mighty but necessary deeds within the sphere of the saving acts of God for his people. For example, the Spirit was in Joseph as in no one else at that time. Consequently, he was elevated to such a responsible position in Egypt that he was able to affect profoundly the course of redemptive history (Gen. 41:38). The Spirit of the Lord came mightily upon Samson, not for his own personal benefit or good, but that he might become the deliverer of Israel (Judg. 15:14). And what is said of Joseph and Samson can also be said of all other saviors of God's people (cf. Judg. 3:10; 6:34; 11:29; 13:25; 14:6, 19; 15:14). Although the Spirit was most frequently conferred upon individuals, it was invariably conferred on them, nonetheless, for the sake of the community.[17]

The king and the prophet are perhaps the most important figures in the redemptive history of the Old Testament. In them the Spirit of God was especially at work. Both king and prophet stood in intimate relationship with the Spirit of God. Both were chosen by God and equipped by the Spirit of God for their special tasks. Of Saul, the first king of Israel, it was said that the Lord had chosen him (1 Sam. 10:24) and that the Spirit of the Lord would come mightily upon him to turn him into "another man" (1 Sam. 10:6; 11:6). When the Spirit did come upon him, he was transformed from being a person with severe inferior feelings about himself, his heritage, and his standing in society (1 Sam. 9:21) and who had consequently dodged his responsibilities to his nation by hiding among the baggage (1 Sam. 10:22), into becoming a great and mighty warrior. He became a powerful king who could command the following of those over whom he reigned and lead them to victory against the enemy (1 Sam. 11:6–11). But when the Spirit of the Lord departed from

Saul (1 Sam. 16:14), then Saul's authority and power to rule as God's vicegerent also departed from him, and his days as king over Israel were numbered.

David, the second king of Israel, left his pastoral duties to become a still mightier leader than Saul, his predecessor. But once again, before David's enthronement is mentioned, his exploits enumerated, or the greatness of his expanding kingdom detailed, the narrator is careful to say that the Spirit of the Lord came mightily upon him (1 Sam. 16:13). The implication of this remark is clear: David's greatness lay not in himself, nor in his heritage, but in the Spirit of God. From the perspective of the Old Testament writers, David would have lived and died a nameless shepherd, unknown to history, were it not that God had chosen him to be king over his people (cf. 1 Sam. 16:9–10, 12), and had put his Spirit upon him in abundance. And although most writers of the Old Testament seem to be saying that the Spirit is something that can be bestowed and removed, given and taken away (as in the instance of Saul and presumably in the experience of the judges of Israel and that of other people as well [cf. Ps. 51:11]), there is nonetheless a note of permanence struck when the relationship of the Spirit to David is referred to. This is the implication of the words, "The Spirit of the Lord came mightily upon David *from that day forward*" (1 Sam. 16:13, italics mine).

What is of special importance in the present study of the Spirit and Jesus is to note that a very close connection existed between the anointing of the king and the coming of the Spirit upon him: "Then Samuel took a vial of oil and poured it on [Saul's] head, and kissed him and said, 'Has not the Lord *anointed* you to be prince over his people Israel? . . . Then *the spirit of the Lord* will come mightily upon you, and you shall . . . be turned into another man'" (1 Sam. 10:1, 6, italics mine). Again, when David had been identified as Saul's successor, the command came to Samuel: "'Arise, *anoint* him . . .' Then Samuel took the horn of oil, and *anointed* him. . . and *the Spirit of the Lord* came mightily upon David . . ." (1 Sam. 16:12a–13, italics mine).[18] It is interesting, too, to notice that the Hebrew verb, *to anoint*, is *māshach*, and the Greek is *chriō*. From the one, via its adjective form, is derived the English word *Messiah*, and from the other, the word *Christ*. The Old Testament kings were messiahs in that they were the anointed of the Lord (cf. 1 Sam. 24:6, passim), and as such they were bearers of the Spirit.

The Old Testament prophets were also persons chosen by God (cf. Jer. 1:4–5). About them, as well as about the kings of Israel, it could be said that there existed a close relationship between the process of their anointing and the coming of the Spirit upon them (cf. 1 Kings 19:16, 19; 2 Kings 2:9, 15). Of all people, the prophet of God could preeminently be described as "the Spirit-bearing person" (*ho anthrōpos ho pneumatophoros*, Hos. 9:7 LXX). It was the prophet who could say, "I am filled with power, with the Spirit of the Lord" (Mic. 3:8). It was the prophet who could affirm with confidence, "The Spirit of the Lord speaks by me, his word is upon my tongue" (2 Sam. 23:2). Thus when the prophet spoke with the Spirit upon him or in him (cf. Ezek. 2:2) he spoke with the authority of God. He was certain that his words were then not his own words but the words of God. And so it is that the phrase, "thus saith the Lord," occurs with such monotonous regularity throughout the writings of the prophets (Isa. 7:7, passim). Undoubtedly it was this fact that prompted J. D. G. Dunn to write:

> The chief characteristic of the biblical prophet is that he is conscious only of a divine power constraining him to speak, of the divine Spirit giving him words to say and compelling him to speak (see particularly Jer. 20:9; Amos 3:8), so that prophetic authority is the authority of inspiration, of divine inspiration, over against the authority either of the institution or of the rationality of his day.[19]

The Spirit catching away the prophet and lifting him up into communion with God, so to speak (cf. Ezek. 3:12–14), was that which gave him his superhuman powers of discrimination so that he could distinguish between the precious and the vile, between the rightness and wrongness in human behavior, in social institutions, and in religious practices. It was the Spirit that gave him his "prophetic immediacy of insight into God's will," so that his hearers recognized in his message an authority unlike that of their merely human advisers or teachers[20]—a message that in reality was the revelation of the mind of God to their minds by a person especially endowed with the Spirit.

The Universal Activity of the Spirit

Always and everywhere, then, the Spirit of God is at work in the world. The Old Testament, as has been pointed out, takes full cognizance of the Spirit's creative activity in the world of nature (cf. Gen. 1:2; Job 26:13; Pss. 33:6; 104:30). But this is a feature of the Spirit's activity that is easily overemphasized, as thoughtful scholars have pointed out.[21] For as the writers of the Old Testament make very clear, it is with persons that the Spirit has most to do[22]—judges, kings, prophets, people of all sorts, but especially those who belong to the community of God (cf. Judg. 3:10; 1 Sam. 16:13; Job 27:3–4; Ps. 51:10–11; Ezek. 2:2). The Spirit of God is seen to be at work within individuals, to be sure, and at work within them for the sake of the larger community, not primarily for their own sakes.[23] But the inspired vision of the prophets was wider than this. They saw the Spirit's activity as not only confined to the experience of individuals, but as reaching out to embrace an entire nation—even a nation that had ceased to be aware of God, that no longer looked up to God to thank him for life and all of its accompanying gifts, that had failed to confess and honor and worship the Lord as God, that in reality was nothing more than a mere assemblage of dry bones. The Old Testament writers foresaw the Spirit as the breath of God breathing new life into this dead assembly, infusing it with spiritual vitality and renewing its awareness of God and of his prior and ultimate claim upon it (Ezek. 37:11–14). These writers understood that the Spirit in this role was the Spirit of judgment and purification, was a cleansing and purifying power (Isa. 30:28; 4:4; cf. also 1QS 3.7–9; 1QH 16.12; 17:26; Mal. 3:2–3),[24] but also that the Spirit was the bringer of life and blessing and prosperity and righteousness (Isa. 32:15–17; 44:3).[25]

The inspired vision of the prophets was wider still. Not only did they envisage the Spirit poured out on individuals and upon the nation of Israel, but they anticipated a time when God would create a new world and inaugurate a new and glorious period in which the Spirit of God would be given freely to everyone—all peoples would be filled with the spirit of wisdom and power and understanding and the fear of the Lord (Joel 2:28–29; see also 3:1–2). The prophets also perceived, however dimly, that the catalyst of this mighty renewal and universal gift of the Spirit was that mysterious messianic figure, the descendent of David par excellence, the Servant of the Lord: "There shall come forth a shoot from the stump of Jesse . . . and the Spirit of the Lord shall rest upon him. . . . His delight shall be in the fear of the Lord . . . with righteousness he shall judge. . . . The wolf shall dwell with the lamb. . . . They shall not hurt or destroy . . . for the earth shall be full of the knowledge of the Lord as the waters cover the sea" (Isa. 11:1–10). And again, "The Spirit of the Lord God is upon me, because the Lord has anointed me to bring good tidings to the afflicted . . . to bind up the brokenhearted, to proclaim liberty to the captives . . . to proclaim the year of the Lord's favor . . ." (Isa. 61:1–2).[26] Notice about this special person: (1) that there is a close connection between his anointing and the Spirit, (2) that his unique powers of wisdom and understanding and his ability to do extraordinary feats are attributed directly to the Spirit that is upon him—he is the supreme bearer of the Spirit, and (3) that his Spirit-heightened powers are not intended for himself but for others, for the reordering of the world, and for the destruction of all that hurts or harms (cf. also 1 En. 62:2, and especially the beautiful passage in Pss. of Sol. 17:21 [23]–38 [43]).*

Summary

What/who is the Spirit of God? His name is "Wind," and like the wind the Spirit is the invisible, irresistible, unpredictable power of God. His name is "Breath," and as the breath of God he breathes life and vitality and being into every one of God's creatures. Always and everywhere the Spirit is present in the world creating, sustaining, maintaining, ordering, renewing, vivifying. His name is "Air-in-Motion," and as such he is motion and action, the exertion of energy at work always for a good end (Ps. 143:10; Jer. 29:11). If it is not possible to say unequivocably that the Old Testament writers thought of the Spirit as a hypostasis (i.e. as a separate person of the Godhead), neither is it possible to say that these writers conceived of the Spirit merely as an impersonal influence exerted by God, distinct from God, less than God. Rather, it appears they are saying in effect that the Spirit of God was in reality God, the vital God, infusing vitality into

* A second verse number in brackets or parentheses signifies a variation in numbering in different editions.

his creation, God present and operative in his world, and especially in the world of human beings. Here in the world of human beings the Spirit is seen calling out particular men and women, heightening and enhancing their natural abilities, providing them with new and additional powers, that is, powers beyond the limits of their own capabilities—physical, intellectual, and psychical—preparing and equipping them uniquely to execute significant roles in the course of redemptive history.

And yet the ultimate (eschatological) dream of the Spirit of God extends beyond any one person, or nation (Ezek. 37:11) to the whole world, to all people (Joel 2:28–29; 3:1–2). It is the dream of the Spirit that he might fall upon all, inspire all, make all alive with spiritual life, awaken within all a new awareness of and a love for God, generate a whole new people of God in a historical situation. This universal coming of the Spirit upon all human beings, and the consequent reordering of this disordered world is in some mysterious way related to a unique Messiah-figure—God's Anointed, God's Chosen One, who was viewed as the supreme bearer of the Spirit of God (Isa. 61:1–4; 42:1–9; 11:1–9), and who thus would be filled with extraordinary powers, equipped for a superhuman task. This then in brief is an overview of the Spirit of God as described in the Old Testament. It will provide for the present study the basis of understanding for the work of the Spirit in the life of Jesus.

The literature that was written between the Old and New Testaments contains many of these same ideas about the Spirit of God and are repeated and reinforced here (cf. Sir. 48:12, 24; Jub. 25:14; 31:12; Pss. Sol. 17:37–38; 18:7; 1 En. 49:3; 62:2) and modified to some extent. For instance, the expression, "the Holy Spirit," occurs more frequently now (4 Ezr. 14:22; Asc. Is. 5:14; cf. Sir. 48:12; Pss. Sol. 17:37; Wis. 9:17; 1QH 7.6, 7; 14:12b, 13; 17:26; CD 2:11–13) but is judged by some not to be a periphrasis for God's name.[27] The spirit of man is seen as coming from God (Gen. 2:7; cf. Ps. 51:10–11), and because of this it is sometimes called the spirit of God or even his Holy Spirit (cf. CD 5:11). And yet it is clear even here in these later texts that the Spirit of God in the true sense is an entity which stands outside of human persons and which comes to them from God in special situations and under special circumstances.[28]

The rabbis believed that the Spirit of God was primarily the Spirit of prophecy inspiring the writing of each Old Testament book. Many of them believed, too, that since this work had been completed, the Spirit had ceased to be active, that prophecy had become defunct, that the voice of God had been stilled. The Holy Spirit had departed from Israel. No longer was there any inspired revelation. No longer was there any *Geistträger*, any "bearer of the Spirit."[29] The pious Jewish people waited expectantly for that new day, the last times, when the Messiah would come and the age of the Spirit would be inaugurated (Isa. 11:2; Joel 2:28–29; 3:1, 2).[30]

Who Was Jesus?

Important Preliminary Remarks

Before beginning this and the following sections, it is judged necessary to remind each reader of the caveats made in the introduction, where some important basic presuppositions were brought out into the open—presuppositions that underlie all that is written here and that, for better or worse, shape the ideas expressed:

In the first place, the present study will proceed by assuming that all the New Testament books are the documents of the church, written under the direction of God, under the inspiration of the Spirit of God, written out of faith and commitment—but not for these reasons without any historical basis—written to record the church's remembrance and understanding of Jesus, written, in all their diversity, to underscore a fundamental unified interpretation of Jesus.

In the second place, this study will make no attempt to test the historicity of the New Testament texts it uses from a critical point of view, nor will it endeavor to arrange them in chronological order with the intent of showing a possible progression of Christological thought from the simple to the complex. If this is a fault, forgiveness is requested and a degree of tolerance is asked for. As indicated in the introduction, other more capable scholars have adequately dealt with such topics, and their works are ready at hand.[31]

And finally, this study, therefore, will confine itself to these New Testament documents as wholes, not to any supposed part of them that may have existed in a preliterary stage. The task at hand will not be to ask where does history end and interpetation begin, but rather, given these documents in their finished form, to ask what they are saying about Jesus and the Holy Spirit, and what precisely does what they say mean to anyone who might choose to read them and reflect on them. What, then, do these texts tell about who Jesus was?

Jesus Was a Human Being

First, and of great importance, the New Testament documents affirm that Jesus was a human being, with all the characteristics of humanness, such as a physical body, intelligence, emotions, will, and so on. Almost from the beginning of the history of the Christian church to the present day devout thinkers about the person of Jesus have been and are reluctant to admit that he was really and truly a human being, a genuine member of the human race, having flesh and bones and blood and soul and mind (cf. Heb. 2:14) as other human beings have. Yet the inspired writers of the New Testament, far from being embarrassed by this admission, embraced it and recognized it as an absolutely essential ingredient of the Gospel.[32] And so it was that the apostle John went immediately on the offensive against very early *pseudoprophētai*, "false prophets," who, with their high Christology, wished to water down the realness of Christ's humanness (1 John 1:1–3; 2:18–22; 4:1–2; 5:6). And so it was, too, that Tertullian later carried on this same battle arguing that

> if Christ's being flesh is discovered to be a lie, it follows that all things which were done by the flesh of Christ were done untruly—every act of intercourse, of contact, of eating, or drinking, yea, his very miracles . . . [even] the sufferings of Christ will be found not to warrant faith in him. For he suffered nothing who did not truly suffer . . . God's entire work, therefore, is subverted. Christ's death, wherein lies the whole weight and fruit of the Christian name, is denied, although the apostle asserts it so expressly as undoubtedly real, making it the very foundation of the gospel, of our salvation, and of his preaching (1 Cor. 15:3–4, 14, 17–18).[33]

The New Testament makes it clear that Jesus was born of a woman (Gal. 4:4; Matt. 1:18–25; Luke 1:26–35; 2:1–7), born in the humblest of circumstances, born like any person is born, accompanied, one must assume, by pain and blood and joy.[34] In exactly the same way as other infants are dependent upon their parents for love, care, sustenance, and protection so was Jesus, unable as he was to fend for himself and unaware, too, of the dangers that threatened his life (cf. Matt. 2:13–15a). The canonical New Testament, therefore, portrays a realistic picture of Jesus as a genuinely human child—a picture quite different from that found in the later apocryphal gospels. In these one reads that Jesus, while still lying in his cradle, says to his mother: "I am Jesus, the Son of God, the Logos, whom thou hast brought forth."[35] And the canonical writings portray, too, a picture very different from that which can be found in the works of more contemporary writers, some of whom are known to exclaim:

> Oh wonder of wonders, which none can unfold
> The Ancient of Days is an hour or two old . . .
> He sleeps in the manger; he reigns on the throne . . .
> A Babe on the breast of a maiden He lies
> yet sits with the Father on high in the skies.[36]

In their zeal to affirm the deity of Jesus, these writers and others like them effectually eliminate the realness of his humanity. But this the New Testament writers do not do. They stand unalterably opposed to such Docetism.

There is little in the Gospels about the childhood of Jesus. But the following information can be gleaned from them: Born in Bethlehem in the last days of Herod the Great (37–4 B.C., cf. Matt. 2:1), Jesus apparently grew up in Nazareth of Galilee (Matt. 2:23; 4:13; 21:11), a mean, contemptible village without status or privilege (cf. John 1:46). Yet interestingly, that village gave to Jesus its name, and by it he thus was to be distinguished from the many other "Jesuses" of his day (cf. Mark 14:67; John 1:45; Acts 2:22).[37] His home, too, was an unpretentious home, and his family poor. Joseph and Mary were able to offer only two turtledoves or two young pigeons as a purification sacrifice after the birth of their child (Luke 2:22–24). They could not afford the one-year old lamb for the whole burnt offering.[38] Jesus may have been the eldest child of a large family,[39] subject to all the pressures that this would involve, if the brothers and sisters referred to in the gospel accounts (Mark 3:32/Matt. 12:46; Mark 6:1–3/Matt. 13:55–56; John 2:12; 7:5;

cf. 1 Cor. 9:5; Gal. 1:19) were indeed his full brothers and sisters, and not children of Joseph by a previous marriage.[40]

Jesus had Joseph as his father for at least twelve years (Luke 2:41–42). In all probability he learned to call him "Abba," "My father" (cf. Luke 2:48), before ever he began to address God as "Abba." From this fact one can infer that Jesus' own understanding of God as Father was powerfully shaped by the sort of person Joseph was as he related both to Jesus and to all the other members of that family. Luke records the story of Jesus in the Temple when he was only a boy, and he does so with good reason. It affords him the opportunity to speak of Jesus' obedience to his parents and to inform Theophilus that this was not a one-time act of obedience on his part, but the steady undeviating set of his will toward them. This indeed is the force of the Greek verb that he used in telling this story—*ēn hypotassomenos* (Luke 2:51), "he was habitually submitting himself [to them]." Is not Luke saying in effect that Jesus' training in obedience to Joseph and Mary was that which fitted him for his lifelong ministry of obedience to the will of God; it was that which developed within him an attitude toward authority that enabled him to obey God, even when to do so meant his own death; it was that which helped him to choose God's way rather than selfishly to choose his own way?

Luke also takes note of the fact that Jesus' childhood was like that of other children. He grew up and grew strong physically, while at the same time he developed mentally, religiously, and socially (Luke 2:40, 52). Subject to all the normal laws of growth and development (cf. 1 Sam. 2:21b), Jesus was not in any way exempt from the stresses and struggles that are commonly involved in that very human process of growing up. In fact, one of the Greek verbs Luke uses to describe this process is the verb *prokoptein* (Luke 2:52), a picturesque word that literally means "to cut one's way forward," as one might chop a path through a forest.[41] It suggests that Jesus experienced no fantastic developments in his early years or easy shortcuts on his way to maturity.

Surely this so-called "silent period" in Jesus' life, between his birth and the start of his mission, was the time when he learned the Law of God, the Torah. He learned it from his devout parents at home and from the rabbis in his synagogue. He learned to read the Law (cf. Luke 4:16). He worked at memorizing it so that he could quote it with ease (Luke 4:3–13; cf. 2:46–47). He loved the Law and filled his mind with it. Its message seemed to have gripped him and shaped his thinking and his life. Like the blessed man of Psalm 1, his delight must have been in the Law of the Lord on which he meditated day and night (Ps. 1:2)—inferences that can be drawn from his youthful but intelligent interaction with the teachers of the Torah in the Temple (Luke 2:46–47). These, too, were the years when he formed good habits that were to last a lifetime. Again it is Luke who provides an example of this, for it is he who notes that on the Sabbath Jesus went to the synagogue "as his custom was" (Luke 4:16), as he was in the habit of doing.

This period was also the time when Jesus learned a trade. He did not spend all his waking hours studying Torah. He followed in the footsteps of Joseph and became a craftsman, more particularly a worker in wood (Mark 6:3; cf. Matt. 13:55).[42] Justin Martyr (mid-second century) says of Jesus that he made ploughs and yokes (*Dial.* 88), skills he gained by apprenticing himself to Joseph and by working alongside him.

Perhaps this is the place to be reminded that the consequence of Jesus' being a truly human person was that he was born into the world at a particular point in time, in a particular geographical location, among a particular people who spoke a particular language or languages, whose intellectual horizons were to a degree limited to their place in space and time. And so, consequently, Jesus "in language, culture and historical circumstance, . . . was a Palestinian Jew of the first century."[43]

It follows, then, that if Jesus can thus be described, his outlook and perspectives on life were conditioned by the outlook and perspectives of his contemporaries, that is, by his parents, his rabbis, perhaps by John the Baptist,[44] the scribes, Pharisees, Sadducees, Herodians, and so on. His knowledge, therefore, of necessity was limited in much the same way as their knowledge was limited. He knew essentially what a village boy might learn who listened to the rabbis and made the best of his opportunities. Certainly the New Testament is not reluctant to intimate that this is so. It does not shrink from saying of Jesus that he grew in wisdom (Luke 2:40), that is to say, he gained his information as other humans gain theirs—through the discipline of diligence and hard work. The New Testament is not afraid to state that Jesus asked questions specifically for the purpose of gaining information (Mark 5:30–33; 9:21; Luke 2:46,

52; cf. 1 Sam. 2:26; Luke 1:80; see also Mark 11:13). It does not back away from saying that he did not know the day nor hour when the end of the world would come (Mark 13:32).

The New Testament is clear on this point, then, that Jesus' knowledge was in some way circumscribed. In the words of Professor Leon Morris, "This seems inevitable if there is to be a real incarnation. It is the essence of human life that we do not know quite a lot of things. . . . Ignorance is an inevitable accompaniment of the only human life that we know."[45] And again Morris writes, "Sometimes one meets people who overlook this aspect of Jesus' life. They picture him as going on a serene way, knowing the thoughts of everyone about him, knowing the outcome of every course of action in which he or they were engaging. If this was the manner of it, then the life Jesus lived was not a human life, even human life at its highest level."[46]

This admission that Jesus was in reality human and limited in knowledge naturally raises the questions of how much did he know or not know, and whether or not he could have been mistaken in what he taught. For many contemporary scholars this is not a problem. They can accept without difficulty the suggestion that Jesus was in error on any number of matters.[47] Other scholars, however, do not wish to say that Jesus could be in error, especially in his teaching, and they call attention to the important but often overlooked factor that there is a significant difference between ignorance and error. Just because Jesus was limited in knowledge does not as a consequence mean that he must be wrong in what he taught.[48] This thorny but important question will be discussed later in more detail, so let it suffice now to conclude with a statement from James Orr:

> Ignorance is not error, nor does the one necessarily imply the other. That Jesus should use language of his time on things indifferent, where no judgment or pronouncement of his own was involved, is readily understood; that he should be the victim of illusion, or false judgment, on any subject on which he was called to pronounce, is a perilous assertion.[49]

By far the largest part of the gospel record is concerned with the ministry of Jesus, and here still the genuineness of Jesus' humanity is stressed. Jesus knows himself to be a truly human person (Matt. 4:4). He identifies himself with the people of Israel and comes with them to the Jordan River to be baptized by John (Mark 1:9). He was tempted by Satan with temptations as real as any temptation that ever came to any other person (cf. Heb. 2:18; 4:15)—temptations that came to him not only at the beginning of his mission (Mark 3:13), but at its end (Mark 14:32–42), and in between as well (cf. Luke 4:13; Matt. 16:22–23).

Jesus began his special mission of preaching and teaching in the fifteenth year of Tiberius Caesar (A.D. 28), during the prefecture of Pontius Pilate (A.D. 26–36), while Annas and Caiphas were the high priests in Jerusalem, and Herod Antipas was tetrarch of Galilee (Luke 3:1–2). His words were human words, spoken into human history at a particular period in that history—spoken with all the limitations of human speech. His illustrations were drawn from human experiences. His pulpit was the mountain, or the roadside, or the lake. His parish was primarily the people of Galilee and Judea. He had the characteristics of an itinerant rabbi and was recognized and addressed as such by those who heard him (Mark 9:5; 11:21; cf. Matt. 8:19; Mark 4:38, passim). His words were astonishing, indeed, and spoken with authority, and his deeds even more so. And yet the people saw before them a man (Matt. 13:55)—a great teacher come from God, to be sure (John 3:2), or a prophet (Mark 8:28/Matt. 21:11; Luke 7:16, 39; John 4:19; apparently even Jesus thought of himself as a prophet [Mark 6:4/Luke 13:33; cf. Matt. 23:31–36]),[50] but a man nonetheless. They did not, they could not, see in him anyone different from other flesh and blood persons they had known or had heard about (see especially Luke 24:19).

The Gospels in their unobtrusive way continue to stress the fact that Jesus was indeed a human being simply by recording that he, too, experienced those things—little and big—that go into making up human existence, such as paying taxes, heartily eating and drinking, climbing into fishing boats, and so on (see Matt. 17:24–26; 11:19; 9:1). They note that he was hungry, thirsty, and weary (Matt. 21:18; Luke 4:2; John 4:6–8), in fact, so weary that he was able to fall sound asleep in the cramped quarters of a small boat in a storm (Mark 4:38). They describe the full range of human emotions that Jesus felt—love, joy, grief, compassion, anger, gratitude, wonder, and desire (see Mark 10:21; John 11:5; Luke 10:21; John 11:33–36; Matt. 20:34; Mark 1:41; 3:5; 8:6; Luke 7:9; 22:15).

The Gospels say, too, that he experienced those darker emotions of a troubled human soul—loneliness, perplexity, alarm, dismay, and despondency (Mark 14:33; Luke 12:50; John 12:27). He may also have experienced the anguish of being tormented by subtle and not so subtle insinuations about his birth, i.e. that he was illegitimate, a child conceived outside of wedlock—people called him "the Son of Mary" (Mark 6:3).[51] In a bitter reply to Jesus' criticism of their conduct the Jews retorted, "*We* (*hēmeis*) were not born of fornication" (John 8:41). And it is known that other scandalous yet worthless allegations were made about his birth.[52] "The scope of these sufferings," B. B. Warfield observes, "was very broad, embracing that whole series of painful emotions which runs from a consternation that is appalled dismay, through despondency which is almost despair, to a sense of well-nigh complete desolation."[53]

And the Gospels also relate that Jesus at times gave way to these emotions and expressed his feelings physically—he wept (John 11:35), he even wailed (Luke 19:41), he sighed (Mark 7:34), he groaned (Mark 8:12), he flashed angry glares at people (Mark 3:5), he spoke with annoyance in his voice (Mark 10:14), or with chiding words (Mark 3:12). On occasion Jesus broke out in a rage (John 11:33, 38 as the Greek makes clear), or openly exulted (Luke 10:21), or cried aloud in utter desolation (Matt. 27:46). "Nothing is lacking [here in the Gospels] to make the impression strong that we have before us in Jesus a human being like ourselves."[54]

The words of C. S. Lewis are apt at this point:

> God could, had he pleased, have been incarnate in a man of iron nerves, the stoic sort who lets no sigh escape him. Of his great humility he chose to be incarnate in a man of delicate sensibilities who wept at the grave of Lazarus and sweated blood in Gethsemane. Otherwise we should have missed the great lesson that it is by his *will* alone that a man is good or bad and that *feelings* are not, in themselves, of any importance. We should also have missed the all important help of knowing that he faced all that the weakest of us face, has shared not only the strength of our

> nature but every weakness of it except sin. If he had natural courage, that would have been for many of us almost the same as his not being incarnate at all.[55]

And, of course, there is everywhere in the Gospels the ultimate mark of Jesus' humanity, namely his mortality. He died! The overwhelming testimony of the New Testament is not that Jesus fainted from fear or swooned from pain, but that he expired from mortal wounds (Matt. 27:50; Mark 15:37; Luke 23:46; John 19:30; Rom. 5:6; 1 Cor. 15:3; 2 Cor. 5:14; 1 Thess. 5:9–10).

The writers of the Acts and the Epistles have as their chief interest the resurrected and exalted Lord of the Church. But they, too, like the writers of the Gospels, are careful to affirm that this very one who now occupies their attention in this new way was truly human. They know him to have been a historical person who was born of a woman, born under the Law (Gal. 4:4), as much so as any of his brothers (cf. Gal. 1:19), a legitimate descendent of David (Rom. 1:3), an Israelite humanly speaking (*kata sarka*, Rom. 9:5), a man from Nazareth (Acts 2:22, passim). They know him to have been one who truly shared their flesh and blood (Heb. 2:14), who experienced their temptations (Heb. 2:18; 4:15), who learned obedience as they did (Heb. 2:10; 5:8–9), who cried out in his distress to God for help (Heb. 5:7). They take note of his human characteristics such as his meekness, gentleness, and humility (2 Cor. 10:1; Phil. 2:6–8; cf. Matt. 11:29). They recall his betrayal (1 Cor. 11:23–25), his crucifixion, death, and burial (1 Cor. 15:3–4; Heb. 5:8–9; 1 Pet. 1:24; 3:18; 5:1). "Whatever exalted view of Jesus the early church had, [these biblical writers] had no doubt that he was a real man. There is nowhere in the New Testament any suggestion that he was so exalted a being that it would not be meaningful to speak of his humanity" (cf. Rom. 5:12–18; 1 Cor. 15:21–22).[56]

Everywhere throughout the New Testament, therefore, it is taken for granted that Jesus was really a human person. Each of the New Testament writers in his own way emphatically affirms this fundamental fact. Already many of the things that they have written about Jesus which point precisely in that direction have been noted above. But there are four things in particular that stand out as unimpeachable proof that, whatever else is true of Jesus, he was genuinely a human being:

1. Jesus prayed to God. He prayed to God by himself in the early morning before the rush of activities and the needs of the many people whom he encountered filled up the hours of his day (Mark 1:35; Luke 5:16). He prayed with his disciples who, upon hearing him, asked him to teach them to pray (Luke 11:1). He sometimes prayed the whole night through, especially before making an important decision (cf. Luke 6:12). He prayed before other crucial events in his life (cf. Luke 3:21; 9:18, 28–29; Mark 14:35) and after the exhilaration of caring for the needs of people (Mark 6:46; Matt. 14:23). He prayed out of his distress in the Garden of Gethsemane, asking to be spared the bitter experience of crucifixion and death (Mark 14:32–39/Matt. 26:36–42; Luke 22:41–44; cf. Heb. 5:7)—his prayers all expressing a genuinely felt sense of dependence on the Father and of trust in the Father. Perhaps, too, as Professor Jeremias has suggested, pious Jew that Jesus was, no day in his life passed without his engaging in the Jewish custom of prayer three times daily.[57] Certainly, however, the Gospels record that Jesus, like other pious Jews of his time, prayed the blessing and offered the thanksgiving over the meals he shared with his friends (cf. Matt. 14:19; 15:36; 26:26–27). And it is very likely that Jesus began every prayer he prayed to God with the familiar and intimate, "Abba," "My Father!" (Mark 14:36/Matt. 26:39; Luke 22:42; cf. Luke 11:1–2). The evidence of the New Testament, then, "indicates that it is more than probable that prayer was Jesus' regular response to situations of crisis and decision." And "he who prays to God, whoever or whatever else he is, is man."[58]

2. Jesus worshipped God. This is a datum noted in the New Testament that is easily overlooked by its readers. Yet it is of singular importance when considering the realness of Jesus' humanity. The principal New Testament text that establishes this point beyond doubt is the temptation narrative, which appears both in Matthew (4:3–11) and in Luke (4:3–13). According to this narrative, the devil took Jesus to an exceedingly high mountain (Matt. 4:8) and showed him all the kingdoms of the world and their glory in a moment of time (Luke 4:5). The devil then said to Jesus that he would give to him all these and the power and authority that accompanied them—for

all this was his to give to whomever he wished (Luke 4:6)—if Jesus would but fall down before him and worship him (Matt. 4:9; Luke 4:7). It is Jesus' reply that is so very significant here. He, of course, refused the devil's attractive offer. But the reason he put forward for refusing was couched in a quotation borrowed from Deuteronomy (cf. Deut. 5:9; 6:13; 10:20), which clearly revealed the current of his mind and heart and the set purpose of his will: "It is written," Jesus quoted from memory, "You shall worship the Lord your God and him only shall you serve" (Matt. 4:10; Luke 4:8). Jesus did not mean by this answer, "Satan, you have it quite backwards! Instead of me worshipping you, you must worship me, the Lord!" Rather he meant, "Satan, I cannot, I will not worship you, for there is only one who has such a claim on my loyalty, and there is only one I can and will worship and serve, and that is God—the Lord God!" God, then, was the sole object of Jesus' worship, and his whole life was set on a course of worshipful service to him.

Another New Testament writer strikes the same chord. In his Letter to the Hebrews, the author makes the point that Jesus, who is God's instrument for "bringing many sons to glory" (Heb. 2:10), identifies himself so completely with those he brings along that both he and they can be said to be of "one stock" (Heb. 2:11, *ex henos*). As such he is not ashamed to call them his brothers, doing so in the words of Psalm 22:22: "I will tell of your name to my brothers; in the midst of the congregation I will praise thee" (Heb. 2:12). Here, then, in the thinking of this writer, Jesus stands on a level with other men and women (cf. Heb. 2:9), takes his place beside them, and raises his voice with them in worship and praise to God.

3. Jesus trusted God. Robert Butterworth rightly criticizes Professor J. A. T. Robinson for thinking that the *sine qua non* of personal existence can only be understood in terms of "the nexus of biological, historical and social relationships with our fellow-men and with the universe as a whole," and that as a consequence Jesus can only be considered human if he was

> a genuine product of the [evolutionary] process, with all the prehistory of man in his genes, [part of the] living stream, . . . linked through his biological tissue to the origin of life on this planet

> and behind that to the whole inorganic process reaching back to the star-dust and the hydrogen atom—as much a part of the "seamless robe of nature" as any other being.[59]

To test the accuracy of this conclusion, Robinson gets off into speculation about the sexuality of Jesus, as if this were the supreme test of the genuineness of his humanity.[60] But such criteria for being human are in reality superficial. "Neither participation in the genetic process nor sexuality are themselves exclusively human."[61] Surely some more personal, some more interior criterion is needed as a test for the full and true humanness of Jesus. This Butterworth finds in the *faith* of Jesus. Professor Robinson, in particular, has neglected to discuss this important element in Jesus' life. Other New Testament scholars and theologians often fail in the same way. "Jesus is so viewed [by them] through the eyes of faith that his own personal faith goes by largely unnoticed."[62] In fact, some, following the lead of Thomas Aquinas, reject the idea that Jesus lived his life in total fidelity to God as incredible. Thomas Aquinas wrote:

> The object of faith is divine reality that is hidden from sight. . . . Now a virtue, like any other habit, takes its image from its object. Hence, when divine reality is not hidden from sight, there is no point in faith. From the first moment of his conception Christ had full vision of God in his essence. . . . Therefore he could not have had faith.[63]

But the New Testament does not allow the faith of Jesus to go by unnoticed nor allow anyone to deny its genuineness. It does not fail to take note of such an important aspect of Jesus' humanness. It boldly says that Jesus confessed, in the words of Isaiah the prophet, "I will put my trust in him," that is, "in God" (Heb. 2:13; cf. Isa. 8:17;12:2).[64] It also boldly describes Jesus as "the pioneer and perfecter of our faith" (Heb. 12:2), that is, as "the man of faith par excellence." This, wrote Philip Hughes,

> seems to be the primary sense of the Greek original [here in Heb. 12:2]. . . [Jesus'] whole earthly life is the very embodiment of trust

> in God (Heb. 2:13). It is marked from start to finish by total dependence on the Father and complete attunement to his will (10:7–10). . . . In looking to Jesus, then, we are looking to him who is the supreme exponent of faith, the one who, beyond all others, not only set out on the course of faith, but also pursued it without wavering to the end.[65]

In thinking still more about the faith of Jesus as a mark of his humanness, there are also those difficult phrases—*pistis Iēsou* and *pistis Iēsou Christou* to be considered. They appear in the letters of Paul and are most frequently translated as "faith in Jesus," "faith in Jesus Christ," or possibly as "the faithfulness of Jesus" or "the faithfulness of God in Jesus."[66] Literally, however, the Greek is "the faith of Jesus" or "the faith of Jesus Christ" (Rom. 3:22, 26; Gal. 2:16; 3:22; Phil. 3:9, Greek; contrast Gal. 3:26; 1 Tim. 3:13; 2 Tim. 3:15 Greek). It may be, then, that this phrase is but one more indication of Jesus' own faith in God, a faith so radical, so all engrossing that Jesus could accept death as a criminal as the will of God for him, confident that God would ultimately vindicate him by raising him from the dead.[67]

4. Jesus depended on the Spirit of God. As the Spirit came upon human beings in the Old Testament in their weakness and limitedness to inspire them to see life as God sees life and to evaluate it with God's valuation, as the Spirit came upon them to equip them for special tasks, superhuman tasks, as the Spirit came upon them to enable them to push back the darkness and bring light, hope, and healing, so the Spirit came upon Jesus (cf. Luke 3:22; 4:1, 18; Matt. 12:28). The Holy Spirit in the life of Jesus is but one additional proof of the genuineness of his humanity, for the significance of the Spirit in his life lies precisely in this: that the Holy Spirit was the divine power by which Jesus overcame his human limitations, rose above his human weakness, and won out over his human mortality. It will be the purpose of the major part of this volume to show how this is so; therefore, these few remarks will be sufficient for the present.

Jesus Was Unique

In response to the question, "Who was Jesus?" one is compelled by the overwhelming testimony of the New Testament texts to say that he was indeed a human being in the fullest sense. But having now said this, one is also compelled by these same New Testament texts to say more than this about Jesus. For the equally emphatic testimony of the New Testament, even that of the synoptic gospels, "where the narrative is most simple and straight-forward,"[68] as well as that of John, the Acts, the Epistles, and the Revelation where theological interpretation is more obvious and plentiful, leads one beyond such a simple verdict as, "Jesus is a man just like us." Emil Brunner is right when he says, "We are also obliged to come to the exactly opposite view and say: He is *not* a Man like ourselves."[69] If then one goes on to ask, "In what way, or ways, was Jesus *not* a man like ourselves? In what way, or ways, was he a *unique* person?" the New Testament provides any number of answers, only four of which will be mentioned here.

1. One answer that must be given is that Jesus was sinless. Whereas the New Testament states without equivocation that all human beings have sinned and are sinners (Rom. 3:23; 5:8), it is equally unequivocable in its assertion that Jesus did *not* sin, nor was he a sinner (2 Cor. 5:21; Heb. 4:15; 7:26; 1 Pet. 1:19; 2:22; 1 John 3:5). According to the New Testament, Jesus knew of no sin in himself, nor of any need for penitence (cf. John 8:46). Hence, although he came from Galilee to the Jordan River to be baptized by John, whose baptism was a baptism of repentance for the forgiveness of sins, it was not because he personally sensed the need to repent of sins he had committed—something else compelled him to come (see the discussion of this in chapter 4). And no other person, friend or enemy, knew of any sin in him so as to be able to point an accusing finger at him (John 8:46). In fact, quite the opposite picture of Jesus is presented. People are made to testify instead to his sinlessness—Judas: "I have betrayed a guiltless person" (Matt. 27:4); Pilate, the Roman procurator: "I can find no fault in him at all" (Luke 23:4; John 18:38; 19:4, 6); the crucifying Roman soldier: "This was a righteous man" (Luke 23:47).

Furthermore, although Jesus was tempted in precisely the same way as all human beings are tempted (*kata panta kath' homoiotēta*, Heb. 4:15a), yet he was never defeated by these temptations (Heb. 4:15b). The temptation narratives in Matthew (4:3–11) and Luke (4:3–13) depict the sureness and naturalness with which Jesus resisted the tempter. There is no situation put forward from his life that could possibly undermine the Christian claim expressed in the words, "He was tempted in every way imaginable, *yet without sin*" (Heb. 4:15). Not even Paul's remark about God sending Jesus "in the likeness of sinful flesh" (Rom. 8:3) can shake this conviction. For Paul's expression, "sinful flesh," was not meant to say that Jesus was a sinner. His carefully chosen Greek word, *homoiōma*, "likeness," makes this clear. "In the *likeness* of sinful flesh" is as far as the apostle wishes to go in speaking of the real humanity of Jesus. There may be ambiguity here in these words about the kind of human nature Jesus possessed—sinful or sinless[70]—but there is no ambiguity in Paul's thinking about whether Jesus himself was a sinner or a person without sin (cf. 2 Cor. 5:21). The words of Emil Brunner again: "We know of no other man in whose life sin plays no part, whose life is pure and unstained, reflecting the holy love of God."[71] Jesus was a human being, yes. But he was unlike all other human beings in that he was sinless. In this, then, he was a unique person.

2. A second answer to the question of how Jesus was a person like other persons yet different from all other persons is that his ministry was unique. It was unique not in that he performed miracles that no one else had performed or could perform, for most, if not all, of the extraordinary things that Jesus did had already been done by people who had lived before him (cf. 2 Kings 4:32–37), or who were to come after him (cf. Acts 9:40–41; 19:11–12). Rather, the ministry of Jesus was unique in what might be termed its prophetic dimension. Jesus was perceived as a prophet by the people who heard what he said and who saw what he did (Mark 8:27–28; Luke 24:19). He even perceived of himself as a prophet (Mark 6:4; Luke 13:33). And yet the Gospels make it quite clear that although Jesus was indeed a prophet, he must nevertheless be distinguished from any other prophet. All earlier prophets merely promised or predicted that the kingdom of God would come. Jesus, however, proclaimed that the Kingdom of God had already come *in himself* in that he cast out demons by the power of the Spirit (Matt. 12:28)—a proclamation he made again and again in many different ways (cf. Matt. 12:29; Mark 3:27; Luke 11:21–23).[72]

Jesus praised John the Baptist for calling him a prophet, and more than a prophet—the greatest of all prophets (Matt. 11:7–11; Luke 7:24–28). And yet the Gospel writers state that there was such a vast difference between Jesus as prophet and John as prophet that the two could hardly be classed together. They see John the Baptist in his prophetic preaching as always directing people's attention away from himself (Mark 1:7/Matt. 3:11/Luke 3:15–16; John 1:24–27). But they see Jesus in his prophetic preaching as centering the revelation in himself and nowhere else (cf. Luke 11:31–32).[73] "In short, *there is a clear sense in which Jesus the prophet was unique*—because in his ministry alone the final revelation, the end time had come (Matt. 13:16–17/Luke 10:23–24; Matt. 12:41–42)."[74] Jesus was a man, a prophet, to be sure, but he was the prophet par excellence, and in this sense he was a person without peer.

3. Still another answer given by the New Testament to this question concerning the uniqueness of Jesus is: Jesus was aware that he had a special relationship with God as a Son to his Father. If what has been said above about the humanity of Jesus is true, this awareness was a developing awareness, an awareness that kept pace with his physical and mental growth and with the gradual unfolding to him of his mission in life (cf. Mark 1:11; 9:7; Luke 2:48–49). It was an awareness that came through prayer and constant communion with God, mediated to him in decisive experiences of revelation and insight by the Holy Spirit. (More will be said about this in chapter 7.)

That Jesus indeed had such a singular relationship to God, as Son to his Father, and was himself aware of this relationship, is made clear by two striking practices of Jesus that the Gospel writers take note of. One of these is that whenever Jesus prayed, he characteristically and habitually addressed God as "Abba," "My Father" (Mark 14:36/Matt. 26:39/Luke 22:42; cf. Matt. 11:25–26/Luke 10:21–22; John 12:27). The other of these is that he taught his disciples to pray using this very same word for God. He taught them to address God with that same wonderfully intimate word that he himself regularly used—"Abba," "My Father" (Luke 11:2). Now in order to more fully understand the significance of these practices it is necessary to expand on them to some degree.

First, Jesus' custom of addressing God as Abba is absolutely extrordinary, for "there is no instance of the use of Abba as an address to God in all the extensive prayer-literature of Judaism."[75] This fact alone, then, that Jesus first addressed God as Abba, is in itself sufficiently strong evidence to demonstrate that he was aware that he enjoyed a special intimacy with God, that he was "Son" of God uniquely. And Jesus' own existential understanding of who God was—supremely good, gracious, loving, all-wise and all-powerful—and who he himself was in relation to this God—unique Son—were the elements that determined for him the whole course of his life. Surely it was such an understanding that prompted within him glad obedience to all that his Father wished him to do, that brought forth from him willing, undeviating loyalty to his Father's purposes, that fortified him with a steady and unswerving "'set' of his will's current in the direction of the Father's will."[76]

Second, Jesus' unique relationship to God, as Son to his Father, and his awareness of this relationship, becomes still more evident from observing that he taught his disciples to address God as *Abba* (Luke 11:2). For in teaching them to do this, Jesus was in essence claiming that he possessed the right to bestow on others a share in his own filial relationship to God, and, furthermore, that it was his mission to do this very thing. These factors distinguish Jesus' Sonship from that of his followers—his was direct and unmediated; theirs was derived from and dependent upon his.[77] Jesus recognized, it appears, that the relationship to God as Abba was not open to any person independently of himself and his mission. Only by becoming his disciple, only in dependence upon him, could one come to know God as Father. Thus Jesus experienced his Sonship as a unique relationship with God in the outworking of his mission. As Bauckham writes, Jesus' "relationship of filial intimacy with God impelled him to a mission of mediating the gracious presence of his Father to others. This sharing of sonship with others belonged to his unique mission as the agent of God's . . . salvation. He was the unique Son through whom the . . . gift of sonship was bestowed on others."[78]

These ideas are all gathered up and made explicit in a saying of Jesus that is found in Matthew and Luke: "All things have been given to me by my Father; and no one really knows [*epiginōskei*] the Son except the Father, nor does anyone really know [*epiginōskei*] the Father except the Son and those to whom the Son chooses to reveal him" (Matt. 11:27; Luke 10:22).[79] Here Jesus knows himself to be *the* Son. He knows that he is the Son of the Father in a special sense. He knows that his relationship to the Father is different from that of other people in that it is his singular privilege and right to represent the Father (cf. Mark 12:6). And furthermore, he knows that it is his mission to make the Father known to others, to mediate to them his knowledge of God as Abba.

But this saying of Jesus taken from Matthew and Luke does not stand by itself. Throughout the synoptic Gospels, for example, not to mention the Gospel of John, there is to be found the continuous repetition of these same themes: (1) Jesus stands in a special relationship to God as Son (Mark 12:6; 13:32; 14:36, cf. Matt. 26:39, 42; Luke 22:42); (2) Jesus himself becomes increasingly conscious of the uniqueness of this filial relationship (Mark 14:61–62, cf. Matt. 26:63–64; Luke 22:67–70; 1 En. 105:2; 4 Ezra 7:28–29; 14:9); and (3) Jesus wishes to share this filial relationship with others (Matt. 11:25–27/Luke 10:21–22; Matt. 17:2–5; 28:19; Luke 2:48–49).[80] Certainly the New Testament presents Jesus as a genuine human being. At the same time, the New Testament makes it clear that mere human categories are inadequate to describe Jesus fully. He was a human being, yes. But he was also a human being who experienced an unparalleled relationship to God. He was Son of God as no one else was Son of God. In this he was unique.

4. Still one more answer to the question of how Jesus was different from all other people is this—he was God become human, or more precisely, he was the preexistent Son of God become the historical person, Jesus of Nazareth. This is the ultimate answer of the New Testament to the question about the uniqueness of Jesus.

To many modern thinkers, however, such an answer as this is inconceivable, and hence no answer at all. Incarnational language is archaic. It is mythological. It belongs to the first century, not to the twentieth. It is part of an ancient intellectual framework, an antiquated way of thinking that is no longer meaningful in today's world. One can with intellectual integrity believe that Jesus was a supremely inspired person, but *not* that he was a preexistent Being become a man.[81] In the words of Professor John Knox, "It is simply incredible that a divine person should become a fully and normally human person. . . . We can have the humanity without the pre-existence, and we can have the pre-existence without the humanity. There is absolutely no way of having both."[82]

Now all this is quite intelligible and logical if the main assertions, (1) that Jesus was really human, and (2) that God, while immanent in his creation, does not invade it from outside, are granted. But if arguments for God invading his world from outside in the incarnation lie both in the earliest statements about Christ in the New Testament as well as in those that appear later, after some years of Christological reflection, then, as Professor Moule suggests, "We may have to admit inability to make a logical system out of the evidence, and be content to hold to, or be held by, both ends of the dilemma, confessing a mystery which cannot be rationalized without doing injustice to some part of the evidence."[83]

The data of the New Testament that points to God's invasion of this world from outside by having sent his preexistent Son into it, provides precisely that evidence—evidence of sufficient magnitude as to require one "to hold to both ends of the dilemma, confessing a mystery which cannot be rationalized." For the testimony of the New Testament is that Jesus is both a man and at the same time more than a man. He is the eternal Son of God become human without the reality of his humanness being destroyed or his divinity being diminished. The earliest Christology which can be securely dated—that found in Galatians, Romans and 1 and 2 Corinthians—is already as high as is any later Christology. But it is not a Christology manufactured out of whole cloth, fabricated out of the air. Nor is it a distortion of the picture of the Jesus presented in the Gospels. Rather, there is "a direct line of continuity between Jesus' self-understanding and the church's christological interpretation of him." Even the idea of the preexistence of Christ, found now so clearly in the letters of Paul, which may look like a tremendous advance on the more primitive Christologies, was in reality implicit in them all along.[84]

Professor Moule, in his important book, *The Origins of Christology*, pursues this same line of thought and demonstrates that the idea of a transcendent Son is already present in the words and practices of Jesus himself. These

> together with the fact of the cross and of its sequel, presented the friends of Jesus, from the earliest days with a highly complex, multivalent set of associations already adhering to the single word

> "Son." No doubt there is a development in perception. No doubt the famous phrase in Romans 1:4, "declared Son of God by a mighty act in that he rose from the dead," reflects . . . the conviction that it was the aliveness of Jesus that had clinched a new understanding of his status. No doubt it was the earliest theologians of the New Testament who first sharpened the terminology. . . . But, although a distinctiveness of status and being begins to become explicit in these various ways, the materials for it seem to be rooted in the traditions about Jesus himself.[85]

Some of the principal texts articulating this idea, that Jesus was indeed the Son of God incarnate, are:

1. "When the time had fully come, God sent forth his Son, born of woman, born under the law, to redeem those who were under the law" (Gal. 4:4–5).

2. "For God has done what the law, weakened by the flesh, could not do: sending his own Son in the likeness of sinful flesh and for sin he condemned sin, in the flesh" (Rom. 8:3).

3. "'The first man Adam became a living being'; the last Adam became a life-giving Spirit. . . . The first man was from the earth, a man of dust; the second man is from heaven [or as some important Greek manuscripts read, 'is the Lord from heaven']" (1 Cor. 15:45, 47).

4. "For you know the grace of our Lord Jesus Christ, that though he was rich, yet for your sake he became poor, so that by his poverty you might become rich" (2 Cor. 8:9).

5. "All . . . is from God, who through Christ reconciled us to himself . . . God was in Christ reconciling the world to himself, not counting their trespasses against them . . . " (2 Cor. 5:18–19).

The most readily understood meaning of these texts is that Paul, from the outset of his ministry, writing at a time before some of the Gospels were written—certainly prior to the fourth Gospel—believed that this Son of God existed beforehand, that God sent him into the world from outside it (note the many instances in the Gospels of Jesus' consciousness of "having come"—e.g. Mark 1:38; 2:17; 10:45; Matt. 5:17; 9:13; 10:34–35; 11:19; 18:11; Luke 6:32; 12:49, 51; 19:10),[86] that this preexistent Son became a fully human being, and that all this happened in the plan and purpose of God so that the

Son might thus destroy sin, redeem/reconcile sinful people, and bring them into life.[87] Other texts in these same early writings argue for an equally high view of Christ's person in Paul's thinking—that he was divine, transcendent, and uniquely one with God (cf. Rom. 1:3–4; 5:10; 8:15–17 [cf. Gal. 4:6]; 8:32; Gal. 1:16 [cf. Matt. 11:27; Luke 10:22]; 2:20).

But the preexistence theme of the Son emerges most clearly in two hymns about Christ from Paul's later letters, Colossians 1:15–20,[88] and Philippians 2:6–11, part of which reads as follows:

> Precisely because he [Christ Jesus] was in the form of God
>   he did not consider being equal with God
>   as grounds for grasping.
> On the contrary, he poured himself out
>   by taking the form of a slave,
>   by being born in the likeness of human beings,
>   and by being recognized as a man.
> He humbled himself
>   by becoming obedient even to the point of
>   accepting death,
>   and that, of all things, death on a cross. . . .

Here is incarnational language par excellence.[89] In beautiful, rhythmic cadences, the hymn describes both the preexistent Christ—he was in the form (*morphē*) of God, sharing the very nature of God, being equal with God—and the incarnate Christ—he emptied himself, taking the form (*morphē*) of a slave, being born in the likeness (*homoiōma*) of human beings, being fully recognized in appearance (*schēma*) as a man. There is then pictured here in these words a person who is both God and human.

The elusive expressions "form (*morphē*) of a slave," "likeness (*homoiōma*) of a human being," and "recognized in appearance (*schēmati heuretheis*) as a man" must never be understood or interpreted in such a way as to weaken the idea of the realness of Christ's manhood. *Morphē* ("form"), *homoiōma* ("likeness"), and *schēma* ("appearance") simply in hymnic fashion are linked together to form a threefold reiteration of one fundamentally important idea, namely, that the preexistent Christ in the incarnation fully identified himself with humanity, that he truly became a human being.[90] (An explanation of how this could be, i.e., how one who was God undiminished could also become a human person to the fullest, and an attempt at explaining the implicataions of the verb, *kenoun*, "to empty," found in this hymn [Phil. 2:7], will be made in chapter 7.)

This conviction that Jesus Christ was the incarnation of the preexistent Son sent by the Father into this world is not confined to the texts already cited. This conviction shows up in almost every part of the New Testament as the following quotations make clear:

1. "The saying is sure and worthy of full acceptance, that Christ Jesus came into the world to save sinners" (1 Tim. 1:15).

2. "In many and various ways God spoke of old to our fathers by the prophets; but in these last days he has spoken to us by [his] Son, whom he appointed the heir of all things, through whom also he created the world. He reflects the glory of God and bears the very stamp of his nature, upholding the universe by his word of power. When he had made purification for sins ['This one statement summarizes the achievement of the Son as man on earth'[91]], he sat down at the right hand of the Majesty on high" (Heb. 1:1–3).

These, perhaps, are among the clearest texts that allude to a preexistent Being entering this world. But they are by no means the only ones. Others that might be overlooked in a hurried reading of the New Testament also exist. For example, 1 Timothy 3:16, 1 Peter 3:18 and 4:1, where in each case the explicit mention of Christ's physical body would be quite unnecessary if he were thought of as simply a man and no more than a man. The reference to Christ's flesh, then, "is meaningful only as a way of emphasizing the fact that the One described . . . became incarnate to die on the cross."[92]

The Gospel of John and the Letters of John together emphasize that the Word, who was in the beginning, who was with God, who was God, who was the agent by whom all things were made, who was life and light, who was the unique Son of God (John 1:1–4, 18; 1 John 1:1–3; 2:22–23), became *sarx*, "flesh," a personal human being (John 1:14; 1 John 4:2–3; 2 John 7). Thus it is not quite fair to John to say that he, in his writings, simply portrays a docetic Christ, a preexistent Son of God only, who strides over the earth like a colossus, no real human person at all.[93] For John sets forth both facts—Jesus as preexistent Son of God *and* Jesus as the Son, the Logos, who accepts human limitations. Without trying to bring these two ideas into a unified system of thought, John nevertheless insists on having it both ways.[94]

As far as the Gospel of Mark is concerned, there is little here that can be called incarnational, unless the term, "Son of Man," which Jesus used of himself, carried within it the ideas of preexistence and incarnation.[95] Matthew and Luke, however, both include as a preface to their Gospels stories relating to the birth of Jesus (Matt. 1:18–21; Luke 1:26–35). Thus they do indeed provide a basis for the doctrine of the incarnation, although neither specifically mentions anything about preexistence. The Acts of the Apostles pictures Jesus both as the Son of God raised from the dead, the judge of all the earth (Acts 9:20; 13:33; 17:31) and as a human being, a man attested by God and anointed with the Spirit of God (Acts 2:22; 10:38). Both ideas—Divine Son and human Jesus—are here held in tension as in other parts of the New Testament with no attempt at resolution.

From this brief survey, then, it becomes clear that ideas of preexistence and incarnation lie very much at the heart of the New Testament and not at its periphery. In the words of Professor Howard Marshall:

> Incarnational thinking about the person of Jesus is of central importance [to the writers of the New Testament who are concerned with theological reflection], and forms indeed the organizing principle of their christology. Moreover, in the case of these writers [there is] found good reason to believe that for them the Son of God, who became incarnate, was a pre-existent Being.[96]

This, to be sure, is the ultimate answer to the question about the uniqueness of Jesus as human. But with this answer it seems that it is no longer meaningful to talk of the realness of Jesus' humanity or even of the uniqueness of that humanity. And yet one must ask about the data of the New Testament: What do they add up to? Surely their sum extends beyond Docetism (Jesus was God masquerading as a man) on the one hand, or adoptionism (Jesus was a mere human being adopted as God's Son) on the other. Thus it may not be possible to bring all the data together into a coherent system. If not, it is "more realistic to hold them together in a paradoxical statement than to force sense upon them by overlooking some phenomena."[97]

And yet one cannot resist trying to resolve the problem and work toward eliminating the paradox. Consequently it will be the burden of the succeeding sections of this book to make this attempt, to undertake this experiment. If the enterprise should end in failure and it is necessary to live finally with paradox, this author wishes to make it clear from the outset that he will then yield to what he presently considers to be the persistent demand of the biblical data, namely, that Jesus was both God and Man, whether or not one can understand how this can be. He agrees with Professor Moule, who wrote:

> It is a familiar fact that the usually accredited test of a realistic doctrine of Christ is whether it yields a realistic doctrine of salvation. Can an inspired person—even with plenary inspiration—achieve what Christians experience in Christ, when they find in him humanity recreated and the new age beginning to be present? If Christ is authentically experienced as not only a teacher but a Savior, one who rescues the human will from its self-centeredness and, when he is allowed to do it, human society from its warped condition, can it be that he is no more than a supremely inspired person? There is no doubt that mainstream Christianity always found in Jesus Christ a Savior and no less—a creator and not an instructor or example only. Information and example may have a limited effectiveness on individuals, given a will and a capacity to respond. But what if this capacity is diminished and the will is warped and what if something more than individual appeal is needed—something as radical as a new creation? Remaking from within by God incarnate seems alone sufficient. This view has been radically questioned; but it is difficult to avoid its force.[98]

NOTES

1. H. Berkhof, *The Doctrine of the Holy Spirit* (London, 1965), 9.

2. See M. Dahood, "Ugaritic *usn*, Job 12:10 and 11QPsªPlea 3–4," *Biblica* 47 (1966), 107–108; idem, *Psalms*, AB (New York, 1970), 3.46.

3. G. von Rad, *Genesis*, trans. J. H. Marks (London, 1961), 47, believes that *Rûach ʾelohim* ("Spirit of God") is better translated in Gen. 1:2 as "Storm of God," i.e. "terrible storm" (cf. the translation of the new RSV, 1990 edition). But see F. Baumgärtel, *TDNT* 6. 363.

4. P. K. Jewett, "The Holy Spirit," *Zondervan Pictorial Encyclopedia*, ed. M. C. Tenney (Grand Rapids 1975), 3. 184.

5. Baumgärtel, *TDNT* 6. 365.

6. W. D. Davies, *Paul and Rabbinic Judaism* (Philadelphia, 1980), 183; see N. H. Snaith, *The Distinctive Ideas of the Old Testament* (London, 1944), 144, 156.

7. A. B. Davidson, "The Spirit of God in the Old Testament," *ExpT* 11 (1899–1900), 21–24.

8. Berkhof, *The Doctrine of the Holy Spirit*, 14; see also E. Schweizer, *The Holy Spirit* (Philadelphia, 1978), 15; G. S. Hendry, *The Holy Spirit in Christian Theology* (Philadelphia, 1956), 12.

9. See F. W. Dillistone, *The Holy Spirit in the Life of Today* (Philadelphia, 1947), 25; A. Richardson, *An Introduction to the Theology of the New Testament* (New York, 1958), 104–105; C. F. D. Moule, *The Holy Spirit* (London, 1978), 4.

10. Davies, *Paul and Rabbinic Judaism*, 182; see also G. W. H. Lampe, "The Holy Spirit and the Person of Christ," *Christ, Faith and History*, ed. S. W. Sykes and J. P. Clayton (Cambridge, 1972), 116; F. Büchsel, *Der Geist Gottes im Neuen Testament* (Gütersloh, 1926), 398, 401–402.

11. But see T. C. Vriezen, *An Outline of Old Testament Theology* (Oxford, 1958), 250; Davidson, *ExpT* 11 (1899–1900), 24.

12. R. W. Crawford, "The Holy Spirit," *Ev Q* 40 (1968), 165, notes this view and argues against it. See also T. Rees, *The Holy Spirit* (London, 1915), 37.

13. But see 1QH 7.6, 7; 14.12b, 13; 17.26; CD 2.11–13.

14. See I. F. Wood, *The Spirit of God in Biblical Literature* (London, 1914), 9, 10, against H. Gunkel, *Die Wirkungen des heiligen Geistes* (Göttingen, 1888), 29, and R. N. Flew, *Jesus and His Church* (London, 1938), 150–51; see Davies, *Paul and Rabbinic Judaism*, 203.

15. Lampe, "The Holy Spirit and the Person of Christ," 116–17.

16. Schweizer, *The Holy Spirit*, 22–23.

17. Davies, *Paul and Rabbinic Judaism*, 203.

18. W. C. van Unnik, "Jesus the Christ," in *Sparsa Collecta: The Collected Essays of W. C. van Unnik*, Supplements to Novum Testamentum, 30 (Leiden, 1980), 263–64.

19. J. D. G. Dunn, "Rediscovering the Spirit," *ExpT* 94 (1982), 10.

20. Davies, *Paul and Rabbinic Judaism*, 219; Dunn, *ExpT* 94 (1982), 10.

21. See A. B. Davidson, *The Theology of the New Testament* (Edinburgh, 1904), 120; Rees, *The Holy Spirit*, 12, 13; Davies, *Paul and Rabbinic Judaism*, 189.

22. Cf. Moule, *The Holy Spirit*, 19.

23. Wood, *The Spirit of God*, 9, 10.

24. See A. R. C. Leaney, *The Rule of Qumran and its Meaning* (London, 1966), 159; M. Black, *The Scrolls and Christian Origins* (New York, 1961), 135.

25. J. D. G. Dunn, *Baptism in the Holy Spirit*, SBT, 15 (London, 1970), 12.

26. See Büchsel, *Der Geist Gottes*, 251.

27. E. Sjöberg, *TDNT*, 6. 381, and fn. 253 for supporting bibliography.

28. Ibid.

29. StrB, 1.127, 2.133. See also Davies, *Paul and Rabbinic Judaism*, 208–15. Davies, after examining the relevant texts and arguments for and against this conclusion, writes: "The evidence, both direct and indirect, of belief in the frequent activity of the Holy Spirit in Rabbinic Judaism is unconvincing. The weight of the evidence suggests that that activity was regarded as a past phenomenon in Israel's history, a phenomenon which had indeed given Israel its Torah, its Prophets, and the whole of its Scriptures, but which had ceased when the prophetic office ended." But see H. Windisch, "Jesus und der Geist nach synoptischer Überlieferung," in *Studies in Early Christianity*, ed. S. J. Case (New York, 1928), 228–29.

30. For a fuller study of the Holy Spirit see also the following important standard works: C. K. Barrett, *The Holy Spirit and Gospel Tradition* (London, 1947); J. Denney, "Holy Spirit," *Dictionary of Christ and the Gospels*, ed. Hastings (Edinburgh, 1906–1908), 1.731–44; J. D. G. Dunn, *Jesus and the Spirit* (London, 1975); M. Green, *I Believe in the Holy Spirit* (London, 1975); G. W. H. Lampe, *The Seal of the Spirit* (London, 1967); H. W. Robinson, *The Christian Experience of the Holy Spirit* (London, 1928); E. F. Scott, *The Spirit in the New Testament* (London, 1923); H. B. Swete, *The Holy Spirit in the New Testament* (London, 1910); idem *The Holy Spirit in the Ancient Church* (London, 1912); B. B. Warfield, "The Spirit of God in the Old Testament," in *Biblical and Theological Studies*, ed. S. G. Craig (Philadelphia, 1952).

31. See Introduction, fn. 10 for bibliography.

32. J. Knox, *The Humanity and Divinity of Christ* (Cambridge, 1967), 93.

33. Tertullian, *Against Marcion*, 3.8. Cf. also these words of Bishop Leo (fifth century): "It is as dangerous an evil to deny the truth of the human nature in Christ as to refuse to believe that his glory is equal to that of the Father" (Sermon 27.1 in J. P. Migne, *Patrologia Latina*, [Paris 1844–55]), 54.216.

34. By the early second century this fact was being denied as too human an element in the experience of Jesus. Note *Odes of Sol*. 19.7, 8: "The Virgin became a mother . . . and she labored and bore the Son *but without pain*" (italics mine; see J. H. Charlesworth, ed., *The Odes of Solomon* [Oxford, 1973], 82).

35. *The Arabic Gospel of the Childhood of Jesus*, a late compilation from *Protoevangelium of James* and the *Gospel of Thomas*, quoted by J. Quasten, *Patrology*, (Utrecht, 1950), 1.125.

36. H. R. Bramley's Christmas hymn in the *English Hymnal*, no. 29, quoted by Robinson, *The Human Face of God*, 110, fn. 47.

37. K. H. Rengstorf, "Jesus Christ," in *The New International Dictionary of New Testament Theology*, ed. C. Brown (Exeter, 1976), 2. 331–33.

38. See J. A. Fitzmyer, *The Gospel According to Luke, I–IX*, AB, 28 (New York, 1981), 426.

39. Some have suggested that Jesus did not begin his ministry before he was thirty years old (cf. Luke 3:23) because Joseph, who, according to the *Protoevangelium of James*, was very old at the time of his marriage to Mary, had died. Jesus, as the eldest son, knew that it was his religious duty to step into his "father's" place and to provide for his mother and younger brothers and sisters until the latter were old enough to take over these responsibilities.

40. J. A. Fitzmyer, a distinguished Roman Catholic scholar, presents a brief but fair discussion of this question of Jesus' "brothers and sisters" in his little book, *A Christological Catechism: New Testament Answers* (New York, 1981), 71–73.

41. LSJ, "*prokoptō*."

42. See C. C. McCowan, "Ho Tektōn," in *Studies in Early Christianity*, ed. S. J. Case (New York, 1928), 173–89; E. Stauffer, "Jeschua ben Mirjam (Mark 6:3), in *Neotestamentica et Semitica*, ed. E. E. Ellis and M. Wilcox (Edinburgh, 1969), 119–28.

43. R. T. France, "The Uniqueness of Christ," *The Churchman* 95 (1981), 202.

44. See J. R. Michaels, *Servant and Son* (Atlanta, 1981), 7–20, who argues engagingly here that Jesus may have learned from John the Baptist and may even have been his disciple.

45. L. Morris, *The Lord from Heaven* (London, 1958), 46–47.

46. Ibid., 47.

47. See R. E. Brown, "How Much Did Jesus Know," *CBQ* 29 (1967), 315–45 [9–39]. To the absolute minimalist, who thinks that Jesus knew no more than any other man, Brown's article will seem forced. To the maximalist, who says that Jesus was God and therefore knew everything, Brown's uncovering of what he considers proof of Jesus' limitation will appear blasphemous. Brown himself believes that to all the nuanced positions in between his study "will offer evidence that must be faced." He is convinced that if the study has the by-product of making Jesus seem more human, then this, too, can be a service to Christian truth.

48. Morris, *The Lord from Heaven*, 48; France, *The Churchman* 95 (1981), 202–203, 212–16; D. Guthrie, *New Testament Theology* (Downers Grove, Ill., 1981), 221–28; E. L. Mascall, *Christ, the Christian and the Church* (London, 1955), 71. I wish to identify myself with these scholars.

49. J. Orr, *Revelation and Inspiration* (London, 1909), 150–51; see also L. Hodgson, *And Was Made Man* (London, 1933), 27; Morris, *The Lord from Heaven*, 48.

50. Dunn, *Jesus and the Spirit*, 84; H. C. Kee, *Community of the New Age: Studies in Mark's Gospel* (London, 1977), 116–19; but contrast E. Fuchs, *Studies of the Historical Jesus* (London, 1964), 22; Schweizer, *The Holy Spirit*, 117; E. Käsemann, *Essays on New Testament Themes*, SBT, 41 (London, 1964), 37–38.

51. See W. L. Lane, *The Gospel According to Mark* (Grand Rapids, 1974), 202–203: "The phrase 'the son of Mary' is probably disparaging. It was contrary to Jewish

usage to describe a man as the son of his mother, even when she was a widow, except in insulting terms" (cf. Judg. 11:1–2).

52. E. Stauffer, *Jesus and His Story* (London, 1960), 24.

53. B. B. Warfield, "The Emotional Life of Our Lord," in B. B. Warfield, *The Person and Work of Christ*, (reprint ed., Philadelphia, 1950), 138; see also 97–138.

54. Ibid., 138–39.

55. C. S. Lewis, *Letters*, in *A Mind Awake—An Anthology of C. S. Lewis*, ed. C. S. Kilby (New York, 1968), 93; contrast Athanasius (ca. 296–373) who held that Christ's body could not have fallen ill or lost any of its strength: The weakness of death came only at the hands of others (*De Incarn*. 21 and 22).

56. Guthrie, *New Testament Theology*, 228.

57. J. Jeremias, *The Prayers of Jesus* (London, 1967), 75. There is not, however, sufficient evidence from the New Testament to give certainty to this suggestion. See Dunn, *Jesus and the Spirit*, 17; P. T. O'Brien, "Prayer in Luke—Acts," *TynB* 24 (1973), 111–27; W. Ott, *Gebet und Heil: die Bedeutung der Gebetsparänese in der lukanischen Theologie* (München, 1965).

58. Dunn, *Jesus and the Spirit*, 21 and 12.

59. R. Butterworth, "Bishop Robinson and Christology," *Religious Studies* 11 (1975), 81. Here Butterworth is quoting from Robinson's *The Human Face of God*, 41–42, 51, 54.

60. Robinson, *The Human Face of God*, 56.

61. Butterworth, *Religious Studies* 11 (1975) 81.

62. Ibid., 81–82; see R. E. Brown, *Jesus, God and Man* (London, 1968).

63. Thomas Aquinas, *Summa Theologiae*, III, q. 7a. 30.

64. According to Philo, trustful hope toward God is *the* essential mark of humanity. See *Quod. det. pot.* 38 (Gen. 4:26): "For what could be found more in keeping with one who is truly a man than a hope and expectation of obtaining good things from the only bountiful God? This is, to tell the truth, men's only birth in the strict sense, since those who do not set their hope on God have no part in a rational nature," in Loeb Classical Library, *Philo*, 2.295.

65. P. E. Hughes, *A Commentary on the Epistle to the Hebrews* (Grand Rapids, Mich., 1977), 522–23.

66. See K. Barth, *The Epistle to the Romans* (Oxford, 1933), 91, 96, for these latter possible translations.

67. See Butterworth, *Religious Studies*, 82–84; M. Barth, "The Faith of the Messiah," *Heythrop Journal*, 10 (1969), 363–70 and bibliography to be found there; Fuchs, "Jesus and Faith," in idem, *Studies of the Historical Jesus*, 48–64; G. Ebeling, "Jesus and Faith," in idem, *Word and Faith* (London, 1963), 201–46; M. D. Hooker, "ΠΙΣΤΙΣ ΧΡΙΣΤΟΥ," *NTS* 35 (1989), 321–42.

68. E. Brunner, *The Christian Doctrine of Creation and Redemption* (London, 1952), 2.324.

69. Ibid.

70. See C. E. B. Cranfield, *A Critical and Exegetical Commentary on the Epistle to the Romans* (Edinburgh, 1975), 1.379–82; R. P. Martin, *Carmen Christi* (Cambridge,

1967), 197–99, 227; J. Schneider, *TDNT*, 5.193–94; K. Barth, *Church Dogmatics* (Edinburgh, 1956), 1.2, 132–71.

71. Brunner, *Christian Doctrine*, 2.324–25.

72. See G. S. Duncan, *Jesus, Son of Man* (London, 1947), 119–31; Brunner, *Christian Doctrine*, 1.325; G. Bornkamm, *Jesus of Nazareth* (London, 1960), 57.

73. Dunn, *Jesus and the Spirit*, 84; see also R. H. Fuller, *The Foundations of New Testament Christology* (London, 1969), chap. 5, especially p. 130.

74. Dunn, *Jesus and the Spirit*, 84, italics his.

75. Jeremias, *The Prayers of Jesus*, 57. For a more detailed elaboration of the implications of this, see also J. Jeremias, *Abba. The Central Message of the New Testament* (London, 1965), 9–30; idem, *New Testament Theology* (London, 1973), 1.65. According to Richard Bauckham the subsequent studies of G. Vermes, *Jesus the Jew* (London, 1973), 211, or of Dunn, *Jesus and the Spirit*, 23, 27–37, do not overthrow this conclusion of Jeremias. See R. Bauckham, "The Sonship of the Historical Jesus," *SJT* 31 (1978), 246, 248. See also Moule, *The Phenomenon of the New Testament*, 50–55.

76. C. F. D. Moule, "The Manhood of Jesus," in *Christ, Faith and History*, ed. S. W. Sykes and J. P. Clayton (Cambridge, 1972), 105–106; but see Brown, *CBQ* 29 (1967), 337–38.

77. Bauckham, *SJT* 31 (1978) 248–49.

78. Ibid., 258.

79. The authenticity of this saying of Jesus has been much debated. Some scholars reject it as inauthentic. Representatives of this position are H. D. Betz, "The Logion of the Easy Yoke and of Rest (Matt. 11:28–30)," *JBL* 30 (1967), 11–20; W. Bousset, *Kyrios Christos* (Göttingen, 1926), 52–57; R. Bultmann, *Theology of the New Testament* (London, 1952), 1.50, 128–33; Dunn, *Jesus and the Spirit*, 27–34 (although to be fair to Professsor Dunn, it must be said that he weighs the arguments for and against and expresses his uncertainty about this saying without actually denying its authenticity); W. Heitmüller, "Zum Problem Paulus und Jesus," *ZNW* 13 (1912), 320–37. Other scholars accept it as authentic. Representatives of this position are Bauckham, *SJT* 31 (1978), 251–57; I. H. Marshall, "The Divine Sonship of Jesus," *Interpretation* 21 (1967), 87–103; idem,"The Development of Christology in the Early Church," *TynB* 18 (1967), 77–93.

80. Cf. R. Abba, "Jesus—Man or Mediator," *ExpT* 55 (1943–1944), 61–62.

81. See J. Hick, ed., *The Myth of God Incarnate* (London, 1977) for a fuller presentation of this point of view; contra M. Green, ed., *The Truth of God Incarnate* (London, 1977) and C. Steads, *Divine Substance* (Oxford, 1977).

82. Knox, *The Humanity and Divinity of Christ*, 98, 106; see also R. E. Brown's review of I. H. Marshall's, *The Epistles of John* (Grand Rapids, 1978) in *CBQ* 42 (1980), 413, who sees incarnational language clearly in John's Gospel, but not in 90 percent of the rest of the New Testament; see also Dunn, *Christology in the Making*, 101–28, who argues that a full-blown doctrine of the incarnation rarely appears in the epistles.

83. Moule, *The Holy Spirit*, 58; see also his *The Origin of Christology*, 138–40.

84. Fuller, *The Foundations of New Testament Christology*, 15, 254, cited by Moule, *Origin of Christology*, 9.

85. Moule, *Origin of Christology*, 30–31.

86. See R. G. Hammerton–Kelly, *Pre-existence, Wisdom and the Son of Man: a Study in the Idea of Pre-existence in the New Testament* (Cambridge, 1973), 64.

87. But see Dunn, *Christology in the Making*, 33–64, 113–28, passim, who after careful exegesis of these texts comes to an opposite conclusion. He writes, "It is . . . likely, indeed probably more likely, that Paul's meaning did not stretch so far, and that at these points he and his readers thought simply of Jesus as one commissioned by God, as one who shared wholly in man's frailty, bondage and sin, and whose death achieved God's liberating and transforming purpose for man" (46). Not to be facetious, but if this is all these texts mean, why could not Paul himself have met these minimal criteria for being God's agent of liberation and transformation of the human race?

88. See P. T. O'Brien, *Colossians, Philemon* (Waco, Tex., 1982), 42–63, for an excellent up-to-date exegesis of this hymn, and see pp. xli–xlix, 40–42 of this same volume for information regarding the authorship of both the letter and the hymn.

89. Against Dunn who denies that this "hymn" is cast in incarnational language, *Christology in the Making*, 114–21.

90. See G. F. Hawthorne, *Philippians* (Waco, Tex., 1983), 75–93, for this translation of the Christ-hymn and an exegesis of its contents.

91. J. H. Davies, *A Letter to Hebrews* (Cambridge, 1967), 20.

92. I. H. Marshall, "Incarnational Christology in the New Testament," in *Christ the Lord*, ed. H. H. Rowdon (Downers Grove, Ill., 1982), 8.

93. E. Käsemann, *The Testament of Jesus* (London, 1968), especially pp. 9–12, 74–78; but see G. Bornkamm, "Zur Interpretation des Johannes-Evangelium" in *Geschichte und Glaube* I (Gesammelte Aufsätze III), (München, 1968), 104–106, who answers Käsemann; see also Moule, "Manhood of Jesus," 100.

94. Moule, "Manhood of Jesus," 100–101.

95. See Marshall, "Incarnational Christology," 12, who thinks that the phrase "Son of Man" may have overtones of preexistence. But he calls attention to Dunn's, *Christology in the Making*, chap. 3, where Dunn rejects Hammerton-Kelly's thesis that "Son of Man" has within it preexistent ideas. See Hammerton-Kelly, *Pre-existence, Wisdom and the Son of Man*.

96. Marshall, "Incarnational Christology," 13. See this article for a more fully developed treatment of the preexistent/incarnational texts of the New Testament than can be provided here.

97. Moule, *The Holy Spirit*, 59.

98. Ibid. See also Knox, *Humanity and Divinity of Christ*, 92, who considers the most appropriate kinds of questions to be, "Who could have saved us but God himself?" and "How could even God have saved us except through a human being like ourselves?" These questions in themselves "while leaving room for all the wonder of the event and all the mystery of Christ, pose no logical dilemma." Note, too, E. L. Mascall, *Who He Is and How We Know Him* (London, 1985).

2. The Spirit in the Conception and Birth of Jesus

The Gospel Narratives of the Conception and Birth of Jesus

In beginning now the study of the Spirit in the life of Jesus, a glance backward will be useful. The Spirit is the Spirit of God. The Spirit is God powerfully present in his world, involving himself primarily in the world of human beings, coming upon people so as to infuse them with new life, new vigor, new vision, new strength, new powers of body and mind in order that each person so infused might play a significant, important, and decisive role in the course of redemptive history.

For centuries, according to many of the rabbis, those teachers who most influenced the thinking of first-century Palestinian Judaism, the Spirit had been silent, his work over, his activity a past phenomenon. The Spirit had indeed given Israel its Torah, its prophets, and the whole of its Scriptures, but having done that his work had ceased.[1]

Suddenly, however, at the very beginning of the Gospel narratives, there is not only renewed interest in the Spirit of God, but the Spirit is said to be once again at work in the lives of human beings. It is as though the writers of these narratives (or at least some of them) wished to awaken within the minds and hearts of their readers an awareness of the present reality of the Spirit and to create within them a new spiritual excitement. Anticipation that something astonishingly great was about to happen was in the air. Not only is it said in the Gospels that the Spirit was active in an extraordinary way at Jesus' birth (Matt. 1:18; Luke 1:35), at his baptism (Matt. 3:16; Mark 1:10; Luke 3:22; John 1:33), at his temptation (Matt. 4:1; Mark 1:12; Luke 4:1), and so on, but there is also running through the early chapters of Luke statements such as: John the Baptist was filled with the Holy Spirit from his birth (Luke 1:15b); Elizabeth was filled with the Holy Spirit and exclaimed about God's new work in the world (Luke 1:41); Zechariah was filled with the Holy Spirit and prophesied of God's goodness (Luke 1:67); John the Baptist, as a child, grew and became strong by the Spirit (Luke 1:80); the Spirit came upon Simeon and gave him special insight and revelation and prompted him to go into the Temple at the right moment (Luke 2:25–26), and so on.

It would appear that Luke especially was proclaiming that the longed-for universal age of the Spirit (cf. Joel 2:28–29) had dawned, the hoped-for new era governed by the Spirit had at last arrived (Luke 4:18–19, cf. Isa. 61:1–3).[2] In this context of excitement because of the renewed activity of the Spirit this study of the Spirit's work, especially in the life of Jesus, is to be begun and carried on. First, then, it is necessasry to begin at the beginning—with the birth of Jesus. The pertinent texts are cited here for ready reference:

The Birth Narratives.

Now the birth [*genesis*] of Jesus Christ took place in this way. When his mother Mary had been betrothed [*mnēsteutheisēs*] to Joseph, before they came together she was found to be with child of the Holy Spirit [*ek pneumatos hagiou*]; and her husband [*anēr*] Joseph, being a just man and unwilling to put her to shame, resolved to divorce [*apolysai*] her quietly. But as he considered this, behold, an angel of the Lord appeared to him in a dream, saying, "Joseph, son of David, do not fear to take Mary your wife [*tēn gynaika sou*], for that which is conceived [*gennēthen*] in her is of the Holy Spirit [*ek*

> *pneumatos hagiou*]; she will bear a son, and you shall call his name Jesus, for he will save his people from their sins." All this took place to fulfil what the Lord had spoken by the prophet [Isa. 7:14]: "Behold, a virgin [*parthenos*] shall conceive and bear a son, and his name shall be called Emmanuel" (which means, God with us). When Joseph woke from sleep, he did as the angel of the Lord commanded him; he took his wife [*tēn gynaika autou*], but knew her not [*ouk eginōsken autēn*] until she had born a son; and he called his name Jesus.
>
> *Matt. 1:18–25*

> In the sixth month [of Elizabeth's pregnancy with John the Baptist] the angel Gabriel was sent from God to a city of Galilee named Nazareth, to a virgin [*parthenon*] betrothed [*emnēsteumenēn*] to a man [*andri*] whose name was Joseph, of the house of David; and the virgin's name was Mary. And he came to her and said, "Hail [*chaire*], O favored one, the Lord is with you!" But she was greatly troubled at the saying, and considered in her mind what sort of greeting this might be. And the angel said to her, "Do not be afraid, Mary, for you have found favor with God. And behold, you will conceive in your womb [*syllēmpsē en gastri*] and bear a son, and you will call his name Jesus. He will be great, and will be called Son of the Most High [*huios hypsistou*]; and the Lord God will give to him the throne of his father David, and he will reign over the house of Jacob for ever, and of his kingdom there will be no end." And Mary said to the angel, "How shall this be, since I have no husband [*andra ou ginōskō*]?" And the angel said to her, "The Holy Spirit [*pneuma hagion*] will come upon [*epeleusetai epi*] you, and the power of the Most High [*dynamis hypsistou*] will overshadow [*episkiasei*] you; therefore [*dio kai*] the child to be born [*to gennōmenon*] will be called holy [*hagion*], the Son of God [*huios theou*]."
>
> *Luke 1:26–35*

These are the texts that tell about the conception and birth of Jesus. What is striking is that only here in the New Testament, in Matthew and Luke, is there any mention of the virginal conception of Jesus. Paul, of course, knows that Jesus traces his ancestry back to David (Rom. 1:3, cf. Matt. 1:20; Luke 1:32) and that Jesus was born of a woman (Gal. 4:4), but nowhere does he make explicit that Jesus was born of a virgin.[3] Mark has no infancy narrative at all, which could mean that he did not know the story of Jesus' birth, or that, if he did, he did not consider it relevant to his purpose. In any case, he begins his Gospel with the ministry of John the Baptist and the baptism of Jesus. John the Evangelist, whose Gospel is later than most of the New Testament writings,[4] and who makes the point that the eternal preexistent Logos became human in Jesus (John 1:1–2, 14; 20:31) shows no awareness of or concern for any account of how this event came about.[5] The greatest part of the New Testament, therefore, is strangely silent about a very important matter—the *how* of Jesus' *genesis*, of Jesus' conception and birth. This fact should make one cautious both about making belief in the virgin birth *the* touchstone of orthodoxy and about wanting to know too much about how the incarnation took place.[6] Nevertheless, these two accounts of the birth of Jesus do exist within the sacred canon, and this fact makes it clear that Matthew and Luke wanted and intended their readers to know as much as they themselves knew and believed about the origin of this extraordinary person. Certainly, then, it is appropriate to examine what they wrote, doing so carefully, cautiously, and reverently.

The Differences in the Gospel Narratives

Matthew and Luke are both equally intent on telling the story of Jesus' conception and birth, and yet each tells it in such a different way that those who read their stories may feel required to say that here are two quite independent and contradictory accounts of the same event. Matthew tells the story as though Joseph, "a model of righteousnesss, mercy and obedience to God,"[7] was the source of his information. Certainly the whole narrative is viewed through Joseph's eyes and felt through his emotions.

Joseph learns that Mary is pregnant. How she became so, he does not yet know. Nor does Matthew say a word about any effort on Joseph's part to find the answer to this question, such as asking Mary for an explanation! He is simply set down in the middle of this disturbing drama ignorant of what really had transpired.[8] But Joseph does know what he must do and how he must do it. As a morally upright person (*dikaios*, Matt. 1:19), he must obey the Law of Moses and at least legally break his engagement to Mary.[9] As a compassionate, merciful, fair-minded (*dikaios*) person, he must do this secretly so as not to expose her to public disgrace (*deigmatisai*).[10] Joseph appears here as a man "torn between his desire to do what was legally correct, and a natural anxiety to protect his betrothed."[11] In reading these words, one thus feels keenly with Joseph those pangs of mental anguish that he felt as he wrestled with the painful problem of what he was to do.

Joseph's decision to "divorce" Mary had hardly taken shape in his mind (this is the force of the Greek aorist participle, *enthumēthentos*, Matt. 1:20), when God quietly and effectively intervened. In Matthew's story the angel of the Lord, the representative of God's will (cf. Gen. 16:7–9; 22:11–12; 2 Kings 1:3; 1 Chron. 21:18; Luke 1:11–17), suddenly appears (*ephanē*) to Joseph at precisely that critical moment of decision. He comes to him in a dream, in a way highly regarded by pious Jews as an important means of divine communication surpassing in importance mere human deliberation (cf. Num. 12:6; 1 Kings 3:5; Jer. 23:25–27; Matt. 2:12–13, 19, 22; Acts 10:9–16). The angel informs him of what has happened, helps him to understand, and orders away his feeling of dread (*mē phobou*).

Here in Matthew's account the angel addresses Joseph, not Mary. He addresses him as "son of David" (Matt. 1:20). This is an exceedingly important piece of information, because Jesus, if he is to be the Messiah, must be able to trace his lineage back through the tribe of Judah to David. He could not do this, however, through his mother's ancestry. Nowhere in the birth narratives is it said that Mary belonged to the Davidic line or that she was in any way herself able to hand on the kingly right to her son. But by being married to Joseph, a true "son of David," Mary could do this. "The absolute oneness in the marriage relation" made it possible for her to be "reckoned as being in very deed that which her husband was,"[12] namely, a descendent of David. She would now, by marriage, be in a position to pass on this ancestry to Jesus, her son.

Furthermore, even though neither of the infancy narratives of the New Testament permits one even to surmise that Joseph may have been the father of Jesus, Matthew, nevertheless, is careful to indicate that Joseph made Mary's child his own child (1) by consummating his betrothal in marriage, taking her home to live with him as his wife[13] before the child was born (Matt. 1:24–25), and (2) by naming the infant at its birth, an act that is tantamount to a formal acknowledgement of Jesus as his legal son. (Notice the significant factor that in this account it is Joseph whom the angel orders to give the child its name [Matt. 1:21].[14]) The carefully worked out genealogy, therefore, with which this Gospel begins (Matt. 1:1–14) becomes significantly more meaningful. It can legitimately be considered "the book of the genealogy of Jesus Christ, the son of David" (Matt. 1:1, see v. 16)—a member of the tribe of Judah, a descendent of David, a rightful heir to the throne.

There is still another possible reason for the angel ordering Joseph to abort his own plans and, in spite of his reluctance, to proceed with taking Mary as his wife. It is that this action may have been designed by God to protect Mary's innocence under the cover of the marriage bond and at the same time to shield her child from base abuse arising from the stigma of illegitimacy. In any case, as Matthew puts it, Joseph, a man sensitive and obedient to the will of God, immediately carries through in precise accord with the command of the angel. He married this already pregnant woman, took her to his home as his wife, and named the child upon his birth (Matt. 1:24–25). Matthew adds that Joseph did more than what was required of him by the messenger of God—he refrained completely from having sexual intercourse with Mary until the child was born (Matt. 1:25).[15]

There are still two other ways in which Matthew's infancy narrative differs from Luke's. The first is that whereas both evangelists agree that the name of the child is to be "Jesus" (Matt. 1:21; Luke 1:31), only Matthew explains why this is so. His name is to be Jesus (the Greek form of the Hebrew name, Joshua—"Yahweh is salvation"[16]), because "he will save his people from their sins" (Matt. 1:21, cf. Ps. 130:8; Judg. 13:5). The second difference follows from the first. Since only God can save from sins, (i.e., forgive sins, cf. Mark 2:7), and since the name *Jesus* means that this one so named is to save his people from their sins, for Matthew, then, Jesus in reality is "God with us" (Matt. 1:23). Matthew shores up and clinches this line of reasoning with a quotation from Isaiah 7:14. He introduces the quote with his special formula that is designed to show a definite continuity between the coming of Jesus and Jewish hopes—"this all happened in order that that which was spoken by the Lord . . . might be fulfilled: 'Behold a virgin shall conceive and bear a son, and his name shall be called Emmanuel'"—that is to say, his name shall be called, "God with us!" (Matt. 1:22–23). For Matthew, then, Jesus was to be nothing less than God with us in saving activity.[17]

On the other hand, Luke begins his story of the birth of Jesus *before* the conception takes place. He casts his account in a form similar to that which he used to describe the birth of John the Baptist (Luke 1:5–25, 57–66). He adds, however, such a wealth of unique features that this new story cannot be considered a mere recasting of any earlier account, or a mere imitation of the story of the Baptist. What is more likely is that Luke, after having gathered his information about both John and Jesus, consciously wove this information together into a basic story pattern that was ready-made for him and borrowed from the Old Testament. It was one that would be easy for him to use and that would be readily understood by his readers. For both he and they were familiar with the Old Testament and its birth accounts of the heroes of Israel's history—Ishmael, Isaac, Samson, etc. (cf. especially Judg. 13:3–25).[18]

Luke does not disclose the source of his information for his story of Jesus' conception and birth. But it is of such an intimate nature that, unless one insists on saying that the whole thing is a theological fabrication,[19] it seems safe to assume that Mary herself was his source, sharing with him her very personal secrets (cf. Luke 1:2; 2:19, 51). Luke's account differs from Matthew's in several ways:

1. Luke says that the announcement about Jesus' conception and birth was made to Mary (Luke 1:26–27). Matthew says it was made to Joseph (Matt. 1:20).

2. Luke identifies the place of the announcement as Nazareth (Luke 1:26). Matthew makes no mention of where the announcement was made.

3. Luke says the announcement came to Mary by an angel who appeared suddenly and directly to her (Luke 1:28). Matthew says the announcement came to Joseph by an angel who came to him indirectly in a dream (Matt. 1:20).

4. Luke names the angel, "Gabriel" (Luke 1:26), a name that means "God is my hero/warrior."[20] He is the very same angel that had

earlier come with God's message to Daniel (Dan. 9:21; cf. 8:16) and to Zechariah, the father of John the Baptist (Luke 1:19), one of the seven angels who stand in the presence of God (Luke 1:19; cf. Tob. 12:15; 1 En. 20; Rev 8:2). Matthew does not name the angel other than to say he was "an angel of the Lord" (Matt. 1:20).

5. Luke has the angel explaining to Mary what is going to happen to her—she is to conceive and bear a son (Luke 1:31), and in effect he asks for her permission to let this happen (cf. Luke 1:38). Matthew has the angel explaining to Joseph what has already happened to Mary with no hint that the angel asked for his consent in the matter (Matt. 1:20–23).

6. Luke says the angel ordered Mary to name her child—in Greek the "you shall call" (*kaleseis*, Luke 1:31) is definitely singular.[21] Matthew says that the angel ordered Joseph to do this (*kaleseis*, Matt. 1:21, see 1:25).

7. Luke tells Theophilus (Luke 1:3) that the child's name was to be "Jesus" (Luke 1:31), but he does not tell why this name was chosen. Matthew agrees that the name was to be "Jesus," but he goes on to say that the reason for this was because this child so named was to be the Savior of his people (Matt. 1:21).

8. Luke records that the angel gave an elaborate description of Jesus—"He will be great, and will be called the Son of the Most High; and the Lord God will give to him the throne of his father David, and he will reign over the house of Jacob for ever; and of his kingdom there will be no end" (Luke 1:32–33). Matthew records that the angel gave only one simple yet significant statement about Jesus: "He will save his people from their sins" (Matt. 1:21).

The differences between these two accounts are considerable. This factor and the somewhat stereotyped forms in which these accounts are presented, have raised questions in the minds of some scholars about their value as history.[22] However important these questions of historicity are—and they are very important—they will not be dealt with here. As was stated in chapter 1, the primary concern of this book is not with matters of historicity, but with trying to discover what the New Testaments texts as they now exist mean. Or more precisely, what are the birth narratives as they presently stand in Matthew and Luke telling people about Jesus and the Spirit? If readers wish to pursue the question of the historicity of these stories, they may easily do so by consulting the abundance of literature on this subject.[23]

The Similarities in the Gospel Narratives

The differences between these two accounts are considerable, to be sure. But for the most part these differences may be looked upon as supplementing rather than contradicting each other. In any case, in spite of their differences, Matthew and Luke do agree on the significant points of this story. They agree that the birth of Jesus occurred during the reign of Herod the Great (Matt. 2:1; Luke 1:5) as though each evangelist wished to stress that this unparalleled event happened in history and could be precisely dated in history. They agree, too, on the *dramatis personae:* Mary, Joseph, Jesus, an angel, and the Holy Spirit. They agree as well on the part that these are to play in the unfolding drama and on the important details that relate to each of them.

Both Matthew and Luke begin their special narratives by introducing Mary and Joseph, about whom they give very little biographical information. They tell only what needs to be told. But it is important to notice that whatever it is they tell now, they tell together. They are in complete agreement on all the following significant matters:

1. They agree that Joseph, whose name means, "May the Lord add [other children]" (Gen. 30:24), traces his ancestry back to David. They say that he is of the house and family of David (Luke 1:27; 2:4; cf. 1 Kings 12:19; 2 Chr. 23:3), that he is a son, a true descendent, of David (Matt. 1:16, 20). This, as was pointed out above, is an essential element in the gospel story. Only in this way could Jesus be legally related to the Davidic dynasty, and himself be reckoned as David's Son (cf. Luke 1:32–33), for nowhere in the New Testament is it said that his mother was of the lineage of David.[24]

2. They both tell that the mother of Jesus was named Mary, a name which probably meant "excellence." They tell that she was "betrothed" to Joseph (Matt. 1:18; Luke 1:27), and they use the same Greek verb, though in different forms, to describe this state—*mnēsteuein.* Although this verb is translated "betrothed" or "engaged," its meaning in first-century Palestine differs vastly from its twentieth-century counterpart, and it is important to understand this. In the first century the engagement of a Hebrew girl was the first part

of a two-part marriage ceremony. It involved a formal promise to marry pledged before witnesses and the paying of the bride price. This gave to the groom legal rights over his betrothed (often a young girl, sometimes as young as thirteen years), who was correctly called his wife from that time on.[25] Even though the girl who was thus "married" continued to live with her own family for a year or more and *not* with her husband, her engagement nevertheless was binding upon her, and it could only be broken by her husband divorcing her (this is the force of Matthew's *apolysai autēn* in 1:19—"to put her away" KJV). Even though the husband was not allowed to have sexual intercourse with his "wife" during this interval, "any violation of his marital rights by her was regarded as adultery,"[26] and would be treated accordingly. After the traditional waiting period was over, however long it was, the marriage proper then took place, and the bride went to live in the home of her husband (cf. Matt. 1:24; 25:1–13). At the time of Jesus' conception, then, it must be reiterated, Jesus' mother was in that first stage of the whole wedding ritual—she was only betrothed to Joseph, no more than this.

3. Matthew and Luke agree in telling that Mary was a virgin. Matthew puts it like this: "Before they [Mary and Joseph] came together she was found to be with child" (Matt. 1:18). In all likelihood his expression, "to come together" (*synelthein*) was not intended by him necessarily to refer to sexual intercourse between these two people but to the fact that Mary, who was engaged to Joseph, had not yet left her father's house to take up residence in that of her bridegroom (cf. Matt. 1:20, 24).[27] Nevertheless, it amounts to the same thing. For Matthew makes it clear that when Joseph learned of Mary's pregnancy, knowing as he did that he had no conjugal rights to her between their engagement and the consummation of their engagement in marriage, he was absolutely certain that *he* was not the father of her child. It is this point that Matthew wishes to drive home to his readers—Joseph had *nothing* to do with the conception of the child that Mary was carrying, nor did any other human male for that matter. To establish this, he quotes Isaiah 7:14 at this place in his narrative and applies it directly to Mary: "A virgin shall conceive and bear a son . . ." (Matt. 1:18–25; cf. Luke 1:34).

Luke immediately identifies Mary as a virgin (Luke 1:27), making use of the same special word (*parthenos*) that Matthew had borrowed from Isaiah to do so—a word with a very narrow meaning. Had Luke intended merely to convey to his audience that Mary was a young girl, and no more than that, there were any number of Greek words at his disposal for such a purpose—words such as *pais* (Luke 8:54), *paidiskē* (Luke 12:45), or *korasion* (Mark 5:41). But he chose *parthenos* instead, because this word carried in itself the clear implication of virginity. And that is precisely the idea that Luke wanted to express. It was not his intent in using this word to disparage the marriage bond in any way whatsoever or to encourage celibacy, but rather to insist rather on the fact that Mary was a pure maiden who had never had sexual intercourse with anyone at any time—neither with Joseph, her betrothed, nor with any other man (cf. Luke 1:34, and note the allusion to Isa. 7:14 in Luke 1:31).[28]

4. Matthew and Luke both agree that the announcement about the birth of Jesus was made to Joseph and Mary by an angel. True, the angel is named in one account (Luke 1:26) and not in the other (Matt. 1:20), and the message of the angel to Mary differs from that to Joseph—as would be expected. But the major significance of the incident of the angel in both accounts, irrespective of the differences, is fourfold: to let people know (1) that the message brought by the angel was a message from heaven with all the authority of heaven behind it, (2) that the child to be born would have no human father (Matt. 1:20–21; Luke 1:28–35), (3) that the name Jesus, which would be given to him, was in effect divinely imposed upon him prior to his birth (Matt. 1:21; Luke 1:31), and (4) that this child to be born would become the Savior of the world (Matt. 1:21; Luke 2:11).

5. There are also other ways in which the birth narratives of Matthew and Luke agree significantly. They agree that Jesus was born only after Mary and Joseph had consummated their engagement in marriage, and Mary had begun to live with Joseph in his house (Matt. 1:24–25; Luke 2:4–7). Both agree that the birth of Jesus took place in Bethlehem of Judea (Matt. 2:1; Luke 2:4–7). And both agree that Mary and Joseph made their home in Nazareth in Galilee and that this was the village where Jesus grew up (Matt. 2:22–23; Luke 2:39–51).[29]

6. The most important point of agreement between these two accounts of the birth of Jesus—at least as far as this particular study is concerned—is that both Matthew and Luke emphatically affirm that

the conception of Jesus must not, cannot, be explained in terms of a natural conception, but only in terms of a supernatural conception—in terms of the activity of the Holy Spirit. Matthew tells only *what* happened to bring about Mary's pregnancy, not at all *how* it happened, even though he very well may have known. And he tells it in the briefest, unadorned fashion possible: Mary "was found to be with child of the Holy Spirit" (*ek pneumatos hagiou*, Matt. 1:18), and again, "that which is conceived in her (*to en autē gennēthen*) is of the Holy Spirit" (*ek pneumatos hagiou*, Matt. 1:20).

Luke's account is fuller than Matthew's and shows more interest in how this event came about. Here the angel tells Mary that she will conceive and bear a son who will be great, who will be called the Son of the Most High, to whom God will give the throne of his father David, whose reign will be over the house of Jacob forever, and whose kingdom will have no end (Luke 1:30–33). To this annunciation Mary responds in perplexity with the question, "How shall this be, *epei andra ou ginōskō*" (Luke 1:34), variously translated, "since I have no husband" (RSV, Moffatt), "since I am a virgin" (NIV), "I am still a virgin" (NEB), or literally, "since I do not know a man" (NAB).

The perplexity of Mary as expressed in her question is matched only by the perplexity of scholars over what appears to be a difficulty raised by that question—why if she was already promised in marriage to Joseph, a marriage that was to have been consummated within a reasonable time, should she have any doubt about the angel's prophecy that she would conceive and bear a son? How could she doubt that what he said would come true, that it was well within the realm of possibility for an apparently normal young woman to bear a child? Without getting sidetracked by the desire to discuss the many suggestions offered to resolve this difficulty,[30] it is sufficient for the purpose at hand to realize that Mary's question brings the angel to the most crucial point in the narrative—that of disclosing, not only to Mary but to all who may chance to read this story, how the conception of this special child was to take place. The angel's words to Mary are significant: "The Holy Spirit [*pneuma hagion*] will come upon [*epeleusetai*] you, and the power [*dynamis*] of the Most High will overshadow [*episkiasei*] you; therefore [*dio kai*] the child to be born [*to gennōmenon*] will be called holy [*hagion*], the Son of God" (Luke 1:35).[31]

The Role of the Holy Spirit in the Birth Narratives

These narratives, which appear in diverse forms, come now to focus clearly on this one central point, namely, that the conception of Jesus in the physical sphere was not by virtue of human paternity, but by the direct intervention of God through the Holy Spirit.

The Holy Spirit in the Birth Narratives

The question now is, what did Matthew and Luke have in mind when they wrote of the Holy Spirit, for both writers used this expression and both used it without the definite article (*ek pneumatos hagiou*, Matt. 1:18, 20; *pneuma hagion*, Luke 1:35). This question must be answered not from the perspective of the fourth century and later, when the doctrine of the Trinity was precisely defined and the Holy Spirit was clearly understood as the Third Person of the Trinity,[32] but from the perspective of the first century, when writers expressed themselves in the categories of the Old Testament with which they were familiar.

This is not to deny the doctrine of the Trinity or to say that in the birth narratives the Holy Spirit was considered merely as an impersonal force at work in the world. For interestingly, as Professor Fitzmyer has pointed out, right here in Luke 1:35 are brought together all of the ingredients necessary out of which the doctrine of the Trinity was later to be formulated—"the Most High," "the Son of God," and "the Holy Spirit."[33] But it is to affirm that the understanding the evangelists had about the Spirit very likely was determined by the teaching of the Old Testament on the Spirit. If, then, the question of what Matthew and Luke meant by the Holy Spirit is answered from the perspective of the first century, it seems self-evident that the Holy Spirit was for them simply another way of speaking about the Spirit of God. Thus, all the richness of meaning that was packed into the old expression (see chapter 1), is crowded now into this new expression—the Holy Spirit is the Spirit of God; the Spirit of God is the Holy Spirit. In sum, the Holy Spirit is God himself at work among his people.

That this is the correct conclusion is especially clear from Luke's account, where the angel is recorded as saying to Mary: "The Holy Spirit will come upon you, and the power of the Most High will overshadow you" (Luke 1:35). Here in a type of Hebrew poetic parallelism (*parallelismus membrorum*), "Holy Spirit" and "power of the Most High" are brought together in such a way that the one explains the other, one identifies the other. In the Septuagint (LXX), the Greek Old Testament, the expression, "the Most High" (*hypistos*), is always a term used of God.[34] Therefore, when the angel spoke of the power of the Most High, he was in reality speaking of the power of God, which then in this passage, because of the poetic form in which it was cast, becomes identical with the Holy Spirit. And as the Spirit in the Old Testament entered upon the scene when God wished to exercise special creative powers affecting for good the lives of individuals who in turn would benefit the community or an entire nation, or when he wished to impart life to his creatures (cf. Ps. 104:30), so here the same is true of the Holy Spirit in these narratives about the birth of Jesus.

Neither the phrase, "the Holy Spirit," nor the phrase, "the power of the Most High," has the definite article in Greek. But this factor does not negatively affect the discussion in any way. For in the first instance, according to Greek usage, the phrase needs no article since it is sufficiently definite in itself,[35] and in the second, according to Semitic usage, no article is to be used since *power* (*dynamis*) is determined/qualified by the genitive phrase, "of the Most High" (*hypsistou*).[36] In any case, each phrase expresses clearly, and both of them together powerfully, "the unmerited, unmotivated, gracious coming of God."[37] The Spirit of God who in the beginning was present in order to bring the first creation into existence (Gen. 1:2) is the same Spirit who comes once again to bring the new creation into being in the conception of Jesus.

Although there is no instance in Judaism of the Spirit's activity in begetting a child,[38] it is clear from Psalm 33:6 and Ezekiel 37:14 that God's Spirit creates new life (cf. Jdt. 16:14; 2 Bar. 21:4). Thus one should not put too fine a point on the distinction between the Spirit "creating" and the Spirit "causing to conceive." For as Professor Ellis has said,

> a barren womb was equated with death (1 Sam. 2:5–6) and life from it was regarded as a creative, miraculous act. . . . Paul in Romans 4:17–19 compares the conception of Sarah with a resurrection from the dead (cf. Gal. 4:27–29 . . .). It is not unlike the case of Mary,

> for Luke does not present the virgin-conception as a "mating" of the Holy Spirit with Mary. Rather God's Shekinah presence "overshadows" her,[39]

and a new life comes into existence.

That Matthew and Luke thought of the Holy Spirit in terms of the Old Testament concept of the Spirit of God is further supported by one of the verbs that Luke uses to record the angel's message to Mary—"The Holy Spirit will come upon [*epeleusetai epi*] you" (Luke 1:35). Certainly, with Josef Ernst, one must reject all attempts at discovering behind this verb and the next ("will overshadow you," *episkiasei soi*) any allusion whatsoever to acts of procreation like those of the mythical marriages of human beings with the gods. Sexual-erotic overtones, typical of the myths, lie completely at a distance from and are especially contradictory to the Old Testament and New Testament pictures of God.[40] Rather, the background for this idea of "to come upon" must be sought in the Old Testament description of the powerful, mighty presence of God, as the Spirit of God, at work in the midst of his people. It is reminiscent of those accounts of the Spirit coming upon (*ginesthai epi/en*) certain chosen ones to enable them to do what they could not do by themselves (cf. Num. 24:2; Judg. 3:10; 2 Chr. 15:1). Perhaps immediately behind Luke's, "the Holy Spirit will come upon you," lies Isaiah 32:15, where the prophet speaks of the barrenness of Israel "until the Spirit is poured out upon us from on high" (*heōs an epelthē eph' hymas pneuma aph' hypsēlou*). Figuratively, this verb, "to come upon," means to come on someone as a stronger comes on the weaker (cf. Luke 11:22), a meaning which helps one to understand its religious and theological use here in Luke 1:35. The Holy Spirit, as the power of God, comes on Mary to enable her to become the mother of a child without the aid of another human being.[41] Thus Matthew and Luke, it would appear, understand the expression, "the Holy Spirit," to be equivalent to the Old Testament expression, "the Spirit of God"—an understanding that would be governed primarily by what the Old Testament had to say about the Spirit.

The Conception and Birth of Jesus by the Holy Spirit

What, then, was the nature of the work of the Holy Spirit in the conception and birth of Jesus? Was it only that the Spirit concurred in the normal action of human generation to make it effectual as many believe he does in the case of all human beings? Is Wheeler Robinson right in his observation taken from his book *The Christian Experience of the Holy Spirit*?

> There is no suggestion in them [the birth narratives] or in the Old Testament preparation for them that a supernatural birth was necessary. . . . The underlying thought of the birth narratives is two-fold, and in both respects it is thoroughly congruous with the thought of the Old Testament. On the one hand there is the mystery of the physiological processes of conception and birth as an appropriate sphere for the divine activity, which controls life from the moment of conception onwards, and in so doing realizes a "thought of God." On the other hand, there is the idea of spirit as acting in and through persons to personal ends, especially to explain the extraordinary and abnormal.[42]

Is it possible, as Dennis Nineham implies, that Matthew and Luke, by adding to their stories genealogical accounts which trace Jesus' ancestry to David (Matt. 1:1–16; Luke 3:23–38), intended thus to say that Jesus' Davidic descent depended wholly on his having a human father in the person of Joseph, and that the work of the Spirit of God, therefore, was such as only to make the Spirit jointly responsible along with Joseph for Jesus' conception and birth?[43] Can it be as the late J. A. T. Robinson suggested, that Matthew and Luke affirm no more than did the author of the Wisdom of Solomon when he penned these words:

> I myself am mortal like to all,
> And am sprung from one born of earth, the man first
>   formed,
> And in the womb of a mother was I moulded into flesh
>   in the time of ten months,
> Being compacted in blood of the seed of man
>   and pleasure that came with sleep.
> And I also, when I was born, drew in the common air,
> And fell upon the kindred earth,
> Uttering, like all, for my first voice the

self-same wail:
In swaddling clothes was I nursed, and with
watchful care.
For no king had any other first beginning;
But all men have one entrance into life,
and a like departure.

Wisdom 7:1–6[44]

Does the earliest Christian witness commit one to say no more than that the way Jesus came into the world and went out again was no different from the path of any king or commoner? Does it require no affirmation other than that Jesus was "a man born like the rest of us, from within the nexus of the flesh, law and sin"?[45]

Indeed the origin of life is a mystery, the beginnings of a human person a great secret, an impenetrable enigma. But given the birth narratives as they are in Matthew and Luke it is not legitimately possible to interpret them simply as allegories illustrative of the natural physiological process of conception and birth. It is not possible to interpret them in such a way that they will allow for Jesus having had Joseph, or some other unknown male,[46] as his father. It is not possible to make them say that Jesus was born as all other humans are born, *totally* within "the nexus of the flesh." It is possible to reject them outright, saying that they were never part of the biblical text, or that they have no basis in history, or that they express outmoded, outdated mythological ideas that are no longer intellectually acceptable. But it is not possible (nor fair) to make them say what they do not say. They say, in effect, that the conception of Jesus was

> a direct act of the creator himself such as never happened before in the case of any other human being. . . . God in his free underivative action, causes Jesus to be born, who entirely under the control of his Spirit will accomplish the saving presence of God. With the affirmation of the Spirit's activity in the birth of Jesus, the mystery of his person is described.[47]

Notice Matthew's account of the *genesis* of Jesus—notice the words he chooses to tell this story and the order in which he arranges them so as to leave no doubt in the minds of his readers as to precisely how he intends them to be understood. At the very beginning of his narrative Matthew makes a point of naming Mary as the mother of Jesus without a corresponding naming of Joseph as his father, although he mentions both Mary and Joseph in the same sentence (Matt. 1:18). Matthew had the perfect opportunity of naming Joseph as the father of Jesus had he wished to do so when he concluded his genealogical sketch with the words: "and Jacob the father of Joseph the husband of Mary, of whom [i.e. 'of Mary,' *ex hēs*] Jesus was born" (Matt. 1:16). The fact is that nowhere in his Gospel does Matthew ever designate Joseph as Jesus' father, although he refers to him seven times (Matt. 1:16, 18, 19, 20, 24; 2:13, 19; cf. Luke 3:23; 4:22; John 1:45; 6:42).

Matthew does say that Mary was betrothed or engaged to Joseph, but he nevertheless is most careful to say that "before they came together she was found to be with child of the Holy Spirit" (Matt. 1:18). The phrase, "before they came together," can mean only one thing: prior to the time Mary went to live in Joseph's house and, by extension, prior to the time these two began to live together as man and wife (i.e., before ever they had opportunity to have sexual intercourse with one another), Mary already had conceived, and a child was forming in her womb. The implication of these words cannot be missed—this conception was *not* the result of human paternity; it was unique and miraculous. But Matthew does not leave the origin of the miracle to one's imagination. He specifies it—Mary was found to be with child "*of* the Holy Spirit" (Matt. 1:18, italics mine). The English preposition *of* used here by the RSV is a translation of the Greek preposition, *ek*, which, among its many usages, often is used to denote the origin, the cause, the reason for something—more precisely, the effective cause by which something occurs or comes to be.[48] This seems to be its most appropriate meaning here.

Although Matthew has used this same preposition, *ek*, several times already in his genealogy of Joseph (Matt. 1:3, 5 [bis], 6, 16) to denote the origin of someone, i.e., to refer to the natural generation of a person born of a particular mother ("Boaz . . . by (*ek*) Ruth," Matt. 1:5), it is not correct to say that his use of *ek* here in Matthew 1:18, "with child of (*ek*) the Holy Spirit," merely echoes that earlier usage.[49] There the mother always was designated as the source from which the child came, the substance out of which the person was formed. Here, however, Matthew does not view the Holy Spirit as the substance out of which the person of Jesus was formed but rather as the active efficient cause by which his humanity was initiated. Implicit in Matthew's "with child of [*ek*] the Holy Spirit" is that the Holy Spirit, not Joseph or any other male, provided the generative force by which Mary's pregnancy occurred and the person Jesus began to be formed.

This idea becomes even more explicit in verse 20, where the angel tells Joseph that "that which is conceived [*to gennēthen*] in her is of [*ek*] the Holy Spirit." Here the Greek passive, *to gennēthen* ("that which was begotten, that which was conceived") is a common enough grammatical construction that often has the male principle of "begetting" introduced by *ek* ("of, from, by"), as Simeon to his children: "I was born *of* Jacob" (*egō egennēthen ex Iakob*, Test. Sim. 2.2).[50] But here in verse 20, precisely where the male principle would be expected to be named after *to gennēthen ek* ("that which is conceived [is] of"), it is *not* named. Matthew instead carefully replaces that with *pneumatos hagiou* ("the Holy Spirit"). No human male, then, is to be thought of as the agent by which Mary's child is begotten; rather the Holy Spirit is that which sets the whole process of this special conception and gestation into motion.

Luke is wholly in agreement with Matthew in this respect. He records that when Mary asked the angel how it would be possible for her to conceive and give birth to a child when she was an unmarried woman (and by implication a *chaste*, unmarried woman), the angel replied that this would be possible because the Holy Spirit (*pneuma hagion*) would come upon her and the power of the Most High would overshadow her (Luke 1:35). In these words Luke also is making the claim that the conception and birth of Jesus was not to be part of the normal course of human events—marriage, intercourse, conception, gestation, birth—but a miracle, the direct intervention of God into the course of human events, so that Mary's child to be born would be a gift of God in the fullest sense.[51]

And the other statement made by the angel and recorded by Luke, "the power of the Most High will overshadow [*episkiasei*] you," is also most significant. For the very same verb in this sentence, "will overshadow" (*episkiasei*), is also found in the LXX in Exodus 40:35, where it describes the overshadowing cloud of God's glory that filled Israel's ancient desert tabernacle, denoting the visible presence of God among his worshipers.[52] And it is used again metaphorically in Psalms 90 (91):4 and 139:8 (140:7) to describe the overshadowing protection that the Power of God affords to those who trust in him.[53] There in the Old Testament the verb *overshadow* (*episkiazein*) symbolized the power and presence of the Almighty with and for his people. Here in Luke its use appears to be an allusion to that same power of God coming now to Mary to make it possible for her to become a mother without help from a husband. The expression, "the power of the Most High will overshadow you," thus points to the Holy Spirit as the creative, powerful presence of the Most High over and around and with Mary. As the tabernacle was full of, contained, the Shekinah glory (i.e., the presence of God, Exod. 40:35), so Mary was to carry within herself the Son of God, the glory of God's people Israel (cf. Luke 2:28–32, esp. v. 32).[54] Luke, like Matthew, is saying in effect that "the conception of Jesus in the womb of the virgin Mary differs from all other conceptions of children by their mothers in that there was no human father."[55] The place of the human father was taken by the Spirit of God, by God Himself. This is not to say "that God appeared in theophany after the analogies of the mythologies of the ethnic religions; but that God . . . in an extraordinary way, unrevealed to us, and without violation of the laws of maternity" nevertheless, enabled Mary to conceive and give birth to a child.[56]

This is an inscrutable mystery. In a sense the overshadowing of Mary hides from view the details of this divine activity. No one can penetrate more deeply into this enigmatic event than the text will allow. Matthew and Luke say just so much and no more. They say (1) that there was a young woman, Mary, who was engaged to be married to a man named Joseph, (2) that she was a virgin, (3) that she conceived a child unaided by Joseph or any other human male, and (4) that the Holy Spirit, the power of the Most High, the Spirit of God, in a free underivative act brought about this conception, setting in motion all the processes necessary to bring into being the full humanity of Jesus.

The Consequences of Jesus' Conception by the Holy Spirit

Matthew and Luke do not conclude their birth narratives simply by stating that the conception of Jesus was the special creative work of the Spirit of God, and leave it at that. They are interested in making known what the effects of such a radical divine action were:

Jesus will be called the Son of God. Luke in particular is concerned to detail the results of the Spirit's work. After he records the words of the angel to Mary—"The Holy Spirit will come upon you, and the power of the Most High will overshadow you," meaning, "and thus you will be enabled to conceive"—Luke immediately continues his narrative by adding two conjunctions together, *dio kai* ("therefore also"). He does so, it would seem, to indicate that that which follows is self-evidently the result of the previously mentioned action. *Dio kai* ("therefore also") are used to establish some connection between the work of the Holy Spirit in the life of the Virgin Mary and the fact that Jesus is to be called the Son of God.

But what is this connection? The answer is not as simple as one might suppose, because Luke 1:35b in the Greek text is not as clear as the English versions make it out to be. It can be and in fact is translated in two very different ways: (1) "Therefore also that holy thing [i.e., that holy child] which shall be born of thee shall be called the Son of God" (KJV, cf. NAB, NEB, NIV), and (2) "Therefore the child to be born will be called holy, the Son of God" (RSV, cf. Moffatt, Phillips). The former translation seems to say, in effect, that Mary's child would be called, or *would be*[57] "Son of God" precisely *because* (*dio kai*) his conception could be traced back to the effective working of the Holy Spirit—"the Holy Spirit will come upon you . . . ; *therefore* [i.e., *for this reason*] also your holy child will be/will be called the Son of God." Such an understanding, however, causes some scholars to raise a caution flag. For in their minds such a translation allows for a Hellenistic interpretation of the text—Jesus is seen thus to be like one of the "divine men," the *theioi andres*, who according to Greek mythology are the result of the sexual intercourse of gods with human women. But such an understanding is alien to the Lucan birth narrative and brings verse 35b into contradiction with what has already been learned about verse 35a (see above, p. 67). Hence, this first translation is rejected by many scholars as misleading.[58]

The second translation still allows for the possibility that what is said in verse 35b is a consequence of verse 35a—that Jesus is to be, or to be called, "Son of God" as the result of the Spirit's creative work upon Mary. But the strict cause and effect relationship of the former translation has been minimized in the latter—"therefore that which will be born will be called holy, The Son of God," because now "Son of God" is a loosely added appositive to *holy*.[59] The question now is, as has been sharpened by these translations, is Jesus the Son of God strictly by virtue of (*dio kai*) the Holy Spirit coming upon a virgin and causing her to conceive, or is something less than this being said? Certainly this much must be conceded by way of a minimal reply—the conjunctions *dio kai* ("therefore also") do bring the two parts of Luke 1:35 together in some way, however slight, and the overshadowing of Mary by the Spirit of God is thereby seen as having set in motion a process by which her child yet to be born can rightly be called "Son of God."

This now raises another question. What does Luke mean when he uses the term, "Son of God"? Does he intend by using it to say no more than that Jesus was to be the Messiah of Israel? Or does he intend to say that Jesus was to be the Son of God in the ultimate sense, that he was to be the incarnation of the preexistent Son, deity incarnate?

For many scholars, "Son of God," like "Son of Man," is simply a recognized designation of the human Messiah, who stands in a relationship to God as his adopted Son.[60] The term is understood by these to be in full accord with the practice of referring to the coming messianic king as God's Son, a practice already seen as present in the Old Testament and in later Judaism (cf. 2 Sam. 7:11–19; Pss. 2:7; 89:26–29; 4QFlor 1.11). According to them, therefore, Luke 1:35 should be interpreted in light of 1:32—Jesus is to be "Son of God" in the sense that he is to be the Messiah, the Davidic king, the heir to the throne of David his father, whose kingdom will last forever.

For other scholars, however, the terms "Son of God" (Luke 1:35) and "Son of the Most High" (Luke 1:32) are to be understood in terms of metaphysical Sonship—Sonship "undoubtedly in its full sense of one begotten of God."[61] Many such scholars are of the opinion that these passages teach the incarnation of the preexistent Son of God, and that even the conjunctions *dio kai* ("therefore also," Luke 1:35) contribute to this understanding of incarnation, hinting, at least, at the idea of the uniting of the two natures, the human and the divine, into one new person. These conjunctions are understood by some to imply both the creative work of the Spirit in producing a perfect human being, on the one hand (*dio*), and also (*kai*) the assumption, the taking, of this humanity to himself by the divine Son, on the other.[62] At this point Professor George Smeaton insists on making a distinction between *being* and *manifestation*. That is to say, the verb used in 1:35b—"will be called" (*klēthēsetai*)—must not be allowed to mean, at this place of all places, that Jesus was *to be* or *to become*[63] the Son of God at his birth, but rather that the one who was eternally "Son" was about to be openly declared, openly manifested, as such to the world.[64] Josef Schmid puts this idea essentially in this way: Not because Jesus was conceived in a miraculous way by his mother without a human father is he the Son of God, but it is quite the other way around—because he is the Son of God (from eternity), his heavenly Father decided upon a miraculous conception and birth for him through the power of the Holy Spirit.[65] "Jesus does not become Son of God by means of his birth from a virgin; he is this already before his incarnation."[66] At the moment of his miraculous conception by the Holy Spirit, however, the eternal Son became a human being; at that time he took to himself genuine humanity.

If scholars are divided over the term, "Son of God," and cannot agree on its meaning, is it not a mark of arrogance to suppose that anyone can say with even a modicum of certainty that he knows what the Gospel writers had in mind when they used it? Certainly it will appear so. Nevertheless, it seems important at least to make an attempt to answer this question—"What did Luke mean when he used the expression, 'Son of God'?"

1. It should be remembered that the idea of a preexistent divine Being becoming human is not at all compatible with the thinking of the modern person. This has been discussed earlier (chapter 1, p. 40, and note 81), and nothing more needs to be said about it here, other than to say that such a world view makes it difficult if not impossible for one to see preexistence or incarnation here in the birth narratives of Matthew and Luke. Expressions referring to Jesus as "Son of God" or "Immanuel" ("God with us") must be explained as mythological statements, or as statements having no metaphysical or ontological meanings whatsoever. They must be explained in other ways—Jesus as Son of God means only that Jesus is the human

Messiah, the Prophet like Moses, the Holy Spirit-inspired person (*der Geistträger*), and so on. Any modern person, on the other hand, whose world view does not demand that the universe be a closed system, and hence, that there can be no possibility of God invading it from outside, of surprising the world as he might wish—that person has a multitude of options open for interpreting this term, "Son of God."

2. Professor Fitzmyer, with the skill and precision that always characterizes his writings, makes it clear that although the terms "Son of God" and "Son of the Most High" (*hypistou*) may indeed have Hellenistic overtones—for example, the title, "The Most High" (*ho hypsistos*), often was used of Greek deities[67]—yet these terms are as much at home in Palestinian Judaism as in the contemporary Hellenistic world of the eastern Mediterranean, if not more so.[68] But—and this is important—Fitzmyer makes it equally clear that the full title, "Son of God," is never found in the Old Testament or other Palestinian texts predicated directly of a future, expected, anointed, Christ-figure.[69] As Hans Conzelmann put it, whom Fitzmyer quotes, the title, "Son of God," just is not "synonymous with Messiah."[70] This studied conclusion, then, can only cast doubt on the statements of those who claim that "Son of God" was a recognized designation of Messiah,[71] and that Luke used it only with this meaning in mind in his narrative of Jesus' birth (Luke 1:35).

3. Admittedly there is no mention of preexistence or incarnation as such in the birth narratives. Admittedly these accounts do not say so in so many words, "This is how the Logos became human, this is how the preexistent Son became a man." But does this necessarily mean that neither Matthew nor Luke had any notion of Jesus' preexistence or any idea of the incarnation when they wrote their Gospels?[72] Only with difficulty can it be put so emphatically. For it is certain that both of these evangelists clearly say that the conception of Jesus was an unusual, even miraculous conception. Both affirm in different ways that as a result of this miraculous event the birth from Mary would bring forth into the world a unique person. Luke, on the one hand, says he will be called, "Son of God" (Luke 1:35). Matthew, on the other hand, echoes this, although in different words. He writes: "This [the miraculous conception of Jesus] took place to fulfil what the Lord had spoken by the prophet: 'Behold, a

virgin shall conceive and bear a son, and his name shall be called Emmanuel' (which means, God with us)" (Matt. 1:22—23). These words, quoted by Matthew, were first spoken to Ahaz, King of Judah, in a time of national crisis (Isa. 7:14). And the birth of the young woman's son at that time was to be a sign to Judah that God was with his people and with the royal line of David to deliver them from their enemy—a sign that was realized in part in Ahaz's day, having its initial fulfilment then. But "whatever may have been the partial fulfilment of the prophecy in the time of Ahaz, [in Matthew's mind] its reference to a different and . . . higher deliverance is undeniable."[73] In his formula for introducing this Old Testament quotation, Matthew uses the verb "to fulfill" (*pleroun*), which can be interpeted to mean that "whatever was foreshadowed in the days of Ahaz by the birth of that Immanuel, *has attained its fullest meaning in this new day* in the birth of this Immanauel." For Matthew, Jesus ("Yahweh helps, Yahweh saves") is by virtue of his conception and birth also Immanuel ("God with us") par excellence.[74] Hence, Matthew and Luke furnish two terms—"Son of God" and "Immanuel"—which at the very least indicate that an extraordinary relationship was to exist between Jesus and the living God. In themselves these terms may not explicitly proclaim the incarnation, but neither do they exclude the possibility that preexistence, and incarnation may have been in the minds of the evangelists as they wrote their accounts of Jesus' birth.

4. When one compares the wording of the highly developed Christology of Paul in his letter to the Romans (1:3–4) with Luke's wording in his Gospel about the birth of Jesus (1:35), it is difficult to conclude that Luke meant something completely different by his use of the term "Son of God" from what Paul meant by his use of that very same term. Notice the verbal parallels between the two texts:

Romans 1:4	*Luke 1:35*
huiou theou (Son of God)	*huios theou* (Son of God)
dynamei (with power)	*dynamis* (power)
pneuma hagiosynēs (Spirit of holiness)	*pneuma hagion* (Holy Spirit)

It would appear that Paul in Romans 1:4 is affirming that the Lord Jesus Christ, who had always been God's Son, was brought by his human birth into a relationship with David as far as his human nature is concerned, and was appointed the glorious Son-of-God-in-Power from the time of his resurrection—a fact attested by the work of the Holy Spirit.[75] If this is so, if here in Romans 1:3–4 Paul is in fact describing the preexistent Son who became the incarnate Son (cf. Rom. 8:3, 32; 9:5), and if the verbal parallels between Luke and Romans are more than mere coincidence, then it is certainly conceivable that Luke, who in all probability composed his Gospel after Paul wrote his letters[76] and in full knowledge of their content and meaning, could indeed have entertained notions of preexistence and incarnation when he thought of and wrote about Mary's child as Son of God.[77]

5. Finally, when the birth narratives are taken together with the Christological statements of other New Testament writers about the person of Jesus, one can with a fair degree of confidence conclude that Matthew and Luke, while not saying explicitly that this is how the eternal Son of God became a man, nevertheless had the incarnation in mind when they wrote their stories. The Fourth Gospel makes no mention of the virginal conception of Jesus, to be sure, yet it clearly affirms the incarnation by saying that "in the beginning was the Word, and the Word was with God, and the Word was God, . . . and the Word became flesh" (John 1:1, 14). Paul, similarly has nothing to say about this miraculous conception, but he also asserts the fact of the incarnation—that the Son of God became a human being. He writes, "When the time had fully come, God sent forth his Son, born of woman, born under the law" (Gal. 4:4; cf. Rom. 1:3–4; 8:3, 15–17, 32; 1 Cor. 15:45, 47; 2 Cor. 5:18–19; Phil. 2:6–11; Col. 1:15–20). As John and Paul, so also Peter (1 Pet. 3:18; 4:1), and the writer of the letter to the Hebrews (1:1–3). All these together, while remaining silent about how the divine became human, nevertheless seem unanimously agreed upon this single important fact that the preexistent Son of God did become human, did become incarnate in Jesus of Nazareth, did become a person born like all other persons—born of a woman. Is it not possible, then, in light of this unified Christian witness, to assume that Matthew and Luke are producing in their birth narratives details about the person

of Jesus which are not touched upon by the other New Testament writers? Is it not possible that they are pressing back to the beginning of things, to the genesis of Jesus? Is it not possible that they are providing the setting for the incarnation, furnishing information about how the eternal Son became a human being, which the other writers either presupposed, or about which they were unaware? (Note that Luke refers to a "birth secret," 2:19, 51.)

If this is correct, then Matthew and Luke are saying at least this much: The Holy Spirit was the energizing factor by which Jesus was conceived within the virgin-womb of Mary; the Holy Spirit was that divine creative element by which the fashioning of Jesus' humanity was begun. From this basic assumption one can go on and take the next step with the writer of Hebrews and say that the body, the humanity that was so carefully and uniquely generated by the Holy Spirit, was the very humanness that the eternal Son made his own and within which he became incarnate—words of the Psalmist placed in the mouth of Jesus: "Sacrifices and offerings thou [O God] hast not desired, but *a body hast thou prepared for me*" (Heb. 10:5). It is in this sense, then, that the words, "The Holy Spirit will come upon you, . . . therefore the child to be born will be called holy, the Son of God" (Luke 1:35), and again, "'Behold, a virgin shall conceive and bear a son, and his name shall be called Emmanuel' (which means, God with us)" (Matt. 1:23) should be understood. Therefore, these words should not be restricted to mean simply that Jesus was only a person inspired by the Spirit of God from his birth as were the prophets and heroes of the Old Testament (cf. Isa. 49:1–5; Jer. 1:5, 7) and no more than this. For this child to be born was to be superior to the prophets, himself "a life-giving spirit" (1 Cor. 15:45). Yet these words are words of mystery transcending one's ability fully to comprehend or express. But they do seem to be saying that the Holy Spirit created the humanity that the Eternal Son made his very own, within which he completely immersed himself. As a result, then, of the creative work of the Holy Spirit in combination with the condescension of the divine Son, the son of Mary is the Son of God! He is Adam's Son and God's![78]

Now to be sure, the narrative form in which the Gospel writers cast these birth stories and the language they use to describe what happened are strange to the modern person. So much so that many people today cannot accept the narratives as historical. Rather, these narratives are considered as the rewriting of the developed Christology of Romans 1:3–4 in story form, theologoumena, *Glaubensaussage*, affirmations of faith but not history.[79] But before finally relegating these accounts to the category of nonhistory, legend, or myth, and thereby running the risk of weakening their theological impact,[80] one will do well to pay heed to the words of Professor Howard Marshall who says the form of a narrative is

> not a crucial factor as regards its historicity. Those who are prepared to accept the possibility of angelic visitations will see no difficulty in a story concerned with such terms. Those who deny the possibility will declare the [stories] to be imaginative. But there is perhaps a third possibility. [In these narratives the writers are] striving to express the ineffable in human terms. It is not surprising if human language breaks down under the strain and recourse must be had to the language of symbolism. The writer has used terms drawn from the biblical tradition to describe a secret mysterious event. It remains possible that this language . . . bears witness to some real event which cannot be described in literal terms and which remains veiled in mystery. Historical and literary investigation can take us thus far and no further.[81]

Jesus will be called "holy." A further consequence of the Holy Spirit overshadowing Mary, so that she might conceive and bear a son, was that her son, Jesus, was to be called "holy" (Luke 1:35). As has been indicated above (see p. 73) the function of the adjective *hagion* ("holy") in the phrase, *to gennōmenon hagion klēthēsetai* (literally, "the being born [one] holy will be called"), is not easily determined. One needs only to examine the translations and to observe how they differ among themselves in order to understand this. For some of these the adjective *hagion* ("holy") is understood as a substantive, a noun, and is made to function as the subject of the verb *klēthēsetai* ("will be called")—"the holy [thing] to be born will be called the Son of God" (cf. KJV). Taken in this way, Luke 1:35 does not assert that Jesus will be or will be called "holy" as a result of the Holy Spirit's coming upon Mary.

But as C. F. D. Moule points out, to take the adjective, *hagion*, in this way, as a substantive in the phrase, *to gennōmenon hagion*, is a distinctly irregular grammatical usage of it.[82] Furthermore, it should be noted that very often (although not always) the thing that is to be called or named is placed before the verb "to call" or "to name" in Greek, while after it in English. Compare the following examples: *prophētēs hypsistou klēthēsē*, "you will be called prophet of the Most High" (Luke 1:76); *hagion tō kyriō klēthēsetai*, "he will be called holy to the Lord" (Luke 2:23); *Nazoraios klēthēsetai*, "he will be called a Nazarene" (Matt. 2:23); *huioi theou klēthēsontai*, "they will be called sons of God" (Matt. 5:9); *elachistos klēthēsetai*, "he will be called least" (Matt. 5:19); *megas klēthēsetai*, "he will be called great" (Matt. 5:19). When these two factors are taken together—Professor Moule's remark about the usage of *hagion* (above), and the New Testament's penchant for putting the appellative before the verb, as *hagion* is before *klēthēsetai* here in Luke 1:35—they combine to favor the translation which indicates that the quality of *hagion* ("holy") is to be attached to Jesus precisely because his conception and birth was to be the result of the creative activity of the Holy Spirit—"The Holy Spirit will come upon you [Mary], and the power of the Most High will overshadow you; therefore also that which will be born will be called holy." Jesus, then, was to be or to be called "holy" because he was to be conceived by the Holy Spirit.

But what did Luke mean when he wrote that Jesus would be holy? The Greek word, *hagios* ("holy"), which he used here in Luke 1:35, has as its fundamental ideas "separation from" and/or "dedication to." It is a religious word, a cultic word, which implies that any person or thing designated as holy is set apart from the profane, removed from the arena of the mundane, consecrated for service to God.[83] Surely Luke had something of these ideas in mind when he thought of the adjective *holy* in reference to Jesus. This is suggested in two ways: (1) When Luke composed his account of Jesus' birth and its consequences, he seemingly purposefully chose to cast it in phrases very like those used with reference to the birth of Samson, one of the chief Old Testament heroes whose life had been dedicated to God. Samson's mother was given these words by the angel of the Lord—they have a familiar ring to them: "Behold you will conceive and will bear a son. . . . Your child will be God's holy one" (*hagion theou estai to paidarion*, Judg. 13:7 LXX). (2) When Luke recorded the purification rites for Mary after the birth of Jesus, he makes it clear that this was in keeping with the Law of Moses, which required that Jesus, like every male child opening the womb for the first time, should be called holy to the Lord, that is to say, consecrated to the Lord, should become the special property of God (Luke 2:23; cf. Exod. 13:2, 12, 15; Num. 18:15–17). "Jesus is holy, therefore, because he was formed (*gebildet wurde*) in his mother's womb by the Holy Spirit. The Holy Spirit made (*gemacht*) him 'holy'"[84] in the sense that the Holy Spirit singled him out and set him apart for a unique ministry for God.

Luke may very well have had in mind a still more profound idea when he thought of and wrote about Jesus as holy. It should be noted that *hagios* ("holy"), as an adjective or substantive, is rarely used of Jesus in the New Testament. But when it is used of him (Mark 1:24/Luke 4:34; John 6:69; Acts 3:14; 4:27, 30; 1 John 2:20; Rev. 3:7, cf. John 10:36), it is used with unusual significance. He is thus viewed as "the Holy One of God" (*ho hagios tou theou*) who stands in opposition to and in authority over unclean spirits (Mark 1:24), and who also deserves and receives the loyalty of people of faith (John 6:69). He is also "the Holy One" (*ho hagios*—the adjective as a substantive now being used absolutely, cf. Isa. 57:15) who bestows an anointing on his people and who gives encouragement to them along with extraordinary promises on which he is able to make good (1 John 2:20; Rev. 3:7). All of this hints at the possibility that in the minds of the writers of the New Testament there was a definite connection between the epithet *holy* as applied to Jesus and his divine origin.[85] Hence, it is possible that Luke, too, in using *hagios* ("holy") of Jesus here in Luke 1:35, included this same idea within the scope of his understanding and within the range of meanings he wished to convey to his readers. That is to say, Luke may have understood that because of the creative work of the Holy Spirit in the conception of Jesus, Jesus was to be holy in the sense that he was to be divine (cf. Pss. 89:5, 7; 111:9). Note that this description of Jesus as holy immediately "culminates in the phrase *huios theou* ['Son of God'], here undoubtedly in its full sense of one begotten by God."[86]

Luke may also have thought of Jesus as holy in the sense that Jesus was himself the bearer of the Holy Spirit (*der Geistträger*). This possibility arises from noticing an extraordinary event that Luke records later in his Gospel. There a man who had an unclean demon (Luke 4:34), or who was held in the grip of an unclean spirit, as Mark's Gospel puts it (1:24), cries out in a loud voice to Jesus: "I know who you are, the Holy One [*ho hagios*] of God." Jesus then confronts the unclean spirit and orders it to be silent and to come out of the man, which it immediately does. This gripping drama powerfully suggests that "there is [here] a mortal antithesis between *pneuma hagion* ['the Holy Spirit'] and *pneuma akatharton* ['the unclean spirit'] which the demons [were able to] recognize."[87] Surely it is so, as will become more clear later on, that Jesus was indeed holy in the sense that he was the bearer of the Holy Spirit, *the* person who, because of his birth by the Spirit, was of all persons the one most fitted to carry the life-creating Spirit into the arena of death to do battle with the destructive forces of evil and death.

The word *hagios* ("holy") has a different meaning still from those suggested above. In usage it quickly shades over into the meaning of "pure" or "clean" in a moral sense—"undefiled," "uncorrupted." Luke might well have had this meaning also in mind as he wrote that Jesus would be holy (Luke 1:35). If so, then Luke would be saying, as Plummer has suggested, that Jesus, as a result of his unique conception, was to be born "free from all taint of sin."[88] This, of course, is not something that can be proved completely by exegesis—only in part. But it may be inferred from (1) the meaning of *hagios* ("holy"); (2) the uniqueness of Jesus' birth—of no one else is it said that his conception was by the Holy Spirit without the aid of a human father; such a statement certainly tends to limit the possible ideas included in the word *holy;* (3) the unified testimony of the New Testament to the character of Jesus, that he was without sin (see chapter 1, pp. 36–37); and (4) the understanding that like begets like (cf. John 3:36)—that is to say, whatever has its origin totally within the natural course of human existence must totally bear the stamp of that existence, including all of the sinfulness that marks it, and all of the weakness and inability to change the situation that characterizes it. There must of necessity be something/someone from outside to break this cycle of sin and death. There must be a new beginning, a new creation. According to this explanation of what it means for Jesus to be holy, that is to be born without the taint of sin, he is as a consequence precisely that—a fresh start for the human race.

Luke, however, does not locate this new beginning in the virgin birth as such, that is, in the fact that no human father was involved in Jesus' conception, as though sin, or the bent toward sinning, could only be passed on to the next generation through the male.[89] Rather Luke locates it in the activity of the Holy Spirit. What is at stake here, as Otto Weber puts it, "is God's new creation."[90] Hence, in spreading his shadow over Mary, in enabling her to conceive without any male counterpart, God the Holy Spirit, regenerator par excellence,[91] provided the human race with a new beginning, gave it a fresh start, a start free of sin and the crippling effects of sin.

But does this interpretation, then, rob Jesus of real humanity? Does it make him so completely different from all other persons that he can no longer be thought of as a real person?[92] The answer to this question is no. One can say that this interpretation effectively denies the genuine humanity of Jesus only if that person is first prepared to say that to be human one must sin, or that sinning is the supreme qualification for being human.[93] Adam, coming fresh from the creative hand of God, was fully human even though at that precise moment he was without sin. He was indeed different from all his descendents at that stage of his existence, but not so different as to make it impossible for him even then to be considered a member of the human race, a true human person. Just so with Jesus. If in fact the creative work of the Holy Spirit at his conception and birth had the effect of bringing into being one who was holy (i.e., spotless, pure, unstained by the sin of generations reaching back to Adam's fall), this does not automatically put him outside the stream of genuine humanity on the one hand, nor on the other hand does it make him holy to such a degree that it automatically puts him beyond the possibility of sinning.

One might say that the Spirit's work at the point of Jesus' conception was to provide him with a human nature that was *initially* unstained by sin—not with one that was henceforth and forever impregnable to sin. Sinlessness, it must be remembered, is a fact of volition, not of nature. Thus, when Jesus was born, he began life with a genuine humanity, but with a humanity that was comparable to that of Adam's before the fall[94]—free from sin but also susceptible to sin. By having been made holy by the Spirit, therefore, Jesus was placed in a position whereby he could fulfill the goal God originally had in mind for all people, that of perfectly obeying God's good and perfect will, should he *choose* to do so. The miraculous conception by the Spirit simply exempted Jesus from the fundamental obstacle of original sin, which is stamped upon all who are born naturally and which prevents them from ever perfectly obeying God. Jesus was holy, but not perfected in holiness. The former was the result of the creative work of the Spirit. The latter was something that only Jesus himself could achieve by the choices he made throughout his life (cf. John 8:29; Mark 14:36/Matt. 26:39/Luke 22:42). He "had to exert at every instant His own free will and devote Himself continually to the service of good and the fulfillment of the tasks assigned to him" in order to advance from the stage of innocence to that of perfect holiness.[95]

Thus, when the writer of Hebrews speaks of Jesus as "having been made perfect" (cf. Heb. 2:10, passim), it is not enough simply to say, as some scholars do, that he was "brought to a certain 'completeness' associated with God's plan" for his life, or that he accomplished and fulfilled "God's purposes for him"[96]—all of which is true. But there must also be seen here in these words, "having been made perfect," the moral and ethical perfection of Jesus as well as the merely functional.[97] This is to say, Jesus won not only for himself, but for all, perfection in holiness by the steady, unswerving, undeviating set of his own will always to do the will of God. And this he did as the whole of the New Testament bears witness (cf. John 8:46; 2 Cor. 5:21; Heb. 4:15; 7:26; 1 Pet. 1:19; 2:22; 1 John 3:5).

In summary, the Holy Spirit's work was to produce a perfect humanity for the eternal Son of God to assume. As a result this humanity was holy. No taint of sin adhered to it. No guilt initially stained it. But it was not holy in the sense that it was incapable of sinning. The New Testament teaches emphatically that Jesus *did not* sin, but nowhere does it say that he was incapable of doing so.

Jesus will be the creation of a new humanity. "The Holy Spirit will come upon you [Mary] and the power of the Most High will overshadow you; therefore the child to be born will be called holy, the Son of God" (Luke 1:35). From these words it is possible to infer still another consequence of the Spirit's work within Mary. It has been alluded to already but bears repeating with some expansion: Jesus' conception by the Holy Spirit was in effect the creation of a new humanity. A radically original event happened when Jesus was conceived and was born. Of no one else has it ever been said that his conception and birth was of the Holy Spirit without the aid of a human father. Just as the Spirit of God in the very beginning hovered over the primal waters and brought order out of chaos, cosmos out of waste and desolation (Gen. 1:2; Ps. 33:6), so the Holy Spirit in the fulness of time (Gal. 4:4) overshadowed the virgin Mary and brought forth a fresh order of humanity in the person of Jesus. Jesus "was a new departure in human life."[98] His birth by the Spirit was that which made him, in the words of Paul, the Last Adam (1 Cor. 15:45), the new Person, the head of a new race.

This inference, drawn from the angel's words in Luke 1:35, is corroborated by numerous statements to be found in other parts of the New Testament that associate the idea of a new beginning for people with Jesus. For example, "if any one is in Christ, that person is a *new creation*; the old has passed away, behold, the new has come" (2 Cor. 5:17). Or, "circumcision is nothing, nor is uncircumcision, but *a new creation*" (Gal. 6:15). Or, "[Jesus] is the first-born from the dead . . . [He] is the prime source, the beginning, of the creation of God" (Rev. 1:5; 3:14), and so on (cf. Col. 1:15–16, 18; Tit. 2:14). All of these statements in different ways "bear witness to a conviction that with Jesus a new humanity had begun."[99]

And yet it must always be kept in mind that the humanness of Jesus was a product of generation, gestation, and birth. Thus he is indissolubly linked with the old creation. The work of the Holy Spirit in fashioning the humanity of Jesus did not break this tie. God was faithful to his promises to David and to Israel by having Jesus, the Christ, the Messiah, born into a Jewish family (cf. John 4:22), whose ancestral line could be traced back to the Davidic monarchy. And God was gracious to humanity in general, for although the Holy Spirit did create Jesus as the prime source of a new humanity, he did this in such a way as not to destroy the connection that united him with the old. Just as God did not create the first Adam *ex nihilo* but chose to form him from the dust of the ground, from the earth he was subsequently to inhabit and over which he was to rule, so the Spirit of God did not create the Last Adam, Jesus, out of nothing but shaped him from the substance of a human mother. He thus maintained the organic connection between the two humanities.

That Jesus was fully and truly human, that he belonged inseparably to the human race is a matter that cannot be stressed too emphatically. "His life lacked nothing which formed part of human historical existence."[100] He had a physical body (cf. Heb. 2:14) and a rational soul (cf. Luke 2:52; Mark 2:8; 14:36), the essentials of humanity, fashioned for him by the Spirit from a woman. He was, therefore, a genuine human being among other human beings, having like them a complete capacity for experiencing fully all the ups and downs of human existence. And yet he was different. He was both one with the human race and paradoxically different from it. And this difference, of course, is the crucial factor. The ancient humanity, caught in the endless cycle of sin and death, could only perpetuate itself in sin and death. It was incapable of ever extricating itself by itself from this fatal cycle. "That which is born of the flesh is flesh" (John 3:6) certainly rang true! Yet from this very flesh, creatively worked upon by the Holy Spirit, came forth Jesus, holy, blameless, unstained by sin (cf. Heb. 7:26), a new departure in human existence, the new humanity, the new Man, "as human as the old, but not sinful like the old."[101] Hence, linked so closely with the old humanity, yet so very different from it, he was able to break its cycle of sin and death, to halt its plunge to destruction and to renew it as he is new.

This idea (cf. Rom. 5:12–19; 1 Cor. 15:21–22, 45) was taken and developed and marvelously expressed centuries ago in Irenaeus's doctrine of recapitulation (*anakephalaiōsis*), the summing up or restoration of fallen humanity to communion with God through the obedience of Jesus, the Son of God incarnate. In other words, the fully divine Son of God became fully human in order to gather up all humanity into himself, rehabilitate it, restore it, so that what was lost through the disobedience of the first Adam might be restored through the obedience of the Second Adam. Jesus Christ comprehended, embraced, summed up in himself the whole of humanity in order that he might undo for everyone the damage done by Adam's sin and their own. The human race was given a new start in Jesus.

One part of Irenaeus's work is worth quoting extensively (while keeping in mind that his word *recapitulate* really means "a summing up," "a gathering up into"):

> For as by one man's disobedience sin entered and death obtained [a place] through sin; so also by the obedience of one man, righteousness having been introduced, shall cause life to fructify in those persons who in times past were dead. And as the protoplast himself, Adam, had his substance from untilled and as yet virgin soil ("for God had not yet sent rain, and man had not tilled the ground"), and was formed by the hand of God, that is by the Word of God, for "all things were made by Him," and the Lord took dust from the earth and formed man; so did He who is the Word, recapitulating Adam in Himself, rightly receive a birth, enabling Him to gather up Adam [into Himself], from Mary, who was as yet a virgin. If, then, the first Adam had a man for his father and was born of human seed, it were reasonable to say that the second Adam was begotten of Joseph. But if the former was taken from the dust, and God was his maker, it was incumbent that the latter also, making a recapitulation in Himself, should be formed as man by God, to have an analogy with the former as respects His origin. Why, then, did not God again take dust, but wrought so that the formation should be made of Mary? It was in order that there might not be another formation called into being, nor any other which should [require to] be saved, but that the very same formation should be summed up [in Christ as had existed in Adam], the analogy having been preserved.[102]

Irenaeus asks, in effect, why God did not scrap the old sinful humanity and start over again by taking a new lump of clay and making a new Adam independent of the other. His answer, though somewhat difficult to follow for the Greek is unclear, is that it was God's gracious purpose to allow a human being to undo the moral tangle created by a human being, to produce a Person from within the human race who would be able to save the human race and give it a new start. It was God's gracious purpose in making a new humanity that that humanity should be the old humanity renewed, and that the catalyst for this renewal should be Jesus of Nazareth, son of Mary, Son of Man, but conceived of the Holy Spirit and therefore holy, spotless, unentangled in the web of sin, the Son of God, the Savior of Mankind.

Jesus will be full of the Holy Spirit from his birth. The promise of the angel to Mary was that because of the work of the Holy Spirit within her, she, while yet unmarried and without having had sexual intercourse with any man, would be enabled to conceive and give birth to a Son. As a consequence of this special creative work of the Spirit, her child, Jesus, would be called holy, the Son of God (Luke 1:35). These two things—that Jesus would be holy, that Jesus would be the Son of God—are the only things clearly stated as being the results of Jesus' virginal conception by the Holy Spirit. And yet it seems possible to infer from this unique event with its extraordinary consequences still additional consequences not specifically mentioned by name. One of these, as argued for above, was that Jesus was to be the creation of a new humanity, a new departure in human existence. Another is that Jesus was to be filled with the Spirit from his conception.

This, of course, is not stated in precisely this way in either of the birth narratives, and it is something Luke calls specific attention to at a later period in Jesus' life (Luke 4:1). Nevertheless, it is said of Jesus' forerunner, John the Baptist, that *he* would be filled with the Holy Spirit while still in his mother's womb (Luke 1:15, *eti ek koilias mētros autou*, cf. Luke 1:41, see Judg. 13:3–5; 16:17; Isa. 44:2). Apparently from the beginning of John's existence (*Dasein*),[103] he was to possess the gift of God's prophetic presence, to be stimulated not by wine but by the supernatural stimulation of the Holy Spirit, to be prepared by inspiration for a work that could not be effected apart from this divine equipping. "Thus in the strongest possible way the divine choice of John for his crucial task is stressed."[104]

If this can be said of the herald of Jesus, is it not reasonable to suppose that it can also be said of Jesus? If it can be said of the lesser figure, can it not also be said of the greater? Luke does not put this idea into just these words, but it does appear probable, although not completely certain, that he wants his readers to understand that this is the way things were. As a result of what he said about the birth of John the Baptist and about the unique activity of the Holy Spirit at the birth of Jesus,

Luke seems to be suggesting that Jesus, too, was to be just as much an object of divine choice and care as John, just as completely prepared for his special mission in life as John, and, therefore, just as full of the Holy Spirit as John—and all this from the very moment of his conception.[105] Jesus, it appears, was to be full of the Holy Spirit from his mother's womb, because the Holy Spirit was to come upon her and the power of the Most High was to overshadow her. Thus from the very beginning of Jesus' existence and onward he was to be endowed by the Spirit with those gifts of the Spirit that would be necessary for his exercise of love, trust, and holy affection (cf. Ps. 22:10). And as Jesus was to grow and develop, just so these gifts of the Spirit would be expanding to meet his ever increasing needs.[106]

NOTES

1. Davies, *Paul and Rabbinic Judaism*, 208–15; StrB. 1.127; 2.133; but see Windisch, "Jesus und der Geist," 228–29. In sectarian Judaism it was not true that the Spirit had ceased to work as the writings of the Dead Sea community testify, e.g. 1QH 7.6, 7; 14.12b, 13; 17.26; 1QS 3.6–8; 4.2–8, passim, CD 2.11–13. See also D. E. Aune, *Prophecy in Early Christianity and the Ancient Mediterranean World* (Grand Rapids, 1983), 103–106.

2. Cf. E. Schweizer, *TDNT*, 6.404–15; H. von Baer, *Der Heilige Geist in den Lukanschriften* (Stuttgart, 1926).

3. But cf. R. J. Cooke, *Did Paul Know the Virgin Birth* (New York, 1926).

4. R. E. Brown, *The Gospel According to John*, AB 29 (Garden City, NY, 1966), lxxxvi; but see J. A. T. Robinson, *Redating the New Testament* (London, 1976), 254–311; idem, *The Priority of John* (London, 1985).

5. This in spite of the translation of the Jerusalem Bible, 1966 edition, of John 1:13—"[he gave power to become children of God to all who believe in the name of him] who was born not out of human stock or urge of the flesh, or will of man but of God himself." This translation was based on extremely weak textual evidence and has subsequently been corrected in the 1985 edition of the Jerusalem Bible.

6. Brunner, *Christian Doctrine of Creation and Redemption*, 2.351.

7. R. H. Gundry, *Matthew* (Grand Rapids, 1982), 20.

8. But see U. Luz, *Das Evangelium Matthäus* (Zürich, 1985), 1.103, who notes the possibility that Joseph may in reality have known how Mary had become pregnant, and for this reason could not bring himself to consummate the marriage, lest he touch her who had been made so holy by God, lest he take to himself her who belonged so

uniquely to God. The angel's command to Joseph not to fear (Matt. 1:20) is thought to point in this direction. The difficulty with this appealing interpretation, however, lies in the words of the angel about the nature of Mary's pregnancy (v. 20). The angel's words do not seem intended to confirm what Joseph already knew and to overcome his objections. Rather they seem intended to inform him of what had happened, to let him in on that of which he knew nothing.

9. According to Deut. 22:23–24, stoning to death was the ancient penalty for adultery. But apparently such severe punishment for this offense was no longer practiced at this time. See StrB 1.51, 52; Mishnah Sotah 1.5; cf. Deut. 24:1–4.

10. A less strict judicial way of handling the matter of adultery existed in New Testament times whereby divorce could be effected privately in front of two witnesses. See D. Hill, "A Note on Matthew 1.19," *ExpT* 76 (1965), 133–34.

11. R. V. G. Tasker, *Matthew*, TNTC (London, 1961), 35.

12. H. Alford, *The Greek Testament* (Boston, 1878), 1.440.

13. Luz, *Matthew*, 104.

14. cf. Mishnah, Baba Bathra 8.6.

15. On whether or not this verse can be used as an argument for or against the traditon of the perpetual virginity of Mary, see the commentaries; see also Fitzmyer, *Christological Catechism*.

16. See M. Noth, *Die israelitischen Personnamen*, BWANT 3/10 (Stuttgart, 1978), 106–107.

17. Gundry, *Matthew*, 24; see also W. C. van Unnik, "Dominus Vobiscum: The Background of a Liturgical Formula," in *New Testament Essays*, ed. A. J. B. Higgins (Manchester, 1959), 270–305.

18. See Fitzmyer, *Gospel According to Luke, I–IX*, 313–16; R. E. Brown, *The Birth of the Messiah, A Commentary on the Infancy Narratives of Matthew and Luke* (Garden City, NY, 1977), 294–97; cf. also W. Wink, *John the Baptist in Gospel Tradition* (Cambridge, 1968), 60, fn. 1; P. Benoit, *Exégèse et Théologie* (Paris, 1968), 3.193–96.

19. C. Burger, *Jesus als Davidssohn* (Göttingen, 1970), 132–35. Others see Luke 1:34–35 as an interpolation introducing the virgin birth motif into an older story. See Bultmann, *History of the Synoptic Tradition*, 295–96; H. K. Luce, *The Gospel According to St. Luke* (Cambridge, 1933); V. Taylor, *Behind the Third Gospel* (Oxford, 1926). But see in contrast, J. G. Machen, *The Virgin Birth of Christ* (London, 1932), 119–68; I. H. Marshall, *The Gospel of Luke* (Grand Rapids, 1978), 62–63.

20. Fitzmyer, *The Gospel According to Luke, I–IX*, 328; but see Brown, *The Birth of the Messiah*, 262, for a different meaning for this name.

21. The fact that the mother was to confer the name is for some an additional indication that the child would have no human father. See H. Schürmann, *Das Lukasevangelium* (Freiburg, 1969), 1.46–47. This is not an especially strong argument in light of the fact that Joseph names the boy in Matthew (1:25), and in light of the fact that the angel of the Lord told Hagar that she was going to bear a son and that she was to name him Ishmael (Gen. 16:11).

22. See for example, D. Hill, *The Gospel of Matthew*, NCBC (London, 1972), 76–77.

23. See especially the detailed study by Brown, *The Birth of the Messiah*, and the bibliograpahy there; Machen, *The Virgin Birth of Christ*; Schürmann, *Das Lukasevangelium*, loc. cit., who traces Luke's account to an intimate family tradition. See also the bibliography listed in BAGD at *parthenos*.

24. This in spite of the fact that some of the early church fathers believed that Mary was of "the seed of David" (cf. Ign. Eph. 18.2; Justin, Dial. 43), perhaps because they wrongly construed the phrase "of the house of David" with *virgin* and not with *Joseph* (Luke 1:27). From Luke 1:5, 36, one may infer that Mary, related as she was to Elizabeth, sprang from the tribe of Levi and was of Aaronic lineage instead of Davidic (cf. G. Maier, *Matthäus Evangelium* [Stuttgart, 1979], 1.23).

25. Those translations that render Matt. 1:20 (cf. 1:26), "Do not fear to take Mary your wife [*Mirian tēn gynaika sou*]," rather than, "as your wife," are thoroughly justified in doing so.

26. Fitzmyer, *The Gospel According to Luke, I–IX*, 343–44; StrB 1.45–47; 2.293, 373–75, 393–98; Mishnah, Ketuboth, 4.4–5; J. Jeremias, *Jerusalem in the Time of Jesus* (London, 1969), 364–67.

27. Maier, *Matthäus-Evangelium*, 1.23; Luz, *Das Evangelium nach Matthäus*, 103.

28. Cf. G. Delling, *TDNT*, 5.834–37; see also 826–37; BAGD, 627.

29. Fitzmyer, *The Gospel According to Luke, I–IX*, 307.

30. For a full discussion of the various answers offered to explain the meaning of Mary's question, see J. M. Creed, *The Gospel According to St. Luke* (London, 1930), 19–20; Fitzmyer, *The Gospel According to Luke, I–IX*, 348–50; Marshall, *The Gospel of Luke*, 69–70.

31. The perplexity of Mary (v. 34) and the idea of a conception without a human father (v. 35) presents difficulties for many. To eliminate these difficulties some critics (e.g. Streeter, Harnack, Bultmann) have argued that Luke 1:34–35 is an interpolation into the text: *b* omits the words, "How can this be, since I know not a man," and transfers the answer of Mary, "Behold the handmaid of the Lord" (v. 38) to this place. It is contended that this reflects an earlier form of the text in which the conception by Mary as a virgin was not implied. Creed, *The Gospel According to St. Luke*, 13–14, answers these critics: (1) the unsupported testimony of *b* is not strong textual evidence; besides the crucial verse—v. 35—stands in *b* as in all other mss and versions; (2) the opening salutation would be impoverished if the succeeding narrative did not foretell Mary's special role in the drama; (3) Mary's concluding words (v. 38) would be weakened to banality—they have no special point if the annunciation were confined only to the destiny of Mary's son; and (4) the narrative as a whole coheres with vv. 34–35 and is maimed by their exclusion.

32. See O. Bardenhewer, *Mariä Verkundigung: Ein Kommentar zu Lukas 1:26–38* (Freiburg, 1910).

33. Fitzmyer, *The Gospel According to Luke, I–IX*, 350–51.

34. G. Bertram, *TDNT*, 8.617.

35. BDF, 255, 257.

36. F. W. Gesenius, *Hebrew Grammar*, ed. E. Kautzsch, A. E. Cowley (Oxford, 1910), 126u.

37. E. Schweizer, *The Good News According to Luke* (Atlanta, 1984), 30.

38. See Barrett, *The Holy Spirit and Gospel Tradition*, 20–24, and Schweizer, *The Good News According to Luke*, 29; see also StrB. 1.48.

39. E. E. Ellis, *The Gospel of Luke*, NCBC (London, 1966), 71–72; cf. M. Dibelius, *Botschaft und Geschichte* (Tübingen, 1953), 28–29; see also E. E. Ellis, "Life," *New Bible Dictionary*, ed. J. D. Douglas (Grand Rapids, 1962), 736.

40. J. Ernst, *Das Evangelium nach Lukas* (Regensburg, 1976), 73; J. Schmid, *Das Evangelium nach Lukas* (Regensburg, 1960), 43.

41. J. Schneider, *TDNT*, 2.681; see also G. Schneider, *Das Evangelium nach Lukas* (Gütersloh, 1977), 53: "Er verdank seine Existenz diesem Gottesgeist."

42. H. W. Robinson, *The Christian Experience of the Holy Spirit* (London, 1947), 128–29; Knox, *Humanity and Divinity of Christ*, 107–108.

43. D. Nineham, *The Use and Abuse of the Bible* (London, 1976), 151–52.

44. Robinson, *The Human Face of God*, 141–42, quoting from R. H. Charles, *The Apocrypha and Pseudepigrapha of the Old Testament* (Oxford, 1913), 1.545.

45. Robinson, *The Human Face of God*, 162 and 50.

46. Ibid., 59–62.

47. Schweizer, *The Holy Spirit*, 54–55.

48. BAGD, 234–35.

49. Cf. Gundry, *Matthew*, 21.

50. For the Greek text of Test. Sim. see R. Sinker, *The Testaments of the XII Patriarchs* (Cambridge, 1869), 134; see BAGD, 155, for additional references for this phenomenon.

51. Cf. Fitzmyer, *The Gospel According to Luke I–IX*, 351.

52. G. Voss, *Die Christologie der Lukanischen Schriften in Grundzügen* (Paris, 1965), 73–76, cautions against being too certain that the verb *episkiazein* has the same connotation here in Luke 1:35 as it does in Exod. 40:35; cf. D. Daube, *The New Testament and Rabbinic Judaism* (London, 1956), 27–36.

53. S. Schulz, *TDNT*, 7.399–400.

54. Ernst, *Das Evangelium nach Lukas*, 73.

55. C. A. Briggs, *The Messiah of the Gospels* (Edinburgh, 1899), 49.

56. Ibid; see also Fitzmyer, *The Gospel According to Luke I–IX*, 351.

57. BAGD, 399, makes the point that often "the emphasis [in the verb, *kalein*, 'to call'] is to be placed less on the fact that the name is such and such, than on the fact that the bearer of the name actually is what the name says about him. The pass., *be named*, thus approaches closely the meaning *to be*."

58. Cf. Schmid, *Das Evangelium nach Lukas*, 43–44.

59. Cf. Ernst, *Das Evangelium nach Lukas*, 73.

60. See A. Plummer, *The Gospel According to Luke*, ICC (Edinburgh, 1901), 25; Schürmann, *Das Lukasevangelium*, 54–55; cf. Schweizer, *Good News According to Luke*, 28–29.

61. Marshall, *The Gospel of Luke*, 67, 71; Schmid, *Das Evangelium nach Lukas*, 44; Ellis, *The Gospel of Luke*, 72.

62. See G. Smeaton, *The Doctrine of the Holy Spirit* (Edinburgh, 1889), 129–30.

63. Against BAGD as quoted in note 57 above.

64. Smeaton, *The Doctrine of the Holy Spirit*, 129–30; N. Geldenhuys, *Commentary on the Gospel of Luke* (London, 1950), 77.

65. Schmid, *Das Evangelium nach Lukas*, 49.

66. Ibid., 44; see also Ernst, *Das Evangelium nach Lukas*, 73.

67. Cf. F. Hauck, *Das Evangelium des Lukas* (Leipzig, 1934), 24; Schürmann, *Das Lukasevangelium*, 1.48, fn. 57; Bultmann, *Theology of the New Testament*, 1.50.

68. Cf. Esther 16:16 LXX; Ps. 82:6 (81:6); Dan. 3:93 LXX; Sir. 4:10; see J. A. Fitzmyer, "The Contribution of Qumran Aramaic to the Study of the New Testament," *NTS* 20 (1973–74) 393–94.

69. Fitzmyer, *The Gospel According to Luke I–IX*, 206–207; idem, *NTS* 20, 393–94.

70. H. Conzelmann, *An Outline of the Theology of Luke* (New York, 1969), 76; Fitzmyer, *The Gospel According to Luke I–IX*, 206.

71. Plummer, *The Gospel According to Luke*, 25.

72. See Creed, *The Gospel According to St. Luke*, 19; Brunner, *Christian Doctrine*, 2.352.

73. Alford, *The Greek Testament*, 1.8.

74. See Luz, *Das Evangelium nach Matthäus*, 105; Gundry, *Matthew*, 25.

75. C. E. B. Cranfield, *Romans, a Shorter Commentary* (Edinburgh, 1985), 7; see also his longer work, *The Epistle to the Romans*, ICC (Edinburgh, 1975), 1.61–65.

76. Fitzmyer, *The Gospel According to Luke I–IX*, 57, dates Luke ca. A.D. 80–85.

77. Cf. Ernst, *Das Evangelium nach Lukas*, 73.

78. In commenting on Heb. 2:11 Moffatt writes: "It is implied, though the writer does not explain the matter further, that Christ's common tie with mankind goes back to the pre-incarnate period; there was a close bond between them, even before he was born into the world; indeed incarnation was the consequence of this solidarity or vital tie (*ex henos*. . .)." J. Moffatt, *A Critical and Exegetical Commentary on the Epistle to the Hebrews* (Edinburgh, 1924), 32.

79. See especially, Brown, *Birth of the Messiah*, 29–32, 134–37, 140–42, 181–83; Fitzmyer, *A Christological Catechism*, 69; but see in contrast to these, Machen, *The Virgin Birth of Christ*; M. M. B. Turner, "Jesus and the Spirit in Lucan Perspective," *TynB* 32 (1981), 3–42.

80. See Barth, *Church Dogmatics*, 1.2.172–202, for the theological necessity of these accounts, especially that of the virginal conception.

81. Marshall, *The Gospel of Luke*, 76. Jean Telemond, the suspect Jesuit scholar, in Morris West's novel, *The Shoes of the Fisherman* (New York, 1963), made a similar comment to that expressed here when he addressed a potentially hostile audience and asked a favor of them: "When you come to record the journey, the new contours, the new plants, the strangeness and the mystery, you find often that your vocabulary is inadequate. Inevitably your narrative will fall short of reality. If you

find this defect in my record, then I beg you to tolerate it and let it not discourage you from contemplation of strange landscapes, which, nevertheless, bear the imprint of the creative finger of God" (p.169).

82. C. F. D. Moule, *An Idiom Book of New Testament Greek* (Cambridge, 1953), 107.

83. BAGD, 9; O. Procksh, *TDNT*, 1.89–91; cf. A. Schlatter, *Erläuterungen zum Neuen Testament*, 3 vols. (Stuttgart, 1928), 1.166, who writes, "That thing is holy, which belongs to God."

84. Schürmann, *Das Lukasevangelium*, 54.

85. A. R. C. Leaney, *A Commentary on the Gospel According to St. Luke* (Edinburgh, 1958), 84.

86. Marshall, *The Gospel of Luke*, 71.

87. Procksch, *TDNT*, 1.101–102.

88. Plummer, *The Gospel According to Luke*, 25.

89. One should not overlook the fact that it is said of Jesus not only that he was formed *in* (*en*) Mary (Luke 1:31) as though she were merely a channel through which he came into this world, but that he was formed *from* (*ek*) her as well (Matt. 1:16).

90. O. Weber, *Foundations of Dogmatics* (Grand Rapids, 1983), 102.

91. The creative, life-imparting activity is often referred to in both the Old Testament and the New Testament. For example, Gen. 1:2; 2:7; Job 27:3; 32:8; 33:4; Pss. 33:6; 104:29–30; 147:18; Isa. 44:3–4; Ezek. 37:1–14; Wis. 7:22–27; John 3:5–6; 6:63; Rom. 1:4; 8:11, 14.

92. This is the view of K. Barth: "There must be no weakening or obscuring of the saving truth that the nature which God assumed in Christ is identical with our nature as we see it in light of the Fall. If it were otherwise, how could Christ be really like us?" (*Church Dogmatics*, 1.2,153).

93. But even those who believe that the humanity which Jesus assumed was fallen humanity are not prepared to say that Jesus sinned. In fact they oppose any suggestion that Jesus, as a human person, ever sinned. See Barth, *Church Dogmatics*, 1.2,152; Cranfield, *The Epistle to the Romans*, 1.380–81.

94. This is the traditional view, e.g., that of Ambrosiaster, *PL*, 17, cols. 117–18; Chrysostom PG, 60, cols. 514–15; Cyril of Alexandria, PG, 74, cols. 817, 820; Aquinas, in *Super epistolas S. Pauli lectura*, ed. R. Cai (Turin, 1953), 1.111; J. Calvin, *The Epistles of Paul the Apostle to the Romans and to the Thessalonians* (Edinburgh, 1961), 159; J. A. Bengel, *Gnomon Novi Testamenti* (London, 1862), 528; C. H. Dodd, *The Epistle of Paul to the Romans* (London, 1959), 136–37; W. Sanday and A. C. Headlam, *Commentary on the Epistle to the Romans*, ICC (Edinburgh, 1902), 193. More recently scholars of erudition and faith have departed from this traditional view. For strong reasons they feel compelled to hold that Jesus assumed fallen human nature. See especially Barth, *Church Dogmatics*, 1.2,153–54, for a listing of such scholars. See also A. Kuyper, *The Work of the Holy Spirit* (New York, 1900), 84–87, and Cranfield, *The Epistle to the Romans*, 1.380–82. For although Cranfield is compelled to say that in the incarnation the eternal Son assumed fallen, human nature, he also feels compelled to say that although this is true, yet "fallen human nature was never the whole of Him—He never ceased to be the eternal God" (1.382). A

remark like this, however, leaves one with the distinct impression that if Jesus remained sinless throughout his entire life (cf. Heb. 4:15)—an idea that Cranfield would readily assent to—it was due to the fact that he was the eternal God, not to the fact that he was fully a man who, as a man, made his choices always for God. Without denying the reality of the incarnation, or that God became a man, it is the purpose of this book, nevertheless, to argue for the reality of Jesus' humanness and that as such he was not aided to rise above and conquer his temptations *as God*, but rather as a man whose will was set to do the will of God. His sinlessness was nothing other than the continued obedience to the Father and to the Father's will.

95. F. Godet, *The Gospel of Luke* (Edinburgh, 1881), 1.94.

96. D. A. Hagner, *Hebrews* (New York, 1983), 26.

97. Against Hagner, *Hebrews*, who writes: "The perfection [here] is not a moral or ethical perfection, for Jesus in this sense was always perfect."

98. C. Gore, *Dissertations on Subjects Connected with the Incarnation* (New York, 1895), 65.

99. Moule, "Manhood of Jesus," 104; cf. G. F. Hawthorne, "The Significance of the Holy Spirit in the Life of Christ," an M.A. thesis submitted to the Wheaton College Graduate School (Wheaton, Ill., 1954), 24.

100. E. Brunner, *The Mediator* (New York, 1942), 317.

101. Moule, "Manhood of Jesus," 104.

102. Irenaeus, *Adv. Haer.*, 3.21.10, in *Antenicene Christian Library*, ed. A. Roberts and J. Donaldson (Edinburgh, 1868), 5.358–59.

103. Ernst, *Das Evangelium nach Lukas*, 60.

104. Marshall, *The Gospel of Luke*, 58.

105. See Dunn, *Baptism in the Holy Spirit*, 24.

106. Ibid.; see also H. G. Marsh, *Origin and Significance of New Testament Baptism* (Manchester, 1941), 103, 105; Swete, *The Holy Spirit in the New Testament*, 35; Geldenhuys, *The Gospel of Luke*, 146–47.

3. The Spirit in the Boyhood and Youth of Jesus

Very little can be learned from the canonical books of the New Testament about the boyhood and youth of Jesus. It is a period of his life cloaked in obscurity. Only two quick glimpses are allowed into it, and both of these are given by Luke. One is found in 2:40, where Luke writes: "And the child [Jesus] was growing up and was growing strong, being filled with wisdom, and the grace of God was upon him." The other is when Jesus was taken to the Temple in Jerusalem as a boy of twelve years of age (Luke 2:41–52). The question now is, "What, if anything, can be legitimately inferred from these texts about the work of the Holy Spirit in these early years of Jesus' life?" That is the task presently at hand.

Luke 2:40. As noted earlier (chapter 2, p. 59) Luke, constructed the prebirth accounts and the accounts of the early years of John the Baptist and of Jesus in a similar fashion. The stories of these two people contain such striking features as the appearance of angels, miraculous births, the activity of the Holy Spirit, extraordinary individuals, the impossible accomplished by God, with whom all things are possible, and so on. Luke continues true to form now as he brings the narrative of the initial period of each of their lives to a close.

The final paragraph in both of these accounts begins in exactly the same way using exactly the same words in exactly the same forms: *to de paidion ēuxanen kai ekrataiouto* ("and the child was growing up and was growing strong," Luke 1:80; 2:40).

Thus, in these few words, especially in the verbs used and their tense (imperfect), Luke once more clearly intends to underscore the realness of Jesus' humanity—as real as was that of John. Jesus like John the Baptist was in every way a normal boy, undergoing normal physical and mental growth, growth and development not at all unlike that of historical figures—Isaac, Samson, Samuel, or any other young child (cf. Gen. 21:8; Judg. 13:24–25; 1 Sam. 2:26). If words have meaning, surely then in this matter of growth to maturity Jesus differed not at all from John. There is no hint here that one possessed omnipotence or omniscience and the other did not. Jesus no less than John had experienced the true human weakness and helplessness of infancy. Now both are said to have experienced the genuine need for growing up and for growing strong from childhood to adulthood in order to cope with life as mature persons.

Nor is there anything in the texts cited here that would deny to either of these persons the common ordinary impediments to growth or to indicate that one in contrast to the other strode through each cycle of development untouched or unaffected by those things whose nature is to retard growth or to bring it to a halt. If Plummer is right in saying that Jesus' humanity "was a perfect humanity developing perfectly, unimpeded by hereditary or acquired defects . . . , the first instance of such a growth in history,"[1] he is certainly basing his remarks on more information than that provided by Luke 2:40. This text does say, however, along with Luke 1:80, that whatever impediments these two persons may have encountered, they nevertheless overcame them and made constant progress toward maturity.

From this point on, however, these two summary paragraphs that bring the birth narratives of John and Jesus to a close (Luke 1:80; 2:40) break away from each other. They no longer describe the boys with identical phrases. The differences are significant, and the words used are carefully chosen to show the great superiority of the one to the other.

Luke now says of John that he was growing strong "in spirit" (*pneumati*, 1:80), but of Jesus he says that he was growing strong "filled with wisdom" (*pleroumenon sophia*, 2:40).[2] He intends with these new expressions to call attention now to growth of a certain kind—intellectual, mental growth. About John the Baptist Luke simply states the fact: "He was growing strong [developing] mentally" (*pneumati*, "in spirit").[3] But about Jesus he prefers to put the emphasis not so much on the fact of growth, but rather upon how this mental growth was to take place and with what result. It is not sufficient, therefore, to translate *ekrataiouto pleroumenon sophia* in the following way: "He became strong; he was filled with wisdom,"[4] as though "becoming strong" and "being filled with wisdom" were two separate and distinct things in the experience of Jesus. They are not. Grammatically the one is subordinate to the other. The one explains the other. That is to say, "being filled with wisdom" is a participial phrase subordinate to and explanatory of the verb *ekrataiouto* ("he was growing strong"). It tells *how* and *with what* Jesus was made strong. In this way, then, Luke draws an important distinction between John and Jesus. John was growing strong mentally, yes. But Jesus was growing strong (mentally) "*by being fillled with wisdom.*"

Crammed into this final phrase, "by being filled with wisdom," are several large ideas that are worth unpacking and spreading out so that they may easily be seen:

1. At its center is a participle in the present tense, *pleroumenon*, a progressive tense in Greek, which describes a steady, continuous, uninterrupted action. Jesus was becoming strong (intellectually) *by being ever more and more filled.*

2. Further, the participle, *pleroumenon*, is in the passive voice—Jesus was being filled *by someone*. That is to say, someone other than Jesus himself was doing the filling. But who? Luke does not say in just so many words who this agent was. One may infer, however, both from what Luke had to say earlier about the agent at Jesus' birth (1:35), and from what he will say later on about the driving force in Jesus' ministry (4:1), that this unnamed agent was none other than the Holy Spirit. Jesus, therefore, was growing strong (in mind) because the Holy Spirit was ever more and more filling him.

3. Finally, that with which Jesus was being filled was *sophia*, "wisdom." In choosing this important word, Luke may have intended to say: (a) that the growth of Jesus' mind was to be such that not

only would he become a highly intelligent person, but a person filled with a knowledge of, a love for, and a commitment to the ways of God—the essence of wisdom (cf. 1 Kings 4:29; 2 Chron. 1:10; Prov. 1:2, 7); (b) that perhaps Jesus was to be the Messiah, for the Messianic hope was bound up in just such a person as this, a person endowed with wisdom by the Spirit of God (cf. Isa. 11:2; Pss. Sol. 17:37; 1 En. 49:3)[5]; and (c) that readers must not be surprised when they come across the story of Jesus sitting, while still a young boy, among the learned teachers of Israel asking them questions and intelligently answering theirs (cf. Luke 2:47)—after all, he was constantly being filled with wisdom throughout these very early years of his life.

This, then, is one striking difference between John and Jesus that can be noted when the two similar summary statements about each of these children are compared (Luke 1:80 with 2:40). Both boys are said to have grown up and grown strong physically, mentally, and spiritually. But more is said of Jesus than of John. Only of Jesus is it specifically stated that his intellectual growth was tempered with an accompanying uninterrupted filling of his mind with wisdom (2:40), presumably superintended by the divine Holy Spirit (cf. James 3:15, 17).[6]

It must be pointed out, however, that Luke's quiet reserve in describing this continuing growth experience of Jesus stands in stark contrast to that of the Jesus to be found in the Apocryphal Gospels of the Infancy.[7] In Luke's Gospel the child Jesus expounds no precocious theses and performs no spectacular feats. Rather, although his mind was ever more and more being filled with wisdom by the Holy Spirit so that he was astonishingly wise (cf. Luke 2:47), it was nevertheless a wisdom in keeping with his years, appropriate to each stage of his human development (e.g."as a child he thought as a child") and thus on through each phase of his life. "So the child grew into the Boy, and the Boy into the Man, the intellectual and spiritual growth keeping pace with the physical."[8]

A second difference to be noted here (in Luke 1:80 and 2:40) is that John, for some unexplained reason, withdraws from normal society for a quiet, secret life in the desert,[9] while Jesus remains in the circle of his Galilean family. This would appear to suggest that the Holy Spirit, in filling Jesus with wisdom, did not work in this instance independently of social structures but through them. That is to say, the Holy Spirit took advantage of every educational instrument that was thus readily available—home, parents, school, Scriptures, life and worship of the synagogue, and so on—to mold the intellectual and spiritual dimensions of this developing personality.[10]

The final difference between Jesus and John to be noted in the summary statements about each of them as children (Luke 1:80; 2:40) is a difference that indicates still further the superiority of the one over the other. Only of Jesus does Luke say, "the grace of God was upon him" (NIV). The key word here, again carefully chosen by Luke, is the word *grace* (*charis*). It has the meanings both of human or divine favor and, more concretely of exceptional gifts bestowed upon a person as a result of divine favor.[11] Surely Luke means at the very least by his phrase, "the grace of God was upon him," that God looked upon this special child with pleasure, that he held him in the highest regard (*complaisance*),[12] for everything about Jesus, even in his youngest years, was of such a quality as to call forth the favor of his Father.

But Luke may have meant more than this. He may also have meant by the words, "the grace of God was upon him," that God was even then in the process of graciously fitting Jesus out with those special powers requisite for the unique role he was to play in redemptive history, bestowing upon him the gifts he would need to be the Messiah, the Savior of the world. If this is so, then perhaps there is here yet another reference to the Holy Spirit in the life of Jesus—a suggestion that becomes very probable when one reflects on what Luke later wrote (in Acts 4:33) about the early church. He then wrote of this Holy Spirit-infused community that the apostles gave their testimony "with great *power* . . . and great *grace* was upon them all," that is, the power of the Spirit was making the apostles' words effective, the grace of God was equipping them with the requisite gifts of wisdom, speech, and courage to carry out their ministry.[13] *Power* (of the Spirit) and *grace* (of God) are in this Acts passage for all practical purposes made identical by a kind of rhetorical parallelism. Thus one may not be far off the mark in supposing that Luke meant by his expression, "the grace of God was upon him," here in 2:40—an expression very similar to that which he used in Acts 4:33, "great grace was upon them all"—that God was in effect equipping Jesus with the gifts of the Spirit even then in his earliest years, preparing him for the ministry he was eventually to fulfil.

In summary, Luke 2:40 makes no explicit reference to the Holy Spirit in the life of Jesus. But it is possible to detect even here in Luke's carefully chosen words the presence of the Holy Spirit steadily at work in Jesus' formative years. The Holy Spirit, it may be assumed, was the one who more and more was filling his mind with wisdom. It was he who was the gracious gift of God bestowed on him from his youth up—"the grace of God was upon him." The Holy Spirit, therefore, was not only God's agent by which Jesus was conceived and brought to birth, but he was God's close presence with Jesus all his life long. The Holy Spirit was the divine influence ever present with him, the one nudging him always in the direction of the fear of God (cf. Prov. 1:7; 3:1–4), the one illuminating his mind with truth and filling it with wisdom, the one drawing him toward love and goodness. The Spirit was not, however, the one to make choices for him or to determine the direction his life would take. Those things Jesus must do for himself.

Luke 2:41–52. The only other glimpse into the boyhood years of Jesus is also given by Luke. And once again the question comes, is there any indication that the Holy Spirit was at work in this new period of Jesus' life? It is the story of Jesus having been taken to Jerusalem by his parents when he was twelve years of age (2:41–52).

From the way in which Luke begins this narrative, it is difficult to say with complete certainty whether or not Jesus had previously accompanied Joseph and Mary on any of their annual pilgrimages to Jerusalem to celebrate the feast of Passover. For the following reasons, however, it may be presumed that he had not: (1) The feast of Passover was one of the three feasts that Jewish adult males originally were ordered by the Law to attend each year (Exod. 23:14; Deut. 16:16), and by New Testament times it was the *only* annual feast required of those males living at a distance from Jerusalem. (2) It was not expected that women should go up to these feasts, and at an early period the presence of women and children was a matter of controversy.[14] (3) According to Mishnaic regulations, which may very well have been in effect in Jesus' time, boys from the age of thirteen on were obliged to make the pilgrimage to Jerusalem at Passover and take their place among the adult males of the Israelite community. It was customary, however, for a child belonging to a devout family to be brought up to this feast at least a year before his thirteenth birthday in order to acquaint the child with the obligation that was soon to fall upon his shoulders.[15] Hence, it is more than likely that this difficult journey to Jerusalem from a village more than sixty-five miles away was for Jesus, a boy of only twelve years, his very first experience in this sacred city.

If this is so, and if one but reflects on the kind of boy Jesus must have been, if one but thinks about the unique circumstances surrounding his birth, if one but considers his extraordinary intellectual and spiritual growth (cf. Luke 2:40), his own deep piety encouraged no doubt by the piety of Joseph and Mary, his own keen knowledge of the Old Testament through diligent study and memorization of its text and reflection on it, his own penetrating perception into the significance of God's redemptive acts in human history, his insight into the meaning of the Jewish feasts and especially of this feast of the Passover (cf. Exod. 12:21–27), his awe at being in the city of Jerusalem, "the city of the great King" (Ps. 48:1–2)—when all this is taken into consideration, one can easily imagine the excitement that surely must have filled Jesus' whole boyish being as he made his way up to Jerusalem for the first time. One can easily imagine the spiritual ecstasy that overwhelmed him as he participated with his family in this his very first Passover feast in this special place and the exhilaration that occupied the whole of his attention as he listened to the words and acts of God being expounded by the learned teachers in the precincts of the Temple. Surely, then, one can easily conceive of the possibility (1) that a person (even a boy) of the religious precocity of Jesus might indeed lose all sense of time, and all sense of responsibility to stay in touch with those with whom he had come, even over an extended period of time, and (2) that a person (even a boy) of his spiritual sensitivity and awareness would wish to be in his "Father's house," the Temple, rather than anywhere else in the world (cf. Gen. 28:10–22, especially v. 17).

And so it was that Jesus came up to Jerusalem with his parents when he was only twelve years old. He became so involved with the events surrounding the feast of the Passover, that when the families from Nazareth began their journey homeward, he was totally unaware of and unconcerned about their departure. And on the other hand, since it was customary for large groups of pilgrims from the villages to travel to and from the festivals in caravans, both for fellowship and for protection from highway robbers (cf. Luke 10:30), and since Mary and Joseph had great confidence in Jesus and thus were not overly watchful of his actions, it is not surprising that they were unaware that he had been left behind until the time came for them to form camp in the evening. But upon discovering that he was missing they immediately retraced their steps in search of him. As Luke tells the story, they finally found him "in the temple" (*hieron*, Luke 2:46), or more precisely somewhere in the precincts of the Temple, in one of the porticoes or rooms where scribes met for discussion (and where women were allowed to enter). On special occasions, such as the seven-day feast of the Passover, the Temple Sanhedrin sat in the Temple area and informally received questions and stated their traditions (Sanh. 88b). It was in some such gathering of teachers as this that this young disciple sat totally absorbed.[16]

Mary and Joseph found him sitting in the middle of these teachers—possibly numbered among them were Symeon, Gamaliel (cf. Acts 22:3), Annas, Caiaphas, Nicodemus, Joseph of Arimathea, and others—not himself as a teacher, but as a learner. He was both listening to what was being said and asking questions for information on the points being debated as did any good pupil in discussions about the law.[17] Jesus astounded everyone by his penetrating questions and his insightful answers. Yet there is nothing in Luke's telling of this event intended to lift him above the human level of the extraordinary child who had been well taught in the Old Testament, who possessed a deep love for the Scriptures and a keen insight into their meaning, and who had a thirst to know more about them (cf. Ps. 119:99–100). It was his unusual knowledge of these sacred things and his eager thirst to learn still more that was astonishing. But Jesus is not presented here as a superhuman child such as appears in the Infancy Story of Thomas, or the Arabic Gospel of the Infancy. In these gospels Jesus puts "to silence the elders and teachers of the people expounding sections of the law and the sayings of the prophets," instructing these learned people also in astronomy, medicine, and physics.[18]

When Joseph and Mary had drawn Jesus aside out of the circle, it was Mary and she alone who addressed him. Her words were both a rebuke and an expression of intense love: "Child (*teknon*), why have you treated us like this? Your father and I have been looking for you agonizingly" (*odynōmenoi*, Luke 2:48). Jesus' reply is itself a rebuke, toned down somewhat by the *you* plurals, and a registering of surprise. In effect he asked, "Why were you searching for me and worrying about me, since you should have known where to find me. Did you not know that I had to be in my Father's house?"[19]

Here in Jesus' words, "it was necessary for me" ("I had to") and "*my* Father"—the first words that he is recorded as having spoken—are found the meaning and purpose of this particular story. The impersonal *dei*, "it is necessary," that Luke uses here expresses not only a general necessity, but that which *had to be* as part of God's saving plan as it involved Jesus.[20] And his "My Father" points to a unique relationship that existed between God and Jesus that even then as a child he was becoming aware of. "It is true that God was the Father of all Israel and that every Israelite in later Judaism was accustomed to speak of Him as such (Tob. 13:4; Sir. 23:[1], 4; Wis. 2:16; ʾ*Abot* 5:30; Yoma 8:9, etc.). Nevertheless, Jesus is . . . understood to use the name with a unique intensity of filial obligation and responsibility. . . . [His] visit to the Temple indicates the seriousness with which he has dedicated himself to the service of the God of Israel. . . . The consciousness of Jesus is in these years moving to the climax" it later was to attain.[21]

Mary's spoken question, "Child, why have you done this to us?" was never answered by Jesus. That fact may have cast a long shadow across her mind, for neither she nor Joseph fully understood what had just happened in this perplexing, even distressing, event (Luke 2:50). While "realizing her son's miraculous birth and his Messianic destiny, [yet Mary] remains ignorant of the true nature of his mission and of his designation, 'Son of God.'"[22] Nevertheless Jesus leaves Jerusalem, with all of its excitement, its religious and intellectual fervor, and goes back home to the almost unimaginable narrow and intellectually stifling environment of Narareth with Mary and Joseph. He submits himself to their authority (*ēn hypotassomenos*, Luke 2:51, an imperfect periphrastic construction that emphasizes a continuous attitude and action on Jesus' part) even though there is that within him that longs to remain there in the exciting environs of this "City of God." In spite of his growing consciousness of being God's Son, or better, precisely because he was becoming aware of being God's Son and the obedience to his will that this entails, he returns for yet many years to Nazareth, wholly subject to his earthly parents. And yet in just such a context as this it is said of him that he steadily made progress in wisdom, stature, and favor with both God and people (Luke 2:52; cf. 1 Sam. 2:26). "Clearly such growth is possible without special education and activity when God gives time for his work"[23] and provides the stimulus for it.

To return now to the main point of interest, after examining in some detail Luke's story of the boy Jesus in the Temple (Luke 2:41–52), is there in this story any indication that the Holy Spirit was at work in Jesus' life during this stage of his development, and if so, what was the significance of this work? Several things need first to be taken into account in order to provide an adequate answer to these questions:

1. There is no specific mention of the Holy Spirit in this Temple narrative. Never once do the words *pneuma*, or *pneuma hagion* ("Spirit" or "Holy Spirit") appear here. One might easily deduce from this that thus the Holy Spirit played no special part in Jesus' life at this time or in this place.

2. Luke calls attention to the religious precociousness of the boy Jesus with a carefully chosen word—*synesis* (2:47). This word may be used to refer to a person's faculty of comprehension, to a person's intelligence, to a person's intellectual abilities. Now the thing that is interesting for this study is that often from a biblical perspective such intellectual faculties are viewed as more than the mere product of heredity. God, or more precisely, the Spirit of God, is seen sometimes to step into the human situation to heighten one's *synesis*, one's intellectual capacities. God, or the Spirit of God, on such occasions enables people to go beyond the intellectual limitations imposed upon them by their heredity, their own fears, or whatever, and to think things and to do things otherwise thought impossible (cf. Exod. 31:3, 6; 2 Chron. 1:10–12).

But *synesis* may also be used in another way as well, namely to refer to one's "understanding of" or "insight into" certain matters, especially religious matters. Once again such insight, from a biblical perspective, is perceived not as mere natural ability, but as something granted people by God.[24] *Synesis* is used, for example, to indicate a correct understanding of divine mysteries, an understanding given by the Holy Spirit (cf. Eph. 3:4–5), or to indicate a spiritual insight into the divine will provided by God himself (Col. 1:9; cf. also 2:2), or to indicate the ability to grasp the meaning of the Christian life—an ability again as a gift from the Lord (2 Tim. 2:7).

Further, it is worth noting that *synesis* is often coupled with *sophia* (Deut. 4:6; 1 Chron. 22:12; 2 Chron. 1:10–11; see Col. 1:9)—*understanding* coupled with *wisdom*. This fact helps one to realize that Luke's comment about Jesus' "understanding" in Luke 2:47 has already been prepared for by his earlier statement in 2:40 that Jesus was being "filled with wisdom." In the previous discussion of 2:40 (see p. 99 above), it was argued that the Holy Spirit was the One who filled Jesus with wisdom.

Putting all this together, then, it seems reasonable to assume that in Luke's choice of *synesis* ("understanding") to describe the boy Jesus in the Temple, he wished to give at least an intimation that the Holy Spirit was at work within him, active within his mind, while he was among the teachers of the Law at this particular Passover occasion. Luke seems to be saying, in a veiled way to be sure, that indeed it was the Spirit of God who enabled Jesus to exceed his human limitations so as to understand the Scriptures in a way that amazed those who heard both his questions and his answers. Here, then, at a very early stage in Jesus' life is an example of that insight into spiritual truth provided by the Spirit of God that was later continuously to astonish those who heard him teach with authority (*exousia*, i.e., an authority granted him by the Spirit, Mark 1:22/Matt. 7:28–29; Mark 1:27/Luke 4:36; cf. Matt. 21:23; Mark 6:2).[25] Here is a glimpse into what Jesus would be like in years to come, about whom it could well be said, "The Spirit of the Lord shall rest upon him, the spirit of wisdom [*sophia*] and understanding [*synesis*]" (Isa. 11:2; cf. Isa. 42:1; Luke 4:18; 11:31).

3. There is yet another especially Lucan word in this narrative that contributes still more strongly to the impression that Luke wanted to convey to his readers the idea that the Holy Spirit was

indeed at work within Jesus at this very early period of his life. It is the verb, *existasthai* ("to astonish," "to amaze")—"all . . . were astonished at His understanding" (Luke 2:47 NKJV). The word *existasthai* is used seventeen times in the New Testament, but eleven of these uses are by Luke alone. He uses it frequently "to express a reaction of wonder or surprise at something in the life of Jesus or the sequel to it" (see Luke 8:56; 24:22; Acts 2:7, 12; 8:13; 9:21; 10:45; 12:16).[26] Or to put it another way, *existasthai* is used to express the reaction of people to the present working of the divine power of the age to come in Jesus. Hence, Professor Ellis is precisely right when, in commenting on this verb in Luke 2:47, he says that it is not intended

> just as a tribute to Jesus' intelligence but as a witness to his relationship to God. . . . The same "Holy Spirit" power, later to be manifested in Jesus' ministry, even now is at work. Jesus interprets the Scripture not from the knowledge gained in rabbinic training but from the "wisdom" given by God.[27]

And it might be added, "given by God through the Holy Spirit."

4. Jesus at twelve years of age is becoming aware of a unique relationship that exists between himself and God.[28] This awareness is intensified for Luke's readers by his juxtaposing Mary's rebuke to Jesus with Jesus' reply to her—"*Your* father and I have been looking for you anxiously" (2:48), with "I must be in *my* Father's house" (2:49). From this interchange it is clear that at this moment Jesus comes to understand that God is his Father in a unique way, and that his obedience to *this* Father must take precedence over all other filial loyalties. "The special way that Jesus speaks of 'his' Father," writes Professor Schürmann, "both in prayer and speech is firmly fixed within the traditon and is also to be seen here in this narrative."[29] Jesus understood himself to be the Son of the Father in a special sense—Son of God uniquely.[30]

Now the question arises as to when and how this awareness came about. While emphatically affirming that Jesus is the eternal Son of God incarnate (see pp. 40–45 above), one needs at the same time to affirm with equal emphasis that in the act of becoming incarnate the divine did not in any way destroy or even diminish the human.

The Word *became* flesh (John 1:14)! The Son *became* human! The Divine *became* a baby, a boy, a man! It is too great a mystery to explain easily, or perhaps to explain at all. But however it is to be explained, it must take into account the fact that here in Jesus is a real twelve-year-old boy. And the way in which Luke tells this story about him—taken by his parents to Jerusalem to the feast of Passover at such a crucial time in his life—strongly implies that the entire experience was a crisis event for him. The very shape of the narrative seems designed to say that here at this special feast, recalling the mighty saving acts of God in Egypt (Exod. 12:1–14), something happened to Jesus that had never happened to him before. "A secret epiphany," as Howard Marshall calls it, took place within him, "a temporary unveiling [to him of his] relationship with his Father . . . a momentary glimpse through a curtain into a private room . . . followed by Jesus' return to normal obedience to his parents on their return home."[31] This is to say that Jesus, at this point in his life, began to understand who he was and what his mission in life was to be, that he received new insight into himself and his mission. If this is so, then it is possible that the Holy Spirit was the One who pulled aside the curtain and allowed Jesus to gain, if only initially and partially, an understanding of who his real Father was, of his divine Sonship, and to whom it was that he owed his total allegiance (Luke 1:35; 3:22; cf. Rom. 8:15–16; Gal. 4:6).[32]

In conclusion, even though Luke does not use the precise words *the Spirit* or *the Holy Spirit* in this particular narrative about Jesus (Luke 2:41–52), there are, nevertheless, sufficient clues embedded in the story to indicate that he surely assumed that his readers would understand that the Holy Spirit in all his power was present in Jesus' life, even when he was a boy of twelve. One may also infer from this account that at every phase of Jesus' life the Spirit was there with him, beside him, upon him, within him to fill him with wisdom and understanding, to guide him in the way of righteousness (cf. Pss. 25:4–5; 43:3), and at the right time to let him, at least to the degree appropriate to his years, in on the secret of who he really was. This, then, was the significance of the Holy Spirit in the life of Jesus during these formative years of his childhood and youth.[33]

NOTES

1. Plummer, *The Gospel According to Luke*, 74; see also P. M-J. Lagrange, *Évangile selon Saint Luc* (Paris, 1948), 93.

2. The majority text does add, "in spirit" (*pneumat.*) in Luke 2:40 after *ekrataiouto* ("waxed strong in spirit," KJV), but it is rejected by most commentators as inauthentic, the result of an attempt to harmonize further this verse with 1:80. See Fitzmyer, *The Gospel According to Luke I–IX*, 432; Lagrange, *Évangile selon Saint Luc*, 93.

3. For this meaning of *pneuma* as the seat of the intellectual functions of a person, see Job 32:8, 18; Ps. 77:6; Isa. 19:14; Dan. 5:12, and see F. Baumgärtel, *TDNT*, 6.361. It is possible but not likely, in light of the parallel nature of Luke 1:80 with 2:40, that *pneumati* here in 1:80 refers to the Holy Spirit (cf. 1:15, 41, 67). Luke would hardly say that John's growth was by the Holy Spirit and make no explicit mention of that fact in the parallel reference to Jesus.

4. See Fitzmyer, *The Gospel According to Luke I–IX*, 419.

5. M. M. B. Turner, "Jesus and the Spirit in Lucan Perspective," *TynB* 32 (1981), 35–36.

6. Cf. 1QH 14.12b–13, where it is said that one receives the Holy Spirit and thus is sent "forward toward thine understanding." Apparently this means that for the members of the Qumran community, the Spirit was the means of enlightenment by which one came to know God and his will. The sectary goes on to say, "And I thy servant, I know by the Spirit which thou hast put in me" (1QH 13.18b–19). The marvelous secrets of God are disclosed to him because of the Holy Spirit (1QH 12.11b–13).

7. See E. Hennecke, *New Testament Apocrypha*, ed. W. Schneemelcher, trans. R. McL. Wilson (London, 1963), 1.363–417.

8. Swete, *The Holy Spirit in the New Testament*, 35.

9. For attempts to explain John's action, see Fitzmyer, *The Gospel According to Luke I–IX*, 388–389; Marshall, *The Gospel of Luke*, 95–96; J. A. T. Robinson, "The Baptism of John and the Qumran Community," *HTR* 50 (1957), 175–91; W. H. Brownlee, "John the Baptist in the New Light of Ancient Scrolls," in *The Scrolls and the New Testament*, ed. K. Stendahl (New York, 1957), 33–53; A. E. Geyser, "The Youth of John the Baptist," *NovT* 1 (1956), 70–75.

10. W. Manson, *The Gospel of Luke* (London, 1930), 23.

11. BAGD, "*charis*."

12. Lagrange, *Évangelie selon Saint Luc*, 93.

13. Cf. E. Haenchen, *The Acts of the Apostles* (Oxford, 1971), 231; I. H. Marshall, *Acts* (Leicester, 1980), 108–109.

14. StrB 2.142; Creed, *The Gospel According to Luke*, 45.

15. See StrB 2.144–47; Mishnah Hagigah 1:1; Fitzmyer, *The Gospel According to Luke I–IX*, 441.

16. Ellis, *The Gospel According to Luke*, 85.

17. Creed, *The Gospel According to Luke*, 45.

18. Hennecke-Schneemelcher-Wilson, *New Testament Apocrypha*, 1.398–99.

19. For this meaning of the obscure Greek phrase, *en tois tou patros mou*, literally, "in the of my Father," see E. R. Smothers, "A Note on Luke II 49," *HTR* 45 (1952), 67–69; see also R. M. Grant, "Papias and the Gospels," *ATR* 25 (1943), 220; P. J. Temple, "What Is to Be Understood by *en tois*, Lk 2,49?" *Irish Theological Quarterly* 17 (1922), 248–63; idem "'House' or 'Business' in Lk 2,49?" CBQ (1939), 342–52.

20. Fitzmyer, *The Gospel According to Luke I–IX*, 443.

21. Manson, *The Gospel of Luke*, 23.

22. Ellis, *The Gospel of Luke*, 86.

23. Schweizer, *The Good News According to Luke*, 64.

24. BAGD, "synesis."

25. Cf. Schürmann, *Das Lukasevangelium*, 135.

26. Fitzmyer, *The Gospel According to Luke I–IX*, 442.

27. Ellis, *The Gospel of Luke*, 85.

28. It is not possible to say that Jesus knew all along, from birth onward, that he was the Son of God, for an omniscient being cannot be truly human. But even though we must say that he did not always know *that* he was God's Son uniquely, we can say, with Austin Farrer, that he did know *how* to be the Son of God in the several situations of his gradually unfolding destiny—such as the situation here in the Temple. "God the Son on earth is a fulness of holy life within the limit of mortality" (A. Farrer, *Interpretation and Belief* [London, 1976], 135).

29. Schürmann, *Das Lukasevangelium*, 137; see also Stanton, *Jesus of Nazareth in New Testament Preaching*, 51; Dunn, *Jesus and the Spirit*, 27; but cf. also Brown, *Jesus, God and Man*, 88–92; C. F. D. Moule, *The Phenomena of the New Testament* (London, 1967), 50–51.

30. To understand precisely how Jesus would have perceived this sonship is complicated by the fact that Israel as a whole thought of God as Father and itself as his son (cf. Exod. 4:22–23; Num. 11:12; Deut. 32:6, 18; Isa. 63:16; 64:7–8; Jer. 31:9, 20; Hos. 11:1; Mal. 1:6; 2:10). The king, too, was thought of as God's son (2 Sam. 7:14; Ps. 89:27–28), as was the Messiah (Ps. 2:7; 1 En. 105:2; 4 Ezra 7:28; 13:32, 37, 52; 14:9), and occasionally individual pious Jews spoke of God as their Father (Tob. 13:4; Sir. 23:1 [=4a]; 51:10; Wis. 2:16). See Ernst, *Das Evangelium nach Lukas*, 125; but see also Manson, *The Gospel of Luke*, 23.

31. Marshall, *The Gospel of Luke*, 129–30.

32. See Dunn, *Baptism in the Holy Spirit*, 24; Turner, *TynB* 32 (1981), 36; G. W. H. Lampe, "The Holy Spirit in the Writings of St. Luke," in *Studies in the Gospels*, ed. D. E. Nineham (Oxford, 1955), 167–68.

33. See Dunn, *Baptism in the Holy Spirit*, 24; Marsh, *New Testament Baptism*, 103, 105; Swete, *Holy Spirit*, 35.

4. The Spirit at the Baptism and Temptation of Jesus

The New Testament is essentially silent about the life of Jesus from birth to baptism, from Bethlehem to the Jordan River. Matthew and Luke tell of the Holy Spirit's active role in the conception and birth of Jesus. But only Luke gives even the briefest of glimpses into the intervening years, showing a child growing and a boy developing in favor with God and people. Luke's glimpses do imply, however, that in fact the Holy Spirit was continuously at work in every phase of Jesus' life, infusing him with wisdom in keeping with his years, pervading all his imagining, suggesting all his decisions, guiding him in the ways of God, providing him with spiritual resources to overcome evil, granting him insight on certain occasions into the meaning of his own existence and destiny, and so on. One might say that the Holy Spirit was continuously with him in his silence and in his speech, in his haste and in his leisure, in company and in solitude, in his play and in his work, in the freshness of the morning and in the weariness of the evening—throughout all the hours and days of those early years of his life.[1]

Apart from the birth narratives, there are relatively few direct or specific references to the Holy Spirit in the life of Jesus in the synoptic Gospels (Mark 1:8, 10/Matt. 3:11, 16/Luke 3:16, 22;

Mark 1:12/Matt. 4:1/Luke 4:1; Mark 3:29–30/Matt. 12:31–32; Luke 12:10; Matt. 12:18, 28; 28:19; Luke 4:14, 18; 10:21; see Mark 2:8; 8:12). This fact may cause some to conclude that the Spirit played a very small part in Jesus' public ministry, that there was but very little connection between what was happening in his life and the influence of the Spirit upon him.[2] But this would be a wrong conclusion to draw, and for these reasons: (1) Even though the direct references to the Holy Spirit in the life of Jesus are few, they are nevertheless significantly impressive and they frame "the beginning and end of the Gospel's picture [of Jesus], appearing both at [his] birth and baptism and again at his promise (or impartation) of the Spirit to his disciples at the close of his earthly ministry."[3] They say, in effect, that in everything Jesus said and did, he was aided in saying and doing by the Holy Spirit working through him. (2) An attempt has been made in chapter 3 to show that there are recorded incidents in the life of Jesus where there is no mention of the Holy Spirit, but where his presence, power, and activity are assumed. (3) The many references in the Gospels to Jesus acting with authority (*exousia*), performing his miracles with power (*dynameis*, *dynamei*), being perceived by the people, even by his closest friends, as a prophet, the bearer of the Spirit, or perceiving himself as a prophet,[4] and so on, indicate that even without using the precise expression, "Holy Spirit," the Gospel writers were nevertheless stating in other ways their conviction that Jesus lived in the environment of the Spirit. (See chart on next page.) They were confident that the Holy Spirit was indeed operative in every experience of Jesus so that the great moments of his life were indeed the result of the Spirit's powerful presence within or upon him.[5] Hence, although the sayings about the Spirit and Jesus in the Gospels are relatively few, the presence and power of the Spirit in Jesus' life is recognized by the evangelists and acknowledged by them throughout their writings.

The task now at hand is to continue to examine as carefully as possible the remaining New Testament texts that include both direct and indirect references to the Holy Spirit in the life of Jesus. This will make possible an answer to the question about the importance of, the need for, the reason why the Holy Spirit was so powerfully

acting with authority (*exousia*)	Mark 1:22/Matt. 7:29/Luke 4:32; Mark 1:27/Luke 4:36; Mark 2:10/Matt. 9:6/Luke 5:24; Mark 11:28–29, 33/Matt. 21:23–24, 27/Luke 20:2, 8
performing his miracles with power (*dynameis*, *dynamei*)	Mark 5:30/Luke 8:46; Mark 6:2/ Matt. 13:54; Matt. 11:20–22; 14:2; Luke 4:14, 36; 5:17
being perceived by the people as a prophet	Mark 6:15–16/Luke 9:8–9; Mark 8:28/Matt. 16:14/Luke 9:19; Mark 14:65/Matt. 26:68; see also Matt. 21:11, 46; Luke 7:16, 39; 24:19
perceiving himself as a prophet	Mark 6:4/Matt. 13:57/Luke 4:24; 13:33; cf. Matt. 23:31–38; Luke 11:47–51

present in Jesus' life, especially in his mission and ministry. Once again readers should be reminded that the aim of this study is not to prove or disprove the historicity of these stories or sayings about the Spirit and Jesus, but, accepting them for what they are—part and parcel of the Gospels, Acts, etc. as these texts now stand—to ask what, for these early Christians, was the essential significance of the Holy Spirit in the life of Jesus?

The baptism of Jesus by John the Baptist and the descent of the Spirit upon Jesus is for Mark the beginning of the Gospel (cf. Acts 10:37–38), so it is here that this study will pick up and continue the discussion of the significance of the Holy Spirit in his life.

The Texts. For convenience sake the Gospel accounts are provided here for ready reference:

Matt. 3:13–4:2	Mark 1:9–13	Luke 3:21–22; 4:1–2	John 1:32
Then Jesus	In those days		
came from	Jesus came		
Galilee to	from Nazareth		
the Jordan to	of Galilee		
John, to be			
baptized by			
him. John			
would have			
prevented him,			
saying, "I need			
to be baptized			
by you, and do			
you come to me?"			
But Jesus			
answered him,			
"Let it be so			
now; for thus			
it is fitting			
for us to			
fulfil all			
righteousness."		Now when all	
Then he		the people were	
consented.		baptized, and	
And when Jesus	and was	when Jesus also	
was baptized,	baptized by	had been baptized	
he went up	John in the	and was praying,	
immediately	Jordan. And		
from the water,	when he came		
and behold, the	up out of the		And John
heavens were	water,		bore
opened and he	immediately he		witness,
saw the Spirit	saw the heavens	the heaven was	"I saw
of God	opened and the	opened, and the	the
descending	Spirit descend-	Holy Spirit	Spirit
like a dove,	ing upon	descended upon	descend
and alighting	him like a dove;	him in bodily	as a dove
on him; and lo,	and a voice	form, as a dove,	from heaven,
a voice from	came from	and a voice came	and it

Matt. 3:13–4:2	Mark 1:9–13	Luke 3:21–22; 4:1–2	John 1:32
heaven, saying,	heaven,	from heaven,	remained on him."
"This is my beloved Son, with whom I am well pleased." Then Jesus was led up by the Spirit into the wilderness to be tempted by the devil. And after he had fasted forty days and forty nights, he then became hungry.	"Thou art my beloved Son; with thee I am well pleased." And immediately the Spirit impelled him to go out into the wilderness. And he was in the wilderness forty days being tempted by Satan; and he was with the wild beasts; And the angels were ministering to him.	"Thou art my beloved Son; with thee I am well pleased." And Jesus, full of the Holy Spirit, returned from the Jordan, and was being led about by the Spirit in the wilderness for forty days, being tempted by the devil. And he ate nothing during those days; And when they had ended, he became hungry.	
And the tempter came and said to him . . .		And the devil said to him. . . .	

The Context. Matthew, Mark, Luke, and John introduce their accounts of the ministry of Jesus first by introducing John the Baptist. Neither Matthew, Mark, nor John the Evangelist, however, provide John the Baptist with any historical setting, personal pedigree, credentials, or authenticating signs to validate his mission. They simply present him without explanation. They do not tell when he arrived at the Jordan, where he came from (other than that he had been sent from God, John 1:6), or who his parents were. Apparently John was sufficiently well known to their audiences so that no introduction was thought necessary, or his person and message and the power with which it came were authentication enough (cf. Luke 1:17; John 1:19–28). He is, they say, the promised "voice of one crying in the wilderness," the one whose job it was to "prepare the way of the Lord" (Mark 1:3; Matt. 3:3; John 1:23; cf. Isa. 40:3).

Luke, on the other hand, helps his readers to understand the important nature of the Baptist's mission by telling them who John's parents were and their devoutness (Luke 1:5–23), of John's extraordinary, miraculous birth (Luke 1:23–25, 41, 57), of his becoming like a Nazirite (Luke 1:15; see Num. 6:1–4), of his life in the wild "until the day he was manifest to Israel" (Luke 1:80), and of the precise time on the world's clock when this manifestation took place (Luke 3:1–2).

Each of these writers makes it clear that John's message was a call for Israel to repent, that is to radically turn or return to the God with whom they had broken faith[6] and to reform their lives accordingly (Matt. 3:1–10; Luke 3:7–9). Each evangelist makes it clear, too, that John's ministry was to baptize those who did so repent and to offer them forgiveness for their sins. In the somewhat awkward words of Mark and Luke, John's message and mission was to preach (and perform) "a baptism of repentance for the forgiveness of sins" (Mark 1:4; Luke 3:3). But this mission was a divine mission and this message a divine message. Whereas Matthew and Mark note only that the Baptist came and preached, Luke says he came and preached in response to the call of God. Like an Old Testament prophet, John spoke out only because the word of God had come to him first, only because God had directed him to do so (Luke 3:2–3, cf. Isa. 38:4; Jer. 1:1 LXX; 13:3). And if there was a note of urgency in John's message, it was because he was certain that the kingdom of heaven (kingdom of God) was at hand. He was convinced that God's sovereign, universal rule was verging on arrival,[7] that God was soon to act definitively to destroy evil and to establish his kingdom of goodness, truth, justice, and love (Matt. 3:2). And he wished Israel to know this and to be ready—he felt it as his burden to prepare this people for the Lord (cf. Luke 1:17).

This urgent message from God, carried by this itinerant desert preacher (Luke 3:3), made a deep impression on those who heard him as is indicated by the exaggerated language of Mark's Gospel: "*All* the country of Judea, and *all* the people of Jerusalem" went out to John. They came to John and confessed their sins and were baptized in the Jordan River (Mark 1:5; cf. Matt. 3:5–6; Josephus, *Ant.* 18.5.2).[8]

One of those who heard the message of the Baptist and who responded by making his way from Nazareth of Galilee[9] to the Jordan and by being baptized was none other than Jesus. Matthew makes this part of the story emphatically more precise. He says that Jesus in leaving Galilee and journeying to Judea had only one thing in mind, and that was to obey the word of God that had come to him through his prophet, John. His action was a positive response to a divine call (cf. Luke 3:2 with Mark 11:30–33/Matt. 21:25–27/Luke 20:4-7)[10]—he came "for the express purpose of being baptized by John" (*tou baptisthēnai hyp' autou*, Matt. 3:13).

But how can this be? Was not John's baptism "a baptism of repentance for the forgiveness of sins" (Mark 1:4)? And was not Jesus not only free from sin, but free from any consciousness of sin (cf. John 8:46, and see pp. 36–37 above)? Why, then, should he come with the specific intent of being baptized with this particular baptism of all baptisms?

To answer this question, all that has been said earlier about Jesus in the previous chapters must be kept in mind: He was the Word become flesh, the eternal Son become incarnate. He was the Son of God, not seeming to be a man nor even inhabiting a man, the New Testament is emphatic on this matter—Jesus was the divine become human. Somehow, someway, beyond one's ability to fully understand or explain, the divine Son limited himself to the confines of the man Jesus. Here in this person God the Son looked at the world with the eyes of Jesus, worked in the world with his hands, walked with his feet, felt with his feelings, loved with his emotions, heard with his ears, thought with his mind, and so on. The eternal Son of God and Jesus were one Person as the result of the incarnation. But above all, it must be repeated, the divine did not swamp the human or even diminish it in the process. Rather, in this gracious act of humility, God fully experienced for himself what it meant to be truly human.

Consequently when Jesus heard John's message, it was a real human being who heard it and responded. Although his birth was miraculously brought about by the Holy Spirit, although his mind was continuously being filled with wisdom by the Holy Spirit, although his conduct in righteousness which pleased both God and people was tended and nurtured by the Holy Spirit, yet the Gospels are careful to describe Jesus as a man who must himself make the choices of life. Hence, here he is now, a carpenter in Nazareth of Galilee, a deeply pious person, steeped in the Old Testament Scriptures, a spiritually sensitive person with a will set to do the will of God, who hears the call of God for all Israel to repent and be baptized. And precisely because the call is indeed the call of God (cf. Luke 3:2), Jesus could not remain aloof from it. He promptly obeys. He leaves Galilee; he comes to be baptized with the baptism of John, *not* because he knows everything about himself and his mission—much is yet to be disclosed to him about these matters.[11] But he comes, it may be presumed, (1) because he was prompted to do so by the Holy Spirit (cf. Mark 1:12), (2) because he held the office and authority of John in highest esteem and acknowledged that his baptism was an ordinance of God to which he wished to submit himself (cf. Mark 9:13; Luke 3:2; 7:24–28; 20:3–4; etc.),[12] i.e., his coming to be baptized was "a moral act of commitment to God's call,"[13] and (3) because although he himself was not conscious of having sinned, he nevertheless was keenly aware that he belonged part and parcel to a nation that had turned away from God and that he shared the heritage and predicament of his people.[14]

As a consequence he does not set himself apart from them and their sins. Rather he stands with them—a sinful people in need of a genuine act of repentance. Jesus, in coming to be baptized with John's baptism, is not unlike Daniel, a man of God, himself above reproach (Dan. 6:4), but who at a time of national crisis fell on his knees before God and made his confession to God as if he were as much at fault as his people. He prayed: "*We* have sinned and done wrong and acted wickedly and rebelled, turning aside from thy commandments and ordinances; *we* have not listened to thy servants the prophets. . . . *We* have sinned against thee. [Yet] to the Lord our God belong mercy and forgiveness" (Dan. 9:3–9, italics mine).

This interpretation harmonizes with Matthew's more elaborate account of Jesus' baptism. Matthew alone notes that John tried to persuade Jesus not to be baptized by him. "I need to be baptized by you," he objects, "and do you come to me?" Jesus' reply was simply, "Let it be so now; for thus it is fitting for us to fulfill all righteousness" (Matt. 3:14, 15). He meant by these words, "I am come to you for baptism because this is what any right-minded person would do in this situation. Israel as a whole needs to repent. I claim membership in this nation. Therefore, I, too, as one with them must heed your call to repent and with them demonstrate corporate contrition by submitting to your baptism."[15] "Jesus thus intended to identify himself with John's message and with the revival movement it had created, to enroll as a member of the purified and prepared people of God. It was this, rather than any need for forgiveness . . . which brought him to join the crowd."[16]

The Baptism of Jesus

Jesus was about thirty years of age (Luke 3:23) when he came to John at the Jordan. It was a mature age, an important age. Some Jewish communities considered that that was *the* time of life when a man could rightfully take his place among the chiefs or leaders of Israel.[17]

Mark presents this event in its simplest form—"Jesus came . . . and was baptized" (1:9). Furthermore, Mark is the only one of the evangelists who says categorically that Jesus was actually baptized by John (*hyp' Ioannou*, Mark 1:9). For some reason all others refrain from stating it quite so precisely, including John the Evangelist (John 1:31–34; cf. Matt. 3:16; Luke 3:21). And yet it may correctly be inferred from what Matthew and Luke say elsewhere—"Jesus came . . . to the Jordan to John, to be baptized *by him*" (Matt. 3:13); "crowds of people came out to be baptized *by him*, (Luke 3:7 NEB, although D and some Old Latin manuscripts have *enōpion autou*, "before him," or "in front of him," instead of *hyp' autou*)—that they, too, mean to say that John was not merely a witness to the fact of Jesus' baptism but the agent by whom it was done.

Luke adds a unique and interesting, even important note. He says that Jesus was baptized only "*after* all the people had been baptized" (Luke 3:21),[18] thus indicating that this particular baptism was in a sense the highpoint, the climax of John's mission and ministry. Although crowds of people had flocked to the river to be baptized in response to his call for repentance (Luke 3:7; cf. Mark 1:5; Matt. 3:5), they apparently had come and gone before Jesus arrived. Jesus was alone with the Baptist. Therefore the baptism of Jesus and the accompanying phenomena did not happen for the sake of the people, but primarily for this special person from Nazareth. One can thus imagine the excitement that that moment contained for Jesus, and how he must have felt as he presented himself to John for baptism. If his experience in Jerusalem at the age of twelve was such an ecstatic experience that he lost track of time and parents, if that incident of sitting among the learned teachers and listening to the Scriptures expounded was so rapturous that even then he began to see that he stood in a unique relationship to God, as Son to Father, how much more ecstatic and rapturous might this event of his baptism be, which was the result of his own deliberate choice to heed the call of God and to go God's way! Luke's singular and teasing remark—"after all the people had been baptized, Jesus was baptized" (Luke 3:21), hints at the possibility that this quiet, uninterrupted event might indeed be a crisis event in his life of spectacular proportions.

And indeed it was! Each of the synoptic Gospels affirms that the baptism of Jesus triggered an extraordinary series of events: (1) the heavens opening, (2) the Spirit, the Holy Spirit, descending as a dove, and (3) a voice coming from heaven. All three evangelists agree upon these main features of the story, although they differ as to details in the telling of them. For example, Luke is the only one to say that these unheard of happenings took place while Jesus was praying (Luke 3:21). Jesus at prayer is a familiar theme in Luke (5:16; 6:12; 9:18, 28–29; 11:1; 22:41; cf. 23:34). But Luke rarely ever lets one know precisely what it was that Jesus was praying for or about (but see Luke 22:41–42; 23:34). And true to form he does not here tell his audience the content of this prayer of Jesus. One might wish to know—Was it a prayer like Daniel's, a prayer of national repentance (cf. Dan. 9:3–9)? Was it one of rededication of himself to God? Was it a prayer of personal submission to the will of God? Was it a prayer for guidance for the future?—but it is not possible to know, for Luke does not say. He simply states that Jesus prayed and thus that he had opened himself and had placed himself in that ideal state in which to receive divine direction, divine revelation. He prayed, and his prayer was particularly efficacious.[19] There was an immediate answer from heaven.

The opening of the heavens. While Jesus was coming up out of the waters of the Jordan River (Mark 1:10), or after he had already done so (Matt. 3:16), the heavens opened. This was the first of the supernatural phenomena that immediately followed Jesus' baptism. Although at least part of what happened was considered to be a visible sign to the Baptist by which he recognized Jesus for whom he really was (John 1:31–34), and although in recounting these events the evangelists wanted to provide their readers with a revelation about Jesus—that he was truly the Son of God—nevertheless, the very way in which they (especially the synoptic writers) tell their story makes clear that Jesus is the point of focus for them, not John, not the crowds, not even the readers. As one studies the synoptics, it is difficult to escape the impression that these Gospels were written for the express purpose of saying that these events were of decisive importance primarily to Jesus.[20] Note the following:

1. There is not a hint here, for example, that any other person saw or heard the things that Jesus saw and heard after his baptism. Mark is explicit in this. He specifically makes only Jesus the subject of the verb *eiden—he saw* the heavens opened; *he saw* the Spirit descending, and so on. (Mark 1:10).

2. Matthew and Luke do not contradict Mark, even though neither of their accounts is quite as explicit as his. Luke writes, "When Jesus also had been baptized and was praying, the heaven was opened, and the Holy Spirit descended . . ." (Luke 3:21–22). Matthew says, "When Jesus was baptized, he went up immediately from the water, and behold, the heavens were opened . . ." (Matt. 3:16; this text may originally have included the pronoun *autō* ["to him"] after the verb, "were opened": "the heavens were opened *to him*",[21] thus corroborating Mark's statement that no one but Jesus saw what had just happened). In any case, Matthew from this point on continues his baptism narrative by making Jesus, and only Jesus, the subject of the verb *eiden*—"and *he* saw the Spirit of God descending . . ." (Matt. 3:16).

3. Nowhere in these accounts of Jesus' baptism is there even the slightest suggestion that bystanders were present or were affected in any way by what happened. There is no word about people being astonished, marvelling, giving glory to God, or being excited to spread abroad the fame of Jesus. All such expressions as these that are often found in the Gospels to describe the reaction of the crowds to some spectacular, miraculous event are absent here (cf. Matt. 9:8, 33; 15:31, and so on).[22] It is Jesus only who sees and hears and is affected by

what he sees and hears. How can one understand these narratives otherwise? Seemingly the evangelists purposed to say that the baptism and its accompanying phenomena were of supreme significance primarily to Jesus, determinative for his life and for his mission in life.

Jesus "saw the heavens opened" (Mark 1:10), more precisely, "Jesus saw that the heavens were being torn apart" (*schizomenous tous ouranous*). Just what this was that Jesus saw is difficult, if not impossible, to explain. It must have been more than a thunderstorm quickly discharging itself, however, or the rapid breaking up of the clouds, otherwise it would never have been recorded here. The language is cosmological—picturing a firmament that separates the abode of God above from the world of human beings below (cf. Gen. 1:6–7) now being broken through so as to eliminate every barrier between the divine and human. The language is apocalyptic—picturing the last times as having dawned, the age of God's salvation as having arrived, the breaking in of the heavenly into the earthly (cf. John 1:51; 3 Macc. 6:18; Test. Levi 2:6; 5:1; 18:6 and 2 Bar. 22:1). The language is prophetic—picturing God as answering the people's plea: "O that thou [O God] wouldst rend the heavens and come down . . . to make thy name known . . ." (Isa. 64:1–2 [LXX 63:19]) and fulfilling his promise: "I will . . . open the windows of heaven for you and pour down for you an overflowing blessing" (Mal. 3:10).[23] Hence, this which Jesus saw was something definitely out of the ordinary, spectacular, miraculous, a phenomenon in the heavens, which must have been understood by him to mean that God was on the verge of doing some great new thing, that God was about to manifest himself in some unusual way and to reveal his purpose in an unmistakable fashion (cf. Ezek. 1:1), that God himself was going to come down and act in power.

The descending of the Spirit. The splitting apart of the heavens was prologue. Important as it was in itself because of the ideas it communicated and the hopes it raised, it was by no means the most important of those events that followed immediately upon the baptism of Jesus. The descent of the Spirit (Mark), the Spirit of God (Matt.), the Holy Spirit (Luke) was far more important and significant for Jesus. The heavens opened and the Spirit came down (cf. Isa. 63:14 [LXX] with 63:19)!

1. As if a dove. Each of the Gospel writers agrees upon likening the Spirit in some way to a dove (*hōs/hōsei peristeran*—Matt. 3:16; Mark 1:10; Luke 3:22; John 1:32). They do this either to stress the outward visible form which the invisible Spirit took, or to emphasize the manner in which he came down out of heaven. Their sentence structure is of such a nature, however, that it is not always possible to determine precisely which of these two ideas is intended. Luke makes one descriptive addition, however, which puts the emphasis upon the visibleness of the Spirit, the reality of what could be seen with one's eyes, and which stresses the realness of the Spirit's presence upon Jesus—*sōmatikō eidei*, "in bodily form" (Luke 3:22).

But why the dove? Why is the Spirit likened to a dove in this story? None of the evangelists gives the answer to this question, perhaps because the imagery would have been immediately understood by those who read their accounts, and, hence, no explanation was necessary.[24] The fact, however, that from earliest times until today differing interpretations of the dove-figure and explanations of its origin have been put forward suggest strongly that it was not immediately understood. The early fathers of the church believed the dove was chosen because it symbolized either innocence, peace, meekness, harmlessness, or pleasantness, or because it "more than any other animal [was] susceptible of love,"[25] and thus it became for them an omen portending the qualities that would characterize Jesus upon whom the Spirit was descending.

Some modern scholars attempt to explain the dove against a Hellenistic background where the descent of a bird, more particularly a dove, upon a person was a sign that that person was chosen by the god (or gods) for special favor or assignment.[26] Other scholars instead interpret it against the larger Near-Eastern tradition, seeing in it an allusion to Oriental myths of the begetting or adoption of the king by a goddess disguised as a dove.[27] Most scholars, however, look for an explanation of the dove in the Old Testament and other Jewish literature.[28] The source of this imagery is found in Genesis 1:2, where the Spirit of God hovering over the primeval chaotic waters was likened by the rabbis to a bird—even a dove—fluttering over its young.[29] Thus the presence of the Spirit as a dove at the baptism of Jesus may be explained as a signal that once again God is about to work a new work. "We have [here] to deal with the creative ability of the Spirit; a new thing was being wrought in the waters of baptism comparable with the creation of heaven and earth out of primeval chaos."[30]

The source of the dove imagery is found also in Genesis 8:8–12, the story of the dove that Noah released and that returned bearing an olive leaf in its beak. Against this backdrop, John's baptism is seen as signifying a coming flood of judgment (cf. Luke 3:7–9), but the descending of the Holy Spirit like a dove as signifying "the end of judgment and the beginning of a new era of grace."[31]

Passages such as Hosea 7:11 and 11:11 are still other places where scholars look for an explanation of the dove. They see the dove as a symbol of the community of Israel and suppose, then, that this association was also in the evangelists' minds. "At the moment of his baptism Jesus is the one true Israelite, in whom the election of God is concentrated. The descent of the Spirit 'as a dove' indicates that he is the unique representative of the new Israel created through the Spirit."[32]

Professor Fitzmyer cautions against being too confident that the dove figure can be identified with certainty, for all of the suggestions that have been mentioned run into difficulties, especially those that rely on rabbinic literature for their interpretation. It is only in the later rabbinical literature that the Spirit has been identified as a dove, literature that is later than the beginning of the Christian era. He thus soberly concludes: "Even if one cannot explain the origin of the symbol, the evangelists have clearly understood it as a sign of the presence of the Spirit to Jesus. Since in the Old Testament the 'Spirit' of God is usually a manifestation of his creative or prophetic presence to human beings, it should be so understood here."[33]

2. Upon/Into Jesus. The heavens were torn open. The Spirit of God descended from them. But the truly important element in this particular episode was that the Spirit came down upon Jesus, not John, nor anyone else. All of the evangelists agree upon this. And they seemingly intend to convey even in the way they word this event an idea of permanence. John the Evangelist makes this point the most forcefully. In his telling of the story, he shifts from using a participle with which he described the descent (*katabainon*, "coming

down") of the Spirit, to a finite verb (*emeinen*, "[it] remained") to indicate the Spirit's abiding presence. His transition from one verb form to another may thus have been deliberate to indicate that although the Spirit came upon the Old Testament heroes sporadically (1 Sam. 16:14; 2 Kings 3:15), the Spirit remained permanently, unchangeably with Jesus.[34] Even Luke's added phrase descriptive of the Spirit's descent, *sōmatikō eidei* ("in bodily form"), has been understood to imply this very same thing, that the coming of the Spirit upon Jesus was in "a manner wholly unlike the often transient inspiration of an ordinary prophet."[35]

But the idea of the permanent presence of the Spirit with Jesus may indeed have reached its most emphatic expression in Mark's Gospel. He is the only evangelist to use the preposition *eis* rather than *epi* when he discusses the outcome of the descent of the Holy Spirit as it relates to Jesus. The preposition *epi* means, "on," "upon," "to." There may have been a deliberate, conscious choice to change Mark's *eis* ("into") to *epi* ("upon") on the part of Matthew and Luke, in order to bring their narratives into harmony with the Old Testament texts that seem to provide the background for this event, especially Isaiah 11:2 and 42:1. These texts predict that the Spirit will rest upon (*epi*) David's descendent, upon (*epi*) the Servant of the Lord. But Mark insists on *eis* rather than *epi* when he writes of the Spirit in relation to Jesus.[36] Although *eis*, like *epi*, may mean "to" or "toward," its primary meaning is "into." And in light of the way Mark uses *eis* in other places throughout his Gospel (cf. 1:9, 14, 21, 29; 2:1; 3:1, 20; 5:1, 12–13; 10:15, 23–25; 12:41, 43, etc.), it is almost certain that he means to say "*into* him" here, that he deliberately preferred *eis* to *epi*,[37] that he wanted "to indicate that the Spirit entered into Jesus and did not merely 'come upon him' externally."[38] In a word, Jesus was now filled with the Spirit as he was never filled before! If like John the Baptist (Luke 1:15) Jesus, too, had been filled with the Spirit from his birth (see above, pp. 89–90), this coming of the Spirit "into" Jesus was something more, something even greater—a greater filling yet. The Spirit had come to him to stay. Jesus was now the permanent bearer of the Spirit. Luke catches up this theme and specifically says of Jesus that immediately after his Jordan experience he was *plērēs pneumatos hagiou*, "full of the Holy Spirit" (Luke 4:1).

The coming of the voice. Immediately after the descent of the Spirit, or perhaps coincident with it, there came a voice from heaven, the voice of God (cf. Deut. 4:12). The close connection between these two distinct events is no accident. One supports the other; one confirms the other; one interprets the other. The Holy Spirit comes down into Jesus; the voice of God directs itself toward Jesus. The voice says to him, "You are my Son . . ." (Mark 1:11; Luke 3:22); the Spirit enables him to respond with "Abba, my Father!" (cf. Rom. 8:15–16; Gal. 4:6). Seemingly then, Jesus' understanding of himself as Son of God, his filial consciousness, was not only the result of the declaration from the Father, it was also the result of the inner prompting or the illuminating work of the Holy Spirit. This link between Jesus' sense of Sonship and the activity of Spirit "is certainly well established in the developed Christological reflection of the earliest church (e.g., John 3:34–35; 20:21–22; Acts 2:33; Rom. 1:3–4; Gal. 4:4–6)."[39] It is thus not an idea illegitimately forced upon the synoptic accounts of the events that happened to Jesus at his baptism. And furthermore, Jesus' understanding of the Spirit's coming down upon him and into him may very well have been the result of the voice from heaven—to borrow Büchsel's phrase: "The word from God to Jesus explains the act of God on Jesus."[40]

Some scholars have likened the voice from heaven to, or identified it with, the *bat-kol* (literally, the "daughter of the voice," i.e., an echo of the voice of God).[41] This was a term invented by the rabbis who believed that when God ceased to speak directly through his prophets, he communicated with his people only through an echo of his voice. They considered the *bat-kol* to be an inferior means of revelation, an inferior substitute for the Word of God given immediately through his Holy Spirit.[42] Although the voice which came from heaven at the baptism of Jesus may be analogous to the *bat-kol*, it cannot be identified with it. For here is no echo, but a direct communication. Here is no "daughter of God's voice," but God's voice. Hence, here is no inferior revelation, but the ultimate—God speaking directly with a human being, the Father from heaven with his Son on earth. Perhaps, then, a nearer analogue to the heavenly voice than the *bat-kol* would be "the imagery . . . employed with regard to Sinai where God spoke directly to the people (cf. Dn. 4:28 [*sic.*; see Deut 5:4, 24]; 2 Bar. 13:1)."[43]

The words of the voice are, *Sy ei ho huios mou ho agapētos, en soi eudokēsa*—"You are my beloved/only Son; in you I am well pleased" (Mark 1:11; Luke 3:22).[44] There are several things here to take special notice of:

1. The voice is directed to Jesus and only to Jesus. The very order of the words in Greek makes this point most emphatically, (a) by using the personal pronoun (*sy*, "you") when it was not necessary to do so for clarity's sake, and (b) by putting both it and its verb in the first position in the sentence—*sy ei [ho huios mou]* (contrast Ps. 2:7 LXX: *huios mou [ei sy]*)—"*You are* my Son."

2. The words spoken from heaven appear to be borrowed principally from two especially significant Old Testament texts, texts that no doubt would have been very familiar to Jesus. The first is Psalm 2:7, "You are my son, today I have begotten you."[45] The second is Isaiah 42:1, "Behold my servant (*pais*) . . . in whom my soul delights."[46]

The first text (Ps. 2:7) may originally have been an enthronement psalm that was chanted during the coronation ceremony when some heir to David's throne was acclaimed king, "God's son," or at an anniversary of this event. In later Judaism the term *my Son* was applied to the Messiah (4 Ezra [2 Esd.] 7:28), as it most certainly was in the New Testament (cf. Acts 13:33; Heb. 1:5; 5:5; 2 Pet. 1:17). This seems to be its meaning here in the baptism narrative. That is to say, the voice from heaven was in essence declaring that Jesus was the Messiah, the Christ—"Son of God" in this sense—thus emphasizing his divine authority rather than his divine nature,[47] thus stressing his status and function as the one commissioned to be God's vicegerent on earth rather than his metaphysical being as one in essence with the Father in heaven.

And yet the voice not only said, "You are my Son," it added an important adjective—*agapētos*, "You are my *beloved* [*only*[48]] Son." With this new word, not found in Psalm 2, the voice seems to take the phrase, "my Son," beyond a mere denoting of Jesus as Messiah. It is intended to designate him also as the unique Son, the one who has a special and unparalleled relationship with the Father, a relationship that is quite unrelated to any official function in history.[49] It may be saying, therefore, that he is God's *only* Son, eternally and essentially so—"You *are* my Son!"[50]

The second text (Isa. 42:1) belongs to a group of prophetic passages known as the Servant Songs (Isa. 42:1–4; 49:1–6; 50:4–9; 52:13–53:12). These songs, which describe the person and work of the Servant of the Lord, begin interestingly with God putting his Spirit upon him (Isa. 42:1), and they conclude with the Servant's suffering and death by which he brings healing and redemption to the people he represents. It is not known for certain who this Servant was. Some scholars believe that he was a historical figure—Hezekiah, Zerubbabel, one of the prophets, perhaps Isaiah himself.[51] Other scholars are certain that he is to be identified with the nation of Israel (cf. Isa. 49:3).[52] The greatest number of Christian interpreters, however, see this Servant figure of the Old Testament as a prophetic anticipation of the incarnate Christ.

3. The voice concludes with *eudokēsa*, an aorist indicative of the verb *eudokein*, "to be well pleased," "to take delight" (cf. Luke 12:32). Since the aorist indicative generally refers to some past time, it has been interpreted by some here as describing "the historical process by which God came to take pleasure in Jesus during his earthly life"[53]—"You are my beloved/only Son in whom I *came to take pleasure*." Everything Jesus had said and done up to this moment, his whole life, was declared not only acceptable but something in which the Father took delight. Such an interpretation of this word and its tense certainly is in harmony with Luke 2:52: "Jesus kept advancing . . . in favor with God and people." Others understand that the aorist is reflecting the influence of Psalm 2:7 and/or Isaiah 42:1, where a past decision is recorded, and may indicate that this prior decision of God is now being revealed. Professor J. A. Broadus writes: "In the depths of eternity, before creation began, God loved, delighted in, his Eternal Son; and now at the baptism . . . he bears witness to him . . . saying: 'This is my Son, the beloved, in whom my soul delighted.'"[54] It is possible, too, that the "pastness" of the aorist indicative should not be pressed, since the aorist indicative often expresses a timeless idea[55] and thus is especially well fitted to reflect the Hebrew stative perfect of Isaiah 42:1. It should be translated accordingly, "I am well pleased" (Luke 3:22 ASV, RSV, NIV), "In thee is my delight" (Moffatt), "on thee my favor rests" (NEB).

Summary and Significance of the Baptism Event

Jesus left Nazareth for the Jordan River. He did so in obedience to the call of God spoken through his prophet, John. Jesus had heard the Baptist's message that sounded out through Judea and Galilee calling Israel to repentance and to demonstrate this repentance openly by being baptized. Jesus heard this divine demand and responded with his "Yes!"

There is, however, nothing in the Gospel accounts to indicate that when Jesus left Nazareth he had anything more in mind than to present himself to John for baptism as other obedient Israelites were doing. There is not the slightest hint that he knew ahead of time that this journey to Judea was to be a final break with his hometown and with his family. In fact, Mark's phrase, "in those days," by which he introduces this story, "In those days Jesus came from Nazareth . . . " (Mark 1:9), meaning, "during the time Jesus had a residence in Nazareth," echoed also by Matthew's, "then" (Matt. 3:13), seems designed to give the impression that Jesus was not at this time pulling up stakes.[56] Hence, it is too much to say that Jesus knew before he left Nazareth that from that moment of departure onward he was destined for a public ministry, or that he viewed his baptism as a conscious act on his part of self-dedication to this ministry.[57]

Nevertheless, as it turned out, this journey of Jesus from Nazareth to John, was indeed for him the end of the old (in more ways than one) and the beginning of the new. Although "all the country of Judea, and all the people of Jesusalem" (Mark 1:5) had come to the Jordan and were baptized confessing their sins, nothing extraordinary is recorded as having happened to them. But the synoptic writers agree that when Jesus came and was baptized, the heavens were torn open, the Holy Spirit descended as a dove, and the voice of God spoke from heaven. And these same writers also affirm that in each case Jesus, especially Jesus, was the one who saw and heard and experienced these unusual events.

Hence, it seems insufficient to claim that the only purpose of the Gospel records was *solely* to provide readers with an initial revelation of Jesus as the Son of God, and that there was no desire whatsoever on their part to attempt to say what effect these events had on Jesus himself.[58] Again, to repeat what was claimed earlier, it is not only in what the evangelists say, but in how they say it, that discloses what they considered to be the significance of an incident in the life of Jesus. Here they present him as one stepping out of obscurity, out from an obscure and inconsequential village, and of a sudden he is launched on the stage of world history, onto a mission of ultimate meaning. The very way in which they construct this story indicates that for them the turning point was the baptism of Jesus and what happened to him at that time. Therefore, it is quite difficult to believe that the baptism was of no decisive importance *to Jesus* himself, for the Spirit descended *into him*, and the voice from heaven came *to him*. From the standpoint of the evangelists, these were his experiences and they must have profoundly affected his own thinking and acting; they could not have been other than of great significance to him.

The part of the baptism event that is of the most importance for this study is the descent of the Holy Spirit into Jesus. What is its meaning, its significance? In brief, it was his anointing. It was his commissioning as *the* Messiah of God.[59] If the Old Testament kings and prophets had to be anointed, not only with oil but with the Spirit, in order that they might be enabled to fulfill their divine mission, and thus in some significant sense could become messiahs (cf. 1 Sam. 10:1–6; 16:12–13; 1 Kings 19:16, 19; 2 Kings 2:9, 15; Hos. 9:7 LXX, and see chapter 1), then it is not surprising to learn that the Messiah par excellence, the long-expected deliverer, the Savior himself had to be anointed with the Spirit of God and thus be equipped with power and authority to carry out his divine mission.

This is not a modern interpretation of the significance of the coming of the Holy Spirit at Jesus' baptism thrust forcefully upon unwilling texts. It is an interpretation as old as Peter's sermon to Cornelius recorded in the Acts. For in that sermon Peter links the baptism of John with God anointing Jesus with the Holy Spirit and power. He said: "The word which was proclaimed . . . beginning from Galilee after the baptism which John preached: how God anointed Jesus of Nazareth with the Holy Spirit and with power; how he went about doing good and healing all that were oppressed by the devil, for God was with him" (Acts 10:37–38).

It is an interpretation as old as Jesus himself, who from that momentous experience at the Jordan (not before) realized that he was the Anointed (the Messiah) of the Lord—at least Luke seems to understand it in this way. For Luke records that Jesus, also in a sermon, quotes Isaiah 61:1–2. "The Spirit of the Lord is upon me because he has anointed me to preach good news to the poor. He has sent me to proclaim release to the captives and recovering of sight to the blind, to set at liberty those who are oppressed, to proclaim the acceptable year of the Lord." And then, Luke continues, Jesus immediately applied these words to himself as he told the congregation, "Today this scripture has been fulfilled in your hearing" (Luke 4:18–19, 21).

According to the Gospel writers, Jesus, from the moment the Spirit descended to him, became aware of a new power within him, a power to save, to heal, to bind the strong man and overturn his evil designs (Matt. 12:29). He became aware of having a new authority to teach and preach (Mark 1:22), to release (*aphienai*; cf. *aphesis* in Isa. 61:1 LXX) those held captive by sin (Matt. 9:6), to command unclean spirits to come out of tortured people (Luke 4:36). He became aware that from this moment a new age had dawned, that the old age was on its way out, that the time (*kairos*), God's time, was now being fulfilled, that the kingdom of God was at hand (Mark 1:15). On one occasion some men who were hostile to Jesus asked him, "By what authority are you doing these things?" referring to his miracles. He did not, would not, answer them because of their attitude and their motive for asking him this question (Matt. 21:23–27). But had he answered, surely he would have said, "I do these things by the power of the Holy Spirit which God has given to me!" According to Matthew, all that Jesus did and taught was to fulfill what was spoken by the prophet Isaiah: "Behold, my servant whom I have chosen, my beloved with whom my soul is well pleased. I will put my Spirit upon him, and he shall proclaim justice to the Gentiles" (Matt. 12:17–18; Isa. 42:1, cf. Isa. 11:1–3; 1 En. 49:2, 3; Pss. Sol. 17:42; Test. Levi 18:2–14; Test. Jud. 24:1–6).

Thus the baptism of Jesus, the descent of the dove, the Holy Spirit coming upon him, into him, was of the utmost significance not only to the readers of the Gospel accounts but to Jesus himself. Born as he was of the Spirit, filled with the Spirit from his birth, nurtured by the Spirit throughout his youth, enabled to grow wise by the Spirit, enlightened by the Spirit concerning his unique relationship with

God (of course, in keeping with his years, in keeping with his growth and development as a truly human person—see chapters 2–3), this event, however, was a climactic event in the life of Jesus.

Neither Matthew nor Luke have forgotten what they wrote about Jesus' birth and the part that the Spirit played in that birth. So when they, along with Mark, tell now in such a vivid way of the Holy Spirit coming down into him at his baptism, surely they are intending to say that a new stage in the experience of Jesus and the Spirit has been reached. They are intending to say more about the Spirit and Jesus than they had already said. They are intending to say that the Spirit was now playing a still more significant role in Jesus' life than ever before.

By coming upon him, into him, at the baptism the Spirit anointed him with power and authority to carry out, fulfill, his mission as Messiah. By coming upon him, into him, the Spirit filled him to an even greater extent (if such is possible) than he had filled him before, permeating his being, pervading his thinking, directing his steps, empowering him (cf. Luke 4:1–2). By coming upon him, the Spirit equipped him for service.

> Our documents, accepting the humanity of Jesus more thoroughly than our boldest theologians, overstep the bounds at which they stop. According to them, Jesus really received, not certainly as Cerinthus, going beyond the limits of truth, taught, a heavenly Christ who came and united Himself to Him for a time, but the Holy Spirit, in the full meaning of the term, by which Jesus became the Lord's anointed, the Christ, the perfect man, the Second Adam, capable of begetting a new and spiritual humanity.[60]

From the moment of the baptism onward Jesus was indeed *der Geistträger*, the unique bearer of the Spirit. There is a sense in which it is possible to say that this one came to the Jordan as Jesus of Nazareth and left it as the Messiah of God.[61] And it was just this—a person filled with the Holy Spirit—that would mark him out to his followers as the Messiah, not any outward activity of a king that he might have displayed. That which lent reality to any messianic claims he might have made was the presence and power of the Holy Spirit within him.

Although the descent of the Spirit into Jesus at the baptism is the most important event for this study, its full significance cannot be understood in isolation from the event that immediately followed—the voice out of heaven. If the coming of the Spirit anointed and equipped Jesus for his mission, the coming of the voice outlined for him what that mission was to be. Interestingly, in light of what has been said above, the voice of God does not address Jesus as "Messiah," "the Christ," nor does it say that he *is* the Messiah. Rather, God says to him, "You are my Son, my only Son; with you I am well pleased" (Mark 1:11/Luke 3:22).

The first thing to notice here is that the wording of the voice is such as to express a "relationship to God that transcends messiahship as it was understood in Jewish thought."[62] It is as the Son of God that Jesus is the Messiah, rather than the other way around. Thus the voice "leads beyond messiahship to that personal relationship with God which is basic for the self-understanding of Jesus."[63]

The second thing is that the voice of the Father is directed to Jesus—"*You* are my Son; with *you* I am well pleased." Matthew and Luke have already made it clear that Jesus' birth was by the Spirit, and Luke that Jesus was "Son of the Most High" from his mother's womb. Luke, too, has made a point of saying that Jesus as a boy of twelve already understood, at least to some extent, that God was his Father in an unparalleled way, that he was God's Son uniquely (see the discussion above in chapter 3). Why, then, was the voice directed to Jesus? Why did he need to be told that he was God's Son? The answer must lie in the fact that Jesus, though he was the eternal Son of God incarnate, was indeed incarnate! He had become human. He had become subject to real human limitations. Hence, his awareness of Sonship was subject to growth and development, perhaps even to a degree of uncertainty, in need of constant illumination and affirmation.

The voice from heaven, then, can be understood as the ultimate confirmation, the ultimate assurance. What Jesus had begun to sense, what he was gradually becoming aware of, what he understood in an increasingly distinct way—that he was God's unique Son—came to him now with much greater intensity and clarity. Thus the coming of the voice did not announce Jesus' adoption as Son and Messiah; it was rather a high point in a growing conviction that he was indeed God's

Son.[64] He was able, therefore, to understand his anointing, his messiahship, if you will, in light of this filial awareness. Adolph Harnack says, "Our Lord's consciousness of Sonship must have preceded in time his consciousness of Messiahship, must indeed have formed a stepping-stone to the latter."[65]

The final thing to notice is that the voice, as noted above, combines Psalm 2:7 with Isaiah 42:1 and thus gives Jesus insight, as he would ponder its words, not only into the nature of his person but also of his mission. As the Messiah he is to be the Servant of the Lord, anointed with the Spirit, thrust into the world not to be served but to serve and to give his life a ransom for many (cf. Mark 10:45). There is contained in these words a panoramic view of the remaining years of Jesus' life, a life lived in obedience to God and in service to people, climaxing, as the suffering Servant of Isaiah 53, in being wounded for the transgressions of others, bruised for their iniquities, cut off out of the land of the living for the sins of his people. Hence, as Jesus hears this voice, he begins to grasp the direction that the course of his life will take. He does not draw back from it, for out of his consciousness of Sonship comes also his sense of mission. Sonship means to Jesus "not a dignity to be claimed, but a responsibility to be fulfilled."[66]

The Spirit and the Temptation of Jesus

Jesus had come to the Jordan as a carpenter from Nazareth. But because of the cataclysmic events that happened to him there, a radical change took place that altered completely the remainder of his life. From a quiet existence in an insignificant Galilean village, he was launched upon a totally new career—that of an itinerant rabbi, travelling the length and breadth of the country, teaching and preaching wherever people would stop to listen, gathering disciples about himself, reaching out to heal the sick, raise the dead, roll back the kingdom of darkness, and inaugurate the Kingdom of God, the Kingdom of light and life. The same Holy Spirit that came upon him, into him, at his baptism, now filled him (Luke 4:1), impelled him forward into this new mission, and empowered him to fulfill it. The first step now in accomplishing all that the Father had given him to do was to leave the Jordan and move immediately into the desert (*erēmos*), probably into the wilderness of Judea.

The wilderness theme is a prominent and an important one in the Bible. It was the place where the Lord God met his people and revealed himself to them. Recall that it was in the wilderness of Horeb that God revealed himself to Moses (Exod. 3:1–3), and to Israel in the wilderness of Sinai (Exod. 19; Deut. 8:2; cf. Hos. 2:14–15; 9:10), and to Elijah in the desert after his forty-day fast (1 Kings 19:4–13). Thus it is possible that the evangelists in calling attention to this particular detail in the life of Jesus were intending to say that here in the solitude of the desert, in the place of quiet meditation and prayer, the Father revealed himself through the agency of the Holy Spirit still more vividly to the Son, opened up before him still more clearly his destiny, helped him to understand yet more fully who he was and what he was to do.

But the wilderness was also known as the home of Satan, the lodging of demons, the location of deadly dangers, the arena of evil forces, of the powers of darkness, of demonic activity, the habitation of wild beasts, poisonous serpents, etc. (Lev. 16:10; Num. 24:1–9; Deut. 8:15; Isa. 13:21–22; 34:13–15; Tob. 8:3; Matt. 12:43; Luke 8:24).[67] It is possible that the synoptic writers have this latter interpretation of the desert experience of Jesus more in mind, perhaps, than the former—not, however, to the exclusion of the former. All of these writers agree that here in the desert Jesus encountered the devil (Matt. 4:1; Luke 4:2), or Satan (Mark 1:13), and Mark takes special note that he was with the wild beasts, that is, he was with wild creatures, which in ancient Jewish thought was in some way associated with the evil one and his demons (cf. Ps. 22:12, 16, 20–21; Ezek. 34:5, 8, 25; Luke 10:19; Test. Benj. 5:2; Test. Napth. 8:4; Test. Isscr. 7:7).[68]

But however these evangelists may have understood Jesus' journey to and stay in the wilderness—whether as a place of divine revelation or demonic activity, or both—they all together specify emphatically that Jesus did not go there by accident or on his own initiative. Rather he went into the wilderness because the Spirit, who had come upon him, into him, directed him to go there (Mark 1:12/Matt. 4:1/Luke 4:1–2). Mark expresses this most clearly. He writes: "The Spirit *drove* him into the desert" (1:12). The verb he chose, *drove* (*ekballei* literally "casts out," "thrusts forth," cf. its use in 9:47; 11:15; 12:8, and elsewhere), indicates at least that the Spirit of God directed Jesus to alter whatever plans he might otherwise have had and to go to this particular place. How the Spirit pointed him off toward the desert, whether by some ecstatic experience (see 1 Kings 18:12; 2 Kings 2:16; Ezek. 3:12, 14; 8:3; Acts 8:39, cf. Ezek. 40:2, and note *anēchthē*, "was led up," Matt. 4:1) or by a quiet but strong inner conviction is not stated. But what is stated is that when the Spirit indicated to Jesus that the acceptance of his Servant vocation must lead him into the wilderness, he surrendered his own plans and followed the Spirit's promptings.

This strong Marcan word, *ekballei* ("thrust forth"), is toned down by both Matthew and Luke. Each uses instead some form of the verb *agein* ("to lead") and in the passive voice. But in so doing they make a significant contribution to the understanding of what is happening here. With Mark they continue to stress the significant role played by the Spirit in bringing Jesus to the desert. Beyond Mark, however, they make it clear that the power of the Spirit "does not infringe upon the personal nature of [Jesus'] inward life; Jesus remains master of his will and consciousness."[69] He is now the subject of the verb, not the object: "*Jesus* . . . was being led by the Spirit . . . in the wilderness" (Luke 4:1–2). But although he remains master of his will and consciousness, he, nevertheless, elects to subject himself to the guiding influence of the Spirit. He chooses to substitute the will of God, made known to him through the Spirit, for his own will. In this very act he continues to win the battle of obedience over disobedience, of choosing the Father's way over his own. "Not my will, but yours be done" was a hallmark of Jesus' life and ministry.

Jesus followed the Spirit's leading. And the evangelists agree that this leading was into the wilderness. Only Matthew indicates that the express purpose of this move was so that Jesus might be tested (*peirasthēnai*, Matt. 4:1). In fact, Matthew so constructs his version of this temptation experience that several scholars have suggested he planned it as a Christian reinterpretation of Deut. 6–8.[70] Just as the Lord God led Israel his "son" (cf. Exod. 4:22–23; Jer. 31:9; Hos. 11:1) in the wilderness for forty years to test and to discipline him (Deut. 8:2–5), so Jesus as the supreme Son of God is led by the Spirit for forty days to be tested at this very point, at the point of his sonship (Matt. 4:3, 6). God had made his covenant with Israel and tested Israel to see if it would be faithful as a son, and Israel, filled with manna, failed the test by rebelling against God (cf. Acts 7:36, 39; Heb. 3:8–9). Now the new covenant has been introduced and the New Israel is tested. Only when tested and proven and the covenant confirmed by his unwavering obedience to the Father can Jesus go forth in his work as Son and Servant for others (cf. Heb. 5:8–9).[71] Jesus, while fasting, was truly and painfully tested, as Matthew (4:2–10) and Luke (4:2–13) explain in detail. But he did not fail the test. He did not rebel against God or tempt or doubt God. He succeeded in winning out over the enemy, in thrusting aside the devil's every temptation—no matter how subtle or appealing—to do his own will regardless of the will of God or of God's express commands. His was a real victory over real temptations to do evil. But his victory "did not result from some automatic necessity of his nature as much as from his moment-by-moment committal of himself to the Father."[72]

Something more needs to be said at this point. Jesus did not emerge victorious from this mortal struggle simply because of his own inner strength or because of the set determination of his will. Every one of the synoptic writers in his own way makes it abundantly evident that Jesus was not alone in this battle. It was under the Spirit's compulsion and by the Spirit's direction that Jesus went to meet Satan. And Luke in particular notes that Jesus, full of the Spirit, not only *was led* by the Spirit *into* (*eis*) the place of testing, but he *was being led* (*ēgeto*) by the Spirit *in* (*en*) that place of testing during the whole time he was there (Luke 4:1). If he was being tempted by Satan for forty days (Mark 1:13), he was being led by the Spirit for those same forty days (Luke 4:1). It is impossible to escape the conclusion that these Gospel writers want their readers to understand that Jesus met and conquered the usurping enemy of God not by his own power alone but aided in his victory by the power of the Holy Spirit. He was fortified in his determination to obey the Father by the strengthening force of the Spirit within him. And it is in this same strength that Jesus was thus able to go forth into Galilee "and to commence a task which include[d] the release of the devil's captives ([Luke] 4:18; cf. 13:6). Thus at the outset of his ministry Jesus is depicted as overcoming the evil one who stands in opposition to the work of the Kingdom of God ([Luke] 11:19, 20)"[73] through the all-sufficient inward energizing power of the Spirit of God.

This point is made most forcefully by Matthew who brings the two phrases "by the Spirit" and "by the devil" into close proximity, thus implying that the Savior's victory over the tempter was due in large part to his being filled with the Spirit. It was the Spirit who enabled Jesus to see the subtle dangers that underlay the seemingly innocent appeals of Satan to exercise his messianic powers on his own authority. And the Spirit empowered Jesus to resist these solicitations to take a course that would run counter to the will of God. In the words of H. B. Swete, "If the human spirit of our Lord detected the true nature of the suggestions which were made to it and repelled them, it did so in the power of the Holy Spirit, and not simply by the force of a sinless human will."[74]

NOTES

1. Some of these words are taken from John Baillie's, *A Diary of Private Prayer* (New York, 1949), 89.

2. Scott, *The Spirit*, 79–81, 245; see G. R. Beasley-Murray, "Jesus and the Spirit," in *Melanges Bibliques en homage au R. P. Beda Rigaux*, ed. A. Deschamps and A. de Halleux (Gembloux, 1970), 464–66, for a summary of those who would eliminate every saying of Jesus about the Spirit. See also Windisch, "Jesus und der Geist," 211.

3. E. E. Ellis, *Pauline Theology* (Grand Rapids, 1989), 28. Cf. Matt. 1:20 with John 20:21–22.

4. Jeremias, *New Testament Theology*, 1.78, although he cautions that *prophet* was not a full description of the task for which Jesus had been sent; G. F. Moore, *Judaism in the First Three Centuries of the Christian Era* (Cambridge, 1946–48), 1.237; StrB 2:127–38.

5. See van Unnik's remarks in this connection, "Jesus the Christ," *NTS* 8 (1961–1962), 266.

6. W. L. Holladay, *The Root "Subh" in the Old Testament* (Leiden, 1958).

7. Gundry, *Matthew*, 44.

8. Does Mark's wording here, emphasizing the universality of this repentance (twice he uses *all—pasa . . . pantes*, 1:5), have theological overtones? There was a belief abroad that when there would be a national repentance, when *all* Israel would turn to the Lord, then the anticipated preparation for the coming of the Lord would have occurred (cf. Isa. 40:3, and see StrB 1.162–65 relating to Matt. 4:17).

9. In Mark's Gospel this is the first mention of Galilee (1:9), a term seen to have theological significance (cf. W. Marxsen, *Mark the Evangelist*, trans. J. Boyce [Nashville, 1969], 93–94). Some have even suggested that Mark included it here at

the initial appearance of Jesus in preparation for the resurrection appearance announced at 14:28 (cf. 16:7): "The parallel is not fortuitous between Jesus from Nazareth in Galilee, baptized in/with the Holy Spirit in 1:9–11, and Jesus who goes before and awaits his disciples in Galilee (16:7) to baptize them with the Holy Spirit in fulfilment of the promise in 1:8" (M. R. Mansfield, *Spirit and Gospel in Mark* [Peabody, Mass., 1987], 26).

10. Jeremias, *New Testament Theology*, 1.55–56; L. Goppelt, *Theologie der Neuen Testament* (Göttingen, 1975), 1.93.

11. Against H. A. Meyer, *Critical and Exegetical Handbook to the Gospel of Matthew* (Edinburgh, 1877), 1.117–18.

12. Manson, *The Gospel of Luke*, 30.

13. Guthrie, *New Testament Theology*, 221; see J. W. Bowman, *The Intention of Jesus* (Philadelphia, 1943), 36–38; H. Johnson, *Humanity of the Savior* (London, 1962), 47.

14. What a contrast the canonical gospels present to the apocryphal gospels. See, for example, *Evang. sec Hebraeos*, part of which remains extant in Jerome's *Contra Pelag.* 3.2 (quoted in K. Aland, *Synopsis Quattuor Evangeliorum* [Stuttgart, 1964], 27): "Behold the mother of the Lord and his disciples said to him: John the Baptist baptizes unto the remission of sin. Let us go and be baptized by him. But he said to them: Wherein have I sinned that I should go and be baptized by him? Unless what I have said in ignorance (=is a sin of ignorance)."

15. Cf. S. E. Johnson, *The Gospel According to Mark* (London, 1960), 38. For a different interpretation as to why Jesus submitted to John's baptism, see Geldenhuys, *A Commentary on the Gospel of Luke*, 146; W. L. Lane, *The Gospel According to Mark* (Grand Rapids, 1974), 54; C. E. B. Cranfield, *The Gospel According to St. Mark* (Cambridge, 1959), 52. The answers these scholars give are surely orthodox. But they seem to be saying too much for the Gospel texts to bear. They seem also to be at variance with Luke's intimation that Jesus' growth in wisdom and understanding was gradual and steady. They all seem to be saying that Jesus at the moment of his baptism knew precisely and fully who he was and what he was going to do, that he knew the whole story, the end from the beginning. Once again a kind of Docetism seems to have crept into the thinking of these writers, which could imply that Jesus was not fully human after all.

16. R. T. France, *Matthew*, TNTC (Grand Rapids, 1984), 94.

17. Cf. 1QS[a] 1.6–13.

18. The construction in Greek is *en tō baptisthēnai* (aorist passive infinitive), not *en tō baptizesthai* (present passive infinitive). The latter construction "would have implied the presence of many other candidates for baptism" (Plummer, *The Gospel According to St. Luke*, 98); the former implies their absence. Cf. JB, RSV, Phillips, against NIV. This construction, *en tō* plus the infinitive is used chiefly in Luke's writings. Normally the present infinitive is found, but Luke also has the aorist, whereby the translation usually shifts from "while" to "after that" (BDF, 404.2). But note Schürmann, *Das Lukasevangelium*, 189, fn. 6; Lagrange, *Évangile selon Saint Luc*, 114; Jeremias, *New Testament Theology*, 1.51.

19. Lagrange, *Évangile selon Saint Luc*, 114.

20. But see F. W. Beare, *The Gospel According to Matthew* (New York, 1981), 99–100; Michaels, *Servant and Son*, 27.

21. See B. M. Metzger, *A Textual Commentary on the Greek New Testament* (New York, 1971), 11.

22. Beare, *The Gospel According to Matthew*, 100.

23. See C. Maurer, *TDNT*, 7.962; H. Traub, *TDNT*, 5.529–30.

24. See H. Greeven, *TDNT*, 6.64–68.

25. For a listing of early patristic interpretations, see W. Telfer, "The Form of a Dove," *JTS* 29 (1928), 238–39, and Thomas Aquinas, *Catena Aurea, Commenatry on the Four Gospels Collected Out of the Works of the Fathers*, 4 vols. (Oxford, 1851), notes on Matt. 3:16 and Luke 3:22. See also F.-L. Lentzen-Deis, *Die Taufe Jesu nach den Synoptikern: Literarkritische und gattungsgeschichtliche Untersuchungen*, Frankfurter theologische Studien, 4 (Frankfurt, 1970), 170–83.

26. See Bultmann, *History of the Synoptic Tradition*, 248–49, for references to those who hold such a view.

27. Cf. P. Gerlitz, *Ausserchristliche Einflüsse auf die Entwicklung des christlichen Trinitätadogma* (Leiden, 1963), 132–38.

28. L. E. Keck, "The Spirit and the Dove," *NTS* 17 (1970–1971), 41–67, has argued convincingly the case for a Palestinian rather than a Hellenistic matrix for understanding the dove symbol in the baptism narratives. See also S. Gero, "The Spirit as a Dove at the Baptism of Jesus," *NovT* 18 (1976), 17–35, for a good survey of the literature on this subject.

29. Cf. Ben Zoma: "I was considering the space between the upper waters and the lower waters. . . . And the Spirit of God was brooding on the face of the waters like a dove which broods over her young" (TB *Hagigah* 15a). And Rashi on Gen. 1:2: "The throne of Divine Glory was standing in space, hovering over the face of the waters by the breath of the mouth of the Holy One, blessed be he, and by his command, even as a dove hovers over its nest" (Rashi, *Commentary on the Pentateuch*, trans. M. Rosenbaum and A. M. Silbermann [London, 1946], 3).

30. Barrett, *The Holy Spirit in Gospel Tradition*, 39; cf. also Lagrange, *Évangile selon Saint Marc*, 13; Creed, *The Gospel According to St. Luke*, 57; V. Taylor, *The Gospel According to St. Mark* (London, 1952),161.

31. Dunn, *Baptism in the Holy Spirit*, 27, n. 13; cf. Lampe, *The Seal of the Spirit*, 36; von Baer, *Der heilige Geist in den Lukasschriften*, 58, 169.

32. Lane, *The Gospel According to Mark*, 57. For rabbinic passages that refer to Israel as a dove, see StrB 1.124–25; cf. A. Feuillet, "Le Symbolisme de la Colombe dans les récits évangéliques du baptême," *RSR* 46 (1958) 524–44. But see Marshall, *Commentary on Luke*, 153.

33. Fitzmyer, *The Gospel According to Luke, I–IX*, 484.

34. See B. F. Westcott, *The Gospel According to St. John* (London, 1908), 1.49.

35. Lampe, "The Holy Spirit in Luke," 148.

36. The majority of Greek mss, including ℵ, A, L, W, do have *epi* in the Marcan text rather than *eis*. But *epi* is rejected in favor of *eis* by modern textual critics because they view *epi* as a late reading intended to harmonize Mark with Matthew and Luke.

37. Dunn, *Baptism in the Holy Spirit*, 29, n. 22.

38. Lampe, "The Holy Spirit in Luke," 168. Notice that codex Bezae has *eis auton* for *ep' auton* in all the synoptics. The scribe of this ms apparently harmonized the texts to bring them into line with many patristic commentaries on this narrative. See E. Nestle, "Zur Taube als symbole des Geistes," *ZNW* 7 (1906), 358–59.

39. Dunn, *Jesus and the Spirit*, 62.

40. Büchsel, *Der Geist Gottes*, 162.

41. See Cranfield, *St. Mark*, 54.

42. See the many references to the *bat-kol* in StrB 1.125–32.

43. Marshall, *Commentary on Luke*, 154.

44. Matthew's wording is essentially the same as that of Mark and Luke, except that he changes the second person ("you are") into the third person ("this is"), so as to turn the whole thing into a proclamation directed out to everyone who will listen: "*This is* My beloved Son, *in whom* I am well pleased" (Matt. 3:17). (NOTE: Matthew quotes the second part of this sentence more fully in 12:18.)

45. Codex Bezae, several OL texts, and some church fathers have the whole of Ps. 2:7 LXX—"You are my son, today I have begotten you"—as the words of the voice in Luke 3:22. Many commentators prefer this reading and consider that it is the correct one. See Fitzmyer, *The Gospel According to Luke I–IX*, 485, for a listing of these commentators; see also Leaney, *The Gospel According to Luke*, 110–11.

46. This assumption that the voice combines Ps. 2:7 and Isa. 42:1 has been challenged by M. D. Hooker, *Jesus and the Servant* (London, 1959), 68–73.

47. Ellis, *The Gospel of Luke*, 91.

48. See G. Schrenk, *TDNT*, 2.740, n. 7, for *only* as being the correct meaning for *agapētos* here; see also C. H. Turner, "Ho huios mou ho agapētos," *JTS* 27 (1926), 113–29.

49. See N. B. Stonehouse, *The Witness of Matthew and Mark to Christ* (Philadelphia, 1944), 16–21.

50. See Lane, *The Gospel According to Mark*, 58. Note that the verb, *ei* ("you are"), is the present indicative of *einai*, the verb "to be," which stresses the state of being. It is not from *ginesthai*, the verb that means "to become," which stresses the "coming into existence" of a thing.

51. Cf. S. Mowinckel, *Der Knecht Jahwäs* (Giessen, 1921).

52. C. R. North, *The Suffering Servant in Deutero-Isaiah* (London, 1948), 240–53, with excellent bibliography; H. H. Rowley, *The Servant of the Lord and Other Essays* (Oxford, 1952), 1–88.

53. E. P. Gould, *The Gospel According to St. Mark*, ICC (New York, 1905), 12.

54. J. A. Broadus, *Commentary on the Gospel of Matthew* (Philadelphia, 1886), 59; cf. Lane, *The Gospel According to Mark*, 58: the verb "implies a past choice for the performance of a particular function in history. The thought may be expressed in the formulation, Because you are my unique Son, I have chosen you for the task upon which you are about to enter." See also Stonehouse, *The Witness of Matthew and Mark*, 18–20; T. A. Burkill, *Mysterious Revelation, An Examination of the Philosophy of St. Mark's Gospel* (New York, 1963), 19–20; Hooker, *Jesus and Servant*, 68–73.

55. J. H. Moulton, W. F. Howard and N. Turner, *A Grammar of New Testament Greek* (Edinburgh, 1908, 1929, 1970), 1.134–35.

56. Cf. Gundry, *Matthew*, 49.

57. C. E. B. Cranfield, "The Baptism of Our Lord—A Study of St. Mark 1:9–11," *SJT* 8 (1955), 63.

58. Beare, *Matthew*, 99; D. E. Nineham, *St. Mark* (London, 1963), 58; E. Haenchen, *Der Weg Jesu* (Berlin, 1966), 61.

59. See van Unnik, *NTS* 8 (1961–1962), 113; F. Schneider, *Jesus the Prophet* (Freiburg, 1973), 165, 189; M. Dömer, *Das Heil Gottes* (Bonn, 1978), 63–65.

60. F. Godet, *The Gospel of Luke* (Edinburgh, 1881), 101; cf. Dunn, *Baptism in the Spirit*, 24–32, who argues strongly and convincingly of the Spirit's role in Jesus' becoming the representative of Israel, the new Adam, a corporate person, who thus was the inaugurator of a new humanity.

61. See Hawthorne, "The Significance of the Holy Spirit in the Life of Christ," 63; cf. also Dunn, *Baptism in the Holy Spirit*, 27.

62. Taylor, *The Gospel of Mark*, 162.

63. Marshall, *Commentary on Luke*, 156.

64. See G. B. Caird, *St. Luke* (Baltimore, 1963), 77; Cranfield, *The Gospel of Mark*, 55; Taylor, *The Gospel of Mark*, 162; A. E. J. Rawlinson, *The Gospel According to Mark* (London, 1925), 10, 254; but see B. H. Branscomb, *The Gospel of Mark* (New York, 1937), 16; Barrett, *The Holy Spirit and Gospel Tradition*, 41–44; Creed, *The Gospel of Luke*, 56; M. Dibelius, *Die urchristliche Überlieferung von Johannes dem Täufer* (Göttungen, 1911), 59, 63.

65. Harnack, *The Sayings of Jesus* (London, 1908), 245, quoted by Taylor, *The Gospel of Mark*, 162.

66. R. H. Fuller, *The Mission and Achievement of Jesus* (London, 1954), 84, as quoted by Dunn, *Jesus and the Spirit*, 39.

67. See StrB 4.515–516.

68. But see U. W. Mauser, *Christ in the Wilderness*, SBT 39 (Naperville, Ill., 1963), 146–49, and E. Best, *The Temptation and the Passion*, SNTS Monograph Series 2 (Cambridge, 1965), 8–10.

69. A. Schlatter, *Der Evangelist Matthäus* (Stuttgart, 1982), 97. Schlatter's own words are: "Diese Macht verletzt aber . . . die personhafte Art des inwendigen Lebens nicht. Jesus bleibt der Herr seines Willens und seiner Bewusstseins."

70. B. Gerhardsson, *The Testing of God's Son* (Lund, 1966); G. H. P. Thompson, "Called-Proved-Obedient: A Study in the Baptism and Temptation Narratives of Matthew and Luke," *JTS* 11 (1960), 1–12; P. Doble, "The Temptations," *ExpT* 72 (1960–1961), 91–93; J. A. T. Robinson, *Twelve New Testament Studies* (Naperville, Ill., 1962), 53–60.

71. Dunn, *Baptism in the Spirit*, 31.

72. L. Morris, *The Lord from Heaven*, 52.

73. Marshall, *Commentary on Luke*, 166; see also Schürmann, *Das Lukasevangelium*, 1.208.

74. Swete, *The Holy Spirit in the New Testament*, 55.

5. The Spirit in the Ministry of Jesus

Jesus left his home in Nazareth for the specific purpose of being baptized by John in the Jordan River. In all likelihood he intended to return to Nazareth after his baptism and resume the work that had previously occupied his time (cf. Mark 6:3). But something happened to him in Judea that changed everything, that radically altered whatever personal plans he may have had for himself.

Immediately after Jesus was baptized, the Spirit descended upon him, entered into him, filled him without measure, and remained within him. The consequence of this crisis event was that the entire course of Jesus' life was forever changed. From this moment onward the directing and empowering impulse of the Spirit of God ordered the way he was to go, the things he was to say and do.

It is clear from the previous chapter that the Spirit inclined Jesus' feet away from any homeward journey, away from the Jordan and the companionship of John, into the desert, into the arena of testing, and triumphantly beyond this into the difficult path of his own unique ministry (cf. Luke 4:1–2). It will become clearer now in this present chapter that this directing work of the Spirit continued throughout the remaining years of Jesus' life. Furthermore, it will become clear also that the Spirit so fully motivated Jesus' speech and actions that the miracles he performed and the words he spoke he spoke and performed, not by virture of his own power, the power of his own divine personality, but by virtue of the power of the Holy Spirit at work within him and through him.

The Witness of the Evangelists to the Spirit in Jesus' Ministry

That Jesus did his mighty works and preached his message with authority because he was enabled to do so by the Holy Spirit is the conclusion to which the Gospel writers came after reflecting on the extraordinary nature of his words and deeds. They expressed this conclusion both explicitly and implicitly.

Explicit References

Matthew 12:17–21

Matthew, for example, tells how Jesus with a word healed a man whose hand was withered (Matt. 12:9–14), and how he cured all (*pantes*) the sick in a crowd of people that followed him (Matt. 12:15). Upon telling this story, Matthew immediately proceeded to quote the words of God from Isaiah 42:1–4 and explicitly to apply them to Jesus. The quotation was, "Look! my servant whom I have chosen, my beloved in whom my soul delights. I will put my Spirit upon him, and he will proclaim justice to the Gentiles" (Matt. 12:17–21).[1]

It should be noted that the Hebrew of this quotation (Isa. 42:1–4) does not identify the individual under discussion,[2] whereas the LXX states that Jacob is this servant and Israel this chosen one. Matthew, however, claims that this specially endowed person, anticipated so long ago by the prophet but not identified by him, is in reality neither an unknown figure of past redemptive history, nor is he Jacob/Israel. Rather he is Jesus. Matthew unequivocably affirms that Jesus is the Servant of the Lord par excellence. Jesus is ultimately the Chosen of the Lord. Jesus is the one upon whom the Spirit rests, and who, as a result, will proclaim justice to the Gentiles. Jesus, thus, is the supreme fulfillment of the divine intention expressed in this Old Testament prophecy.

Now it is possible to infer that Matthew used Isaiah 42:1–4 primarily to emphasize the pacifism of the servant as reflected in Jesus' withdrawal from the scene of controversy.[3] The correctness of this inference should not, however, overshadow another equally valid inference, namely that Matthew also used it to direct attention to the source of Jesus' wonder-working power—the Holy Spirit. This additional inference can be sustained not only by considering where Matthew places the quotation from Isaiah—sandwiched in between an unspecified total number of Jesus' acts of healing (Matt. 12:9–14, 15–16, 22–23)—but especially by taking note of the particular Greek word he uses for *servant* when he cites this Old Testament passage, perhaps following the lead of the LXX at this point. It is the word *pais*, a word which can mean "child" or "boy" (Tyndale), as well as "servant" (KJV). The Hebrew word (*ʾebed*), which underlies it, however, unambiguously means "servant" (*doulos*).

It is important now to realize that the Greek word *pais*, not *doulos*, became *the* special word picked up and used by the earliest Christians whenever they wished to refer to Jesus as the Messiah, the Anointed of the Lord, the Son, the One who truly fulfilled the prophecies about the Servant, or when they talked about his powerful deeds and God-pleasing life. Here are excerpts from their words as recorded in Acts: "The God of our fathers glorified his servant (*pais*) Jesus . . ." (Acts 3:13). "Sovereign Lord . . . they were gathered together against your holy servant (*pais*) Jesus, whom you anointed" (Acts 4:24, 27). "O Lord . . . you stretched out your hand to heal, and as a consequence signs and wonders happened through the name of your servant (*pais*) Jesus" (Acts 4:30; cf. 3:26). Clearly Matthew stands in the tradition of these earliest Christians. He with them saw in the works of Jesus the fulfilment of Isaiah 42. For him Jesus was the ultimate Servant/Son, the Chosen One loved by God, anointed and equipped by the Spirit of God, sent forth to do the will of God in the power of the Spirit of God.

Matthew 12:28–29

For a discussion of this explicit reference to the Spirit in the ministry of Jesus see below, pages 169–72.

Luke 4:14

Luke, as well as Matthew, makes explicit the source of Jesus' ability to fulfill his mission. He, following Mark, recites in order the stories of the baptism of Jesus, the descent of the Spirit upon him, and his temptation in the desert. Then, still following Mark, Luke states that Jesus returned to Galilee, to that region from which he had come, not, however, to resume his former occupation, but to inaugurate his new vocation—that of the Christ, the Anointed One, the Servant of the Lord. But unlike Mark (or Matthew) Luke provides his readers with a most significant preface to this fresh phase of Jesus' life. He writes: "Jesus returned to Galilee *in the power of the Spirit*" (4:14a).

With this extraordinary prefatory remark Luke makes it clear that, as far as he understood things, Jesus did not begin to preach, to teach, or to perform miracles, nor did he continue to do such things (cf. 4:14b, which presupposes an extended ministry) on his own initiative or by virtue of his own skills or because he possessed inherently some power for healing or exorcising. Quite the contrary. Luke precisely identifies Jesus' power as the power of the Holy Spirit,[4] and thus attributes those things Jesus did, which caused people to spread his fame far and wide (4:14b), to the *dynamis*, "the power," of the Spirit. Jesus, who had received the Spirit at his baptism (Luke 3:21–22) and by the Spirit's power was tested and found true to God (Luke 4:1–12), now by that same power begins his work of binding the strong man, Satan, and of spoiling his goods (Luke 11:21–22).[5] Clearly, then, for Luke the Holy Spirit, who is to be distinguished from Jesus, is that divine power from outside of Jesus which comes down upon Jesus, which stands over him, which is at work within him and through him, which both inspires and empowers him. Jesus thus begins his mission armed with the Spirit and goes forward to accomplish that mission in the power of the Spirit.

Luke 10:17–22

Still another explicit reference on the part of the evangelists to the influence of the Spirit upon the person of Jesus is found in Luke 10:21a: "In that very hour [Jesus] rejoiced in the Holy Spirit, and said. . . ."[6] Here in one bold remark Luke makes it clear that even the emotions of Jesus were in some powerful sense affected by the Spirit. The extreme joy that Jesus felt at that particular moment was inspired by the Spirit of God (cf. Gal. 5:22).

But there is more yet to be said about this Lucan remark. It is a strange statement, unique in the New Testament, curiously placed by Luke immediately after the story of the return of the seventy/seventy-two (Luke 10:17–20), and immediately before a transcript of an extraordinary prayer and declaration of Jesus (10:21b–22). It is placed purposefully, it would seem, in between both of these two pericopes in order to explain certain aspects of each more fully.

1. In the first of these the seventy/seventy-two had been sent out by Jesus on an extended missionary journey. They had been commissioned by him to go into every city and place where he himself would follow (Luke 10:1) and had been authorized by him[7] to trample down all the powers of the evil one (10:19). When they had finished their tour and had come back, they reported to Jesus with joy and surprise that even the demons were subject to them in his name (10:17). According to Luke, Jesus' first response to this report was to say, "I saw Satan fall like lightning from heaven" (10:18).

The question now is, when and how did Jesus see Satan fall? Did this happen before Jesus' birth? Is this a veiled reference by him to his preexistence when in the age of eternity past he witnessed Satan's sudden and swift ("like lightning") expulsion from the presence of God?[8] Or is this figurative language? Was Jesus simply making use of an ancient idea of the fall and defeat of Satan[9] "to express symbolically the significance of [his disciples'] exorcism of the demons"?[10] Was Jesus saying in effect, "I see, I understand, that these exorcisms signify the end of Satan's rule"? Or is this the language of ecstasy? Do these words refer to a supernatural sight that Jesus had contemporaneously with his disciples' mission? Is Jesus hereby recounting a visionary experience?[11]

It would be presumptuous to say unequivocally which of these answers is the correct answer. Nevertheless, there is good reason to believe that the last of these is to be preferred over the others: (1) The verb translated, "I saw," is the Greek verb *theorein*. Its meaning is not limited to seeing with one's physical eyes (cf. Luke 21:6; 24:39), but it extends its meaning to embrace ideas of mental perception, of seeing with the eyes of the mind (cf. John 4:19; Acts 27:10), even to that of contemplating mystically through the agency of the Holy Spirit (see Clem *Str.* 6.18).[12] (2) The tense of this verb is imperfect (*etheōroun*), a tense that is regularly used to refer to a continuous or repeated action. But since the verb *theorein* is virtually confined to the present and imperfect tenses in the New Testament—its aorist form occurs only four times out of its fifty-eight appearances (Matt. 28:1; Luke 23:48; John 8:51; Rev. 11:12)[13]—and since the Aramaic language that lies behind the Greek has only one past tense,[14] it is not out of the realm of possibility to understand the action described here as a simple past act, such as might take place in a vision, rather than as a repeated or continuous action—"I saw," not, "I was observing." (3) "The wording of the saying with its comparison of Satan's fall in its swiftness and conspicuousness to a flash of lightning suggests a visionary experience more strongly than a figure of speech."[15] (4) Finally, Luke's seemingly deliberate decision to place his remark that Jesus exulted in the Holy Spirit immediately after his remark that Jesus saw Satan fall from heaven is still another indication that the latter experience was an ecstatic one, the agent of which was the Spirit. Just as the Holy Spirit moved Jesus "to an extraordinary height of emotion"[16] in the one instance, so quite likely in the other—the Spirit caught Jesus up in ecstasy during the absence of the seventy/seventy-two and showed him in a vision, in a moment of time, the conquest of Satan (at least the dawning of this conquest) through his disciples' ministry. Thus the very positioning of the saying about Jesus rejoicing in the Spirit can be used to shed light upon Jesus' experience of seeing the downfall of the devil—an experience not unlike that which happened some years later to one of his own Spirit-inspired prophets (Rev. 12:7–12; cf. 1:10–12; 4:1–2; 17:3; 21:10). In other words, the Spirit, who filled Jesus with ecstatic exultation, did so by showing him in a vision who the victor was and who the vanquished.

2. The second pericope, now placed by Luke immediately after the saying, "Jesus rejoiced in the Holy Spirit," contains an extraordinary prayer of Jesus and an equally extraordinary declaration by him. First the prayer: "I praise you, Father, Lord of heaven and earth, because you hid these things from the wise and clever and revealed them to infants. Yes, Father, I praise you because this was desired and willed by you." And then the declaration: "All things were handed over to me by my Father, and no one knows who the Son is except the Father, or who the Father is except the Son and anyone to whom the Son chooses to reveal him" (Luke 10:21b–22/Matt. 11:25–27).

The extraordinary element in these words is that Jesus at this point in life seems to know in the fullest sense who he is and what his mission involves—Son of God uniquely and the exclusive revealer of the Father. But how does this square with the fact that Luke intends, as do the other evangelists, in writing about Jesus to describe a fully human life? Whence came this consciousness within Jesus of a mutual knowledge between himself and the Father of the kind that is indicated here? Whence came to him such an awareness of his singular relationship to God? Was this consciousness, this awareness, an awareness that was his throughout his life? Did he possess from birth an unbroken and sustained knowledge of himself as the unique Son? Could this be? Would such a fact be in harmony with his genuine humanity?

It is in answer to these questions that Luke's saying about Jesus rejoicing in the Holy Spirit may again prove exceedingly helpful. By placing it precisely here, it is as though Luke were saying that just as at the baptism of Jesus the Spirit was closely associated with Jesus' personal awareness of being the divine Son, and as the Spirit was also closely associated with him in the crucial experiences of the temptation in the wilderness when his Sonship was being challenged, so now this joyful ecstasy inspired by the Holy Spirit leads Jesus to yet another fresh, still more profound, understanding of himself and his relationship with the Father. "We cannot think," writes Vincent Taylor, "that Luke was mistaken when he prefaced his version of the . . . saying, 'I thank thee, O Father, Lord of heaven and earth' (v. 21), with the words, 'In that same hour he rejoiced in the Holy Spirit and said.'"[17]

One may correctly infer, therefore, from this account and from others within the synoptic Gospels, that Jesus' consciousness of being in a unique relationship to God, as Son to the Father, was a developing one in keeping with his years and in keeping with his ability to understand and make use of it, spurred on by extraordinary events (e.g. baptism, temptation, transfiguration), by his own constant meditation on the meaning of certain key Old Testament passages (e.g. 2 Sam. 7:8–16; Isa. 42–53; Dan. 2:31–35; 7:9–14; Zech. 9),[18] *and* by the illuminating activity of the Holy Spirit.

> The impression we receive from the Synoptics is that there were times when, as it were, the curve of [Jesus'] filial consciousness suddenly swept up above the normal experiences of His conscious

> life. . . . [At these times] the Father reveals Himself as pre-eminently *His* Father and Jesus perceives that He is *His* son and that He is acknowledged as such by the Father. So far as we are able to judge from the Synoptic narratives, these experiences are occasional. They leave an abiding sense of Sonship which is the undertone of the work of Jesus as healer, exorcist, and teacher, and above all of His mission as the Suffering Son of Man. But they do not always throb at their highest intensity, and Jesus rarely speaks of them.[19]

When these exceptional experiences did occur, however, the Spirit was present in them to interpret their significance to Jesus, and from them to illumine Jesus as to his person, as to who he was indeed. The very same Spirit which bears witness with our spirits informing us of our identity, telling us we are God's children (cf. Rom. 8:14–16), was also the Spirit present within Jesus, seemingly to inform him in like manner of his identity, to tell him that he was God's Son as no other person was God's Son. Surely this is the implication of Luke's purposeful positioning of the statement in 10:21a, "[Jesus] rejoiced in the Holy Spirit and said," immediately before he told his readers what it was that Jesus said, "I thank thee, Father . . ." (10:21b).

John 3:34–35

In words reminiscent of Luke 10:22, John the Evangelist writes, "The Father loves the Son, and has given all things into his hand" (3:35). And also reminiscent of Luke, John prefaces this extraordinary declaration with a reference to the Holy Spirit and Jesus: "He whom God sent speaks the words of God, for it is not by measure he gives the Spirit" (3:34; cf. Luke 10:21a).

In the Greek text this last clause, translated above in a quite literal fashion, is somewhat problematic because there is no expressed subject for the verb *gives*. Hence, the interpreter must decide who it is who gives and who it is who receives, and provide a subject for the verb. Is the one whom the Father sent—that is, the Son—the subject? Is it the Son who gives the Spirit, presumably to those who receive his testimony (John 3:32)? Is he who speaks the words of God to be recognized as God's spokesman because he imparts the Spirit without measure? To explain the text in this way would surely be consistent with Johannine thought (John 7:37–39; 20:22, cf. 1 John 3:24; 4:13) and in harmony with both ancient and some modern interpreters.[20]

But to do so would be to do violence to the context. It would be to import an idea foreign to it, to go against what John is attempting to prove here, namely that the words of Jesus are to be identified with the words of God for the precise reason that Jesus receives the Spirit in no measured degree. God, therefore, must be understood as the subject of *gives* and be supplied to make the translation clear—"He whom God sent speaks the words of God, for *God* sets no measure as he gives him the Spirit" (cf. TEV, JB, NEB, NIV).[21]

The meaning then is clear—Jesus, this particular messenger sent by God, excels all other such messengers. Other messengers, as people supposed, received the Spirit in a measured fashion so that they were able to reveal the mind and will of God, but only partially, since they simply had the ability to prophesy one prophetic book or at the most two.[22] Jesus, however, is given the Spirit without measure, superabundantly, bountifully, completely (*ouk ek metrou*). God gives the Spirit in unlimited fulness to this his last envoy, to Jesus the Son, so that the revelation this one brings is sufficient, complete, in need of no further explanation or amplification (cf. Heb. 1:1–2).[23]

The Holy Spirit that descended on Jesus at the baptism to be with him, to remain in him, to be fully active in his life (John 1:33–34) is the Spirit who now in his fulness inspires Jesus and enables him to speak the words of God with power, to speak words that are in fact the very words of God. The conclusion of the matter is this: the teaching ministry of Jesus was inspired by the Holy Spirit. Jesus spoke as the Spirit filled his mind with new insights prompting him to speak (cf. Mark 13:11). His words came forth with authority through the enabling power of God's Holy Spirit.

Luke writes similarly about the Spirit and Jesus in his preface to the Acts: "The first narrative I composed was all about what Jesus began and continued to do and teach during his earthly life up to his ascension, having given to the apostles whom he chose charges/commandments through the Holy Spirit" (Acts 1:1–2). Here it is stated unequivocably that Jesus gave commands through the Holy Spirit. If this was true of Jesus in his postresurrection ministry, it was certainly all the more true of him in his earthly ministry prior to his resurrection.

From these passages in John and Acts, therefore, it becomes clear that Jesus depended on the Spirit to supply him with insights into the mind of God, so as to shape the message he was to speak. The Spirit of God communicated the words of God to the Son of God incarnate, so that they might become words of life to those who heard. He spoke as no other person had spoken (John 7:46). His words confounded the learned teachers of the Law, so that they did not dare ask him any more questions (Mark 12:34). The audience at Nazareth testified to the graciousness of his words (Luke 4:22). Multitudes of people crowded around him to hear what he had to say (Matt. 5:1–2). But the attractiveness of Jesus' teaching, or its novelty, "lay not so much in the substance of what he taught as in the spiritual force with which his message was delivered."[24] This force was the Holy Spirit through which God's message was communicated to Jesus, and by which it was expressed to the world—"He whom God sent speaks the words of God, for God does not give the Spirit to him sparingly" (John 3:34).

These, then, are the explicit remarks of the Gospel writers about the Spirit as the source of Jesus' power for both his deeds and words. Although their number is not large, their intent is clear. They say in no uncertain terms that, from the perspective of the evangelists, the source of Jesus' ability to do the miraculous and to speak with divine authority was to be found in the Holy Spirit who had come down upon him and had filled him with his fulness. The relatively small number of these explicit statements cannot be used to invalidate this conclusion,[25] for in addition there are also numerous implicit statements throughout the Gospels to this same effect.

Implicit References

Frequent Use of the Word *Power* (*dynamis*)

The word *power* (*dynamis*), which is often used to refer to Jesus and to his works and words, is one of the implicit allusions to the power of God, the Holy Spirit. It has already been noted that in some contexts *power* (*dynamis*) is in fact a synomym for *spirit/Spirit*. For instance, the angel said the following to Zechariah about his son, John, who was yet to be born: "He will go before [the Lord] in the spirit and power . . ." (*en pneumati kai dynamei*, Luke 1:17). Here the words *power* and *spirit* are linked closely together, if not identified. A clearer example, however, is the words of the angel of the Lord to Mary, "The Holy Spirit (*pneuma hagion*) will come upon you, and the power (*dynamis*) of the Most High will overshadow you" (Luke 1:35). Here, by means of poetic parallelism, *power*, the power (*dynamis*) of God, is not merely linked to but is equated with the Spirit, the Holy Spirit (*pneuma hagion*). The Spirit and power are thus indissolubly related and constitute God's creative, effective force present in the world and available to human beings.[26]

It is not surprising, therefore, to learn that Jesus went away from the Jordan back into Galilee "in the power of the Spirit" (*en dynamei tou pneumatos*, Luke 4:14). That is to say, Jesus' life from the baptism onward was filled with extraordinary power because Jesus was filled with the Holy Spirit (Matt. 12:18, Luke 4:1). Thus, when the evangelists write, "the power of the Lord was with [Jesus] to heal" (Luke 5:17), or that everyone wanted to touch Jesus "because power was coming forth from him and was healing all" (Luke 6:19), or that Jesus sensed that power had gone out of him to heal (Mark 5:30, Luke 8:46), they intended to say that the power of God, the Holy Spirit, was present in Jesus and that this power was operative through him to cure the ills of the people. It was a *dynamis* ("power") for healing that originated with the Spirit. Here is to be found the source of Jesus' ability to restore people to wholeness and health—the Holy Spirit!

Is it extraordinary, then, that the miracles of Jesus were designated by the evangelists as "powers" (*dynameis*, Matt. 11:20–23/Luke 10:13; Matt. 13:54/Mark 6:2/Luke 4:36; Matt. 13:58/Mark 6:5; Luke 19:37)? These writers were certain that the powerful Spirit of God was with Jesus to make it possible for him to reverse the effects of the destroyer. They believed that the power of God was in him to heal all that were oppressed by the devil (cf. Acts 10:38). Hence, for them such miraculous deeds of his could be nothing other than powers (*dynameis*),[27] because they were in fact effected by the power of God, the Holy Spirit. The miracles of Jesus were but the actualization of the Spirit's power.[28] Jesus was the bearer of power in the absolute, for he was the bearer of the Holy Spirit (*der Geistträger*) in the fullest sense, in unmeasured fashion (John 3:34). He was able to do such signs and miracles, so testified Nicodemus, only because God was with him (John 3:2; 9:33; cf. 5:19; Acts 10:38).

The Frequent Use of the Word *Authority* (*exousia*)

The use of the word *authority* (*exousia*) in the Gospels to describe the words and works of Jesus is still another implicit reference to the Holy Spirit present and at work in him. That this is true becomes apparent from Mark's brief account about Jesus' preaching in the synagogue at Capernaum. When the people there heard him speak, they were astonished, struck quite out of their senses (*exeplēssonto*) because, unlike the scribes, the learned doctors and teachers of the Law, Jesus taught them with authority (Mark 1:21–22/Luke 4:31–32; cf. Matt. 7:28–29).

Instilled in the minds of these people was the idea that, with the disappearance of the Old Testament prophets, inspiration ceased and any activity of the Spirit was confined to what had been written in the Torah and the other canonical writings.[29] They understood that their rabbis, their teachers, could only interpret the Scriptures and pass on the traditions. They could not offer any new revelation from God. They lacked the authority to speak directly from or for God, because they lacked the inspiration of the Spirit to give authority to what they said. Thus, the explosive testimony of the people in Capernaum recorded by Mark, that Jesus taught with authority (*exousia*), is significant. It meant that here in the voice of Jesus these people were themselves hearing the voice of prophecy so long silent in Israel. They were certain that his words had the ring of truth to them, that these words possessed the same authentic value as the words of the ancient prophets who had their commission directly from God. For them Jesus' words were powerful words, inspired words, authoritative words, because they were words that had the force and authority of the Holy Spirit behind them. [30]

While still in the synagaogue at Capernaum, Jesus encountered a person under the control of an unclean spirit or demon. Jesus exorcised the demon with the briefest of commands, without magical incantations or manipulations of any kind. "Silence!" he said, "Come out of him!" And the demon came out (Mark 1:23–26). As before, the evangelists record the reaction of the people who observed this miracle. They were amazed. To be precise, they were so astonished (*ethambēthēsan*) that they stumbled over their words: "What is this? A new teaching? With authority [*exousia*]? He gives a command to the unclean spirits and they obey him!" (Mark 1:27); "What is there in this man's words? For with authority [*exousia*] and power [*dynamis*] he gives a command to the unclean spirits and they come out!" (Luke 4:36).

In telling this story, both Mark and Luke make it clear that the reason for this astonishment of the people was not the sheer newness of Jesus' teachings nor the spectacular nature of his actions but that these were said or done with authority (*exousia*). The use of this word echoes its earlier use (Mark 1:22; Luke 4:32; cf. 4:14; 9:1) and underscores again the idea that the power by which Jesus worked this miracle was in fact a power accompanied with an authority that came from the Holy Spirit. Thus, "Jesus is the Spirit-guided agent vested with the power of God who now dominates the world of evil opposition."[31] His command was supercharged with an authority the like of which these bystanders had never before witnessed. "Here was a teaching qualitatively new in the authority with which it laid hold of [people]."[32]

The appearance of this same word, *authority* (*exousia*), in the story of the paralytic helps significantly in explaining the events detailed in that story (Mark 2:1–12/Matt. 9:1–8/Luke 5:17–26). The evangelists agree that Jesus spoke two words to the crippled man who had been brought to him for healing. The first word was, "My child, your sins are forgiven!" And the second was, "Get up, take up your mat and walk!" But between these two words came the accusation of the scribes (and Pharisees in Luke): "This fellow blasphemes! Who has the ability to forgive sins except one person, and that person is God?" The second word of Jesus, "Get up and walk!" the word that healed the man of his paralysis and sent him on his way home, was, according to the Gospel writers, spoken in order to make it clear that the Son of Man, Jesus himself, indeed could forgive sins on earth because he possessed the authority, the *exousia*, to do so (Mark 2:10/Matt. 9:6/ Luke 5:24).

But what was this authority? What was the source of this authority? Contrary to what the scribes and Pharisees chose to believe about Jesus (Mark 2:7), he was not acting "in violation of the power and authority of God,"[33] he was not usurping God's prerogatives but was in fact speaking and acting for God. It can be inferred from the narrative that in this instance Jesus' authority to forgive sins was not an intrinsic authority but a delegated authority, not one inherent in him by virture of his own divine nature, but one given him by God, an authority that was his by virtue of a prophetic gift bestowed on him, the gift of the Holy Spirit to him (cf. John 5:19, 27, 30; see also 2 Sam. 12:13; John 20:22, 23). Matthew makes this explicit by concluding his account of this story with these words: "The crowd was awestruck and they praised God *who had given such authority [exousia] to people*" (Matt. 9:8).[34]

Although the word *exousia* itself does not appear in Mark 2:23–28 (Matt. 12:1–8/Luke 6:1–5), where Jesus declares that human beings were not brought into existence for the benefit of the sabbath, but quite the other way around, and that the Son of Man (Jesus himself, cf. Mark 2:5 with 2:10) is master of the sabbath, it is clear, nevertheless, that the authority motif is present here as well. For if Jesus is Lord of the Sabbath and is therefore entitled to abrogate the regulations concerning it if he wishes, then he possesses an authority that is at least equal to that of the Mosaic Law, a law which was not of human origin but was given by God himself.[35] "And the reader's recall should be immediate: this authority was an authority bestowed on Jesus by the Holy Spirit who resides permanently within him (Mark 1:10–11) as the Son of Man."[36]

This idea of pneumatic-prophetic authority (*exousia*) also figures prominently in the narrative of the cleansing of the Temple (Mark 11:15–17, 27–33/Matt. 21:12–13, 23–27/Luke 19:45–46; 20:1–8). There Jesus drives those buying and selling within the temple area out of its precincts, overturns the tables of the money changers and of the dove dealers, permits no one any longer to carry merchandise through the Temple courts, and begins to teach the people about the true purpose of God's house.

Such dramatic, prophetlike action meets with severe resistance from the chief priests, the scribes and the elders of the people. They wish to discredit Jesus in the eyes of the crowd and eventually to destroy him, both because of his violent invasion of their domain, ejecting vendors whom they had licensed, and because of his teaching that the sacred significance of the Temple was being violated by this merchandizing that they were permitting. In pursuing their hostile goals they asked two questions, the answers to which are profoundly important to the central issue of this book: "What sort of authority do you have for acting in this way?" (Mark, Matt., Luke), and "Who gave you this authority?" (Mark, Luke).

Jesus, however, counters with a question of his own: "The baptism of John, was it from heaven [i.e. from God] or from human beings? Answer me!" After debating among themselves how best to answer him—"If we say John's baptism was from heaven, he will say, 'Why did you not believe him?' And if we say it was from human beings, the people will stone us, for they are convinced John was a prophet"—these religious leaders decided the best reply was no reply and they took refuge in feigned ignorance. "We do not know," they said.

Since they would not answer his question, Jesus would not answer theirs. As a consequence there then exists no explicit explanation about the nature and source of his authority! Nevertheless an explanation can be inferred from studying the story more closely. What needs to be noted is that Jesus made his answer to the question of the scribes and Pharisees about his authority depend entirely on their answer to his question about John's authority—John the Baptist, who was a prophet and more than a prophet (Matt. 11:9; Luke 7:26). Their decision about John, in other words, would determine their decision about him.[37] For had they been prepared to acknowledge that John's authority, although it had no hierarchical warrant, was nevertheless genuinely from above, attested by its results, they would have been in a proper frame of mind correctly to assess the question of Jesus' authority. Reflecting on this it is possible to say (1) that Jesus firmly believed that John's authority was prophetic in nature with its origin from God, mediated to him by the Spirit of God, and (2) that since Jesus here had consciously aligned himself with John, he was therefore implicitly claiming that the nature and source of his own authority was the same as that of the Baptist. This is to say, had Jesus directly answered the question concerning his authority he would have said that, like John's, his authority for doing what he did and for saying what he said was that of a prophet like John. His was an authority based on a profound sense of divine inspiration, an authority originating with God and with God's gift to him of the Holy Spirit. Once again it seems that Jesus recognized his authority to be a delegated authority and that he looked not within himself but outside himself to God, to the Spirit of God, for his authorization to speak and act. In the words of the fourth Gospel, he did nothing on his own initiative or by his own authority (John 5:30).

Such an inference, that Jesus' authority was a pneumatic-prophetic authority, is corroborated by still another incident from his life. The evangelists tell of Jesus' return to his hometown of Nazareth (Mark 6:1–6; Matt. 13:53–58; cf. Luke 4:16–30). On the sabbath he began to teach in the synagogue where he had grown up. Those who heard him, however, were filled with indignation at him and asked an important question, quite like the one asked by the scribes (see above)—"Where did this fellow get this wisdom and these miraculous powers? Who gave these things to him?" They did not wait or wish for an answer, for being quite confident in themselves that they knew what the answer was, based on their knowledge of his humble origins and of the fact that he had had no training in the rabbinical schools, they quickly took offence at what he said and refused to listen to his words.

But had Jesus been give an opportunity to reply to their questions, what would he have said? Would he have said that this wisdom was his own wisdom, that is, the wisdom of a divine person, or that his miraculous powers were due to his own divine nature? The final part of this story answers this question with a negative. For here Jesus' words, as recorded by the evangelists, are: "A prophet is not without honor, except in his own home town." These words say, in effect, that Jesus recognized that his wisdom was the wisdom of a prophet, wisdom inspired by the Spirit of God, and that his miraculous powers were of a similar nature, produced by that same Spirit.

The People's Perception of Jesus as a Prophet

Still one more implicit reference to the presence and power of the Spirit in Jesus' life is the Gospel record of the people's perception of Jesus as a prophet. Prophets were people who spoke and acted under divine inspiration, who spoke and acted as they were moved to do so by a divine impulse. They were ambassadors of God, revealers and interpreters of the mind of God, authoritative instructors of the people (Num. 12:6; 1 Sam. 3:19–21; 1 Kings 16:7–12; Jer. 1:5–7; Ezek. 2:3–5). They owed their authority and power to the inspiration of the Spirit of God (Ezek. 2:2; 11:5; Dan. 5:12 LXX; Zech. 1:6 LXX; 2 Pet. 1:21). So when rumors spread abroad about the extraordinary things

Jesus taught, the authoritative manner in which he taught (Mark 1:22, 27; Matt. 7:29; Luke 4:32–36), the amazing things he did, and the powerful manner in which he did them (Mark 6:14; Matt. 14:1; Luke 9:7), it is not surprising to learn that some of those who observed all this were convinced that he was a prophet like one of the prophets (Mark 6:15; 8:28; understood by Luke to mean like one of the classical Old Testament prophets, Luke 9:8), or *the* prophet, that is, the prophet-like-Moses (Deut. 18:15, 18) who belonged to the end time of salvation (John 6:14; 7:40; cf. 1QS 9:11), or even as one of the ancient prophets *redivivus* (Matt. 16:14).

When Jesus raised to life the dead son of the widow from Nain, the crowd was awestruck. They praised God and, reflecting no doubt on the Elijah story (1 Kings 17:8–24), said: "A great prophet has arisen among us" (Luke 7:16).

When Jesus entered Jerusalem for the last time, the whole city was shaken because upon asking, "Who is this person?" it received the reply from the crowd: "He is the prophet from Nazareth of Galilee" (Matt. 21:11; cf. 21:46).

When Jesus told a woman whom he met for the first time about her private life and the many husbands she had had, her immediate response to what she considered supernatural insight was, "Sir, I see that you are a prophet!" (John 4:18–19).

When five thousand people were fed by Jesus from a very meager supply of food, they inferred from this miracle that he truly was *the* long-expected prophet (John 6:14).

When the crowds who attended the great celebration of the feast of tabernacles listened to Jesus' teaching and heard his claims, they had only one response: "This person is truly *the* prophet" (John 7:40; cf 7:52).

When the blind man was asked about Jesus who had given him his sight, he answered with similar words: "He is a prophet!" (John 9:17).

When two of Jesus' disciples who had been with him to the end of his ministry and who had observed him at close hand were asked about him, they testified to the fact that they themselves and others like them were certain that Jesus had been a prophet powerful in word and deed before God and all the people (Luke 24:19).

Even the scepticism of the Pharisees, including both their doubt about Jesus' ability to supernaturally perceive the true character of a stranger (Luke 7:39) and their demand for a sign from him (Mark 8:11/Luke 11:16), points to the fact that everyone else was certain that he was a prophet. And it was as a prophet (a false prophet) that Jesus was arrested and accused. The cry of the guards, "Prophesy!" (Mark 14:65/Matt. 26:68/Luke 22:64), which was not part of the usual games played by the Roman soldiers with the condemned person, makes this quite certain.[38] Such was the recorded testimony of those who came in contact with Jesus.

Yet even when the evangelists do not use the word *prophet* in their description of Jesus, the nature of the incidents they record from his life serve simply to strengthen the conviction that he was considered by the people to be a prophet. For example, like the Old Testament prophets it is said that Jesus gave to the people both promises (Mark 10:29–30) and threats (Matt. 23:13–29/Luke 11:42–52). Like them he had visions (Mark 1:10; Luke 10:18) and ecstatic experiences, at which times he would be caught away by the Spirit (Luke 10:21). He, too, like the ancient prophets, was given power to discern the hidden thoughts of people, to see and know the hidden motives which governed their lives (Mark 2:5, 8; 10:21; 12:43; Luke 6:18; 9:47; 19:5; 20:23). He, as the Old Testament prophets, knew the future and could predict events ahead of their happenings. He foresaw and predicted what would happen to himself (Mark 8:31; 9:31; 10:32–34; 14:18, 27, 30), to his disciples (Mark 10:39; 13:9–11), to the Temple, and to Jerusalem (Mark 13).[39]

In summary, Jesus was recognized by many, including his own disciples, as a prophet whose ministry was to the poor and the helpless (cf. Luke 7:16). This evaluation of Jesus must then have led these people to a belief that the source of his power, authority, and insight—his ability to speak and act for God—was similar to, if not identical with, that of the Old Testament prophets, namely, the Holy Spirit. They must certainly have believed that Jesus as a prophet was bearer of the Spirit, that he too was *pneumatophoros* (cf. Hos. 9:7 LXX).

The Witness of Jesus Himself to the Spirit in His Ministry

That the Holy Spirit was present and active in the life and ministry of Jesus providing him with the wisdom and power, the authority and insight necessary to carry his ministry to completion is affirmed by no less a person than Jesus himself! So say the evangelists. One cannot, therefore, avoid coming to the conclusion that as far as they were concerned, Jesus traced his ability to teach and to heal back to the Spirit at work within him. The evidence for this conclusion is clear and strong.

1. The Gospel writers record that Jesus perceived himself as a prophet, that is, as one who speaks and acts under inspiration of the Spirit of God (see above, p. 160). Note, for example, the story that Luke tells of Jesus' return to his hometown of Nazareth (Luke 4:16–30). There, according to Luke, Jesus went into the synagogue on the sabbath. It had been his custom to set the seventh day apart from labor and to give himself "to the learning of [Jewish] customs and laws."[40]

On this occasion Jesus apparently was invited to read the assigned passage from the prophets[41] and to give the sermon based on that reading. His text, which he stood up to read, was Isaiah 61:1, 2a (with some words from Isa. 58:6). When he had finished reading, he rolled up the scroll, handed it back to the attendant, sat down, and began to teach.[42] Now although Luke does not give the content of this teaching, one may correctly infer that Jesus explained the text he had just read in detail and that he then proceeded to apply it to himself. For Luke does record Jesus as saying, either as an introduction to this sermon or as its conclusion, "Today this scripture has been fulfilled in your hearing!" meaning that "at this moment in history whatever was true in a limited sense about the prophet Isaiah has now reached its ultimate meaning in me: 'The Spirit of the Lord is upon *me*, because he anointed *me* to preach good news to the poor. He sent *me* to proclaim release to the prisoners, recovery of sight to the blind, to set the oppressed free and to proclaim the year of the Lord's favor'" (Luke 4:18–19).

It is true that some commentators understand Luke to be presenting Jesus here as one who viewed himself as the Servant of the Lord,[43] or, because of the reference to the anointing, as the kingly or priestly Messiah.[44] But this is hardly possible and for these reasons:

a. The Isaiah passage quoted here is not part of the Song of the Servant, and hence that idea should not be imported into this text.

b. Kings or priests were not the only prominent Old Testament figures to be anointed (cf. 1 Kings 19:16; 2 Kings 2:9, 15). Therefore, the mere mention of an anointing cannot prove that such a Messiah is intended here, especially when this passage makes no mention of a royal or priestly function belonging to Jesus.

c. The Old Testament also designated prophets as anointed ones, as the anointed of the Lord (1 Chron. 16:22; Ps. 105:15), and interestingly the Targum of Isaiah 61 is introduced with the words, *ʾamar nebîyyaʾ*, "the prophet said," implying that the very prophet who sketched for Israel the summit of its glory in chapter 60 is now in chapter 61 looking up in gratitude and praise to the Lord for giving him such an exalted commission.[45]

d. This "idea of prophets as anointed servants of Yahweh emerges in later pre-Christian Palestinian Judaism, e.g. in Qumran literature (see CD 2:12; 6:1; 6QD 3:4). Moreover, the 'herald' . . . of good news in Isaiah 52:7 appears in 11QMelch 18 precisely as one 'anointed with the Spirit.'"[46]

e. Jesus, in the immediate context of this synagogue sermon, places himself among the prophets. His sermon was given with such power and authority that those who heard it, those who had known him from childhood and had known his humble origins, were both astonished at his words and incensed with him because he dared teach them (Matt. 13:54; Mark 6:2; Luke 4:22). Hence, instead of welcoming him and accepting his message, they were repelled by him and rejected both him and what he had to say (Matt. 13:57; Mark 6:3; Luke 4:29). Jesus' response to them came in the form of a familiar proverb: "No prophet is welcome in his own country" (Luke 4:24).[47] To be sure, Jesus made use here of a proverbial saying, but nevertheless by quoting it and by applying it to himself he accepted the popular estimation of who he was and of what he was doing (cf. Matt. 16:14; 21:11, 46; Mark 6:15), and had no hesitation at all about identifying himself with the prophets.[48]

f. Finally, to understand this anointing as a prophetic anointing "makes it intelligible why Jesus is compared to Elijah and Elisha in the verses toward the end of the episode. Elisha in particular is introduced as 'the prophet'; implicitly, Jesus is suggested to be such too."[49]

Still another example, strengthening the presumption that Jesus thought of himself as a prophet, is the extraordinary formula, "Amen, I say to you." What is astonishing about this expression is that (1) no exact Hebrew equivalent to it has as yet turned up,[50] (2) it is found only in the Gospels, in all of the Gospels,[51] and (3) it was always and only spoken by Jesus as an introduction to and an endorsement of his own words—never, as in the Old Testament, as a response affirming the words of someone else! Hence, it is a completely new way of speaking, "a highly characteristic mode of speech for which there is no parallel."[52]

But what did Jesus intend by this "new way of speaking"? What was the significance of this formula? Luke, who retains *amen* as the *only* foreign word in either his Gospel or the Acts, and who uses the amen formula most sparingly of all the evangelists (only six times), may provide a clue to aid in answering these questions. It is instructive to note where he places the very first instance of Jesus speaking these extraordinary words, "Amen I say to you." He places them in the context of the Nazareth synagogue sermon discussed above, where Jesus consciously identifies himself with the prophets, and his words and works with theirs (Luke 4:24; cf. Matt. 13:57; Mark 6:4). Thus, by using the amen formula initially as an introduction to Jesus' saying that "no prophet is ever welcome in his native place"—a saying by which Jesus set himself squarely among those prophets who were rejected by their own people—Luke seems to understand the formula as a pattern of speech characteristic of such prophets. This is to say, that Jesus' introductory expression, "Truly [Amen], I say to you," although recognizably different in form, may nevertheless have been viewed by Luke as similar in meaning to that introductory formula of the Old Testament prophets—"Thus saith the Lord"—by which the word of the Lord came to the people.

Such an understanding seems to be confirmed by Mark. For his very first use of the amen formula comes at the end of a section where Jesus repeatedly laid claim to being a person who possessed the Spirit—and in the Judaism of Jesus' time to possess the Spirit was almost always a mark of prophetic inspiration.[53] "'Truly [Amen], I say to you, all sins will be forgiven the sons of men . . . but whoever blasphemes against the Holy Spirit never has forgiveness' . . . for they had said, 'He has an unclean spirit'" (Mark 3:28–30; cf. Matt. 12:31–32; Luke 11:14–15, 17–23; 12:10). Hence, although the amen sayings are unique and point to the uniqueness of Jesus, they at the same time are in harmony with the "Thus saith the Lord" of the prophets and point to his unity with them.

Long ago the prophet Micaiah perfectly defined the scope of prophetic authority when he stated: "What the Lord says to me, that will I speak" (1 Kings 22:14). Thus, Jesus' "Amen, I say to you," should not be understood to mean, "I say this," that is "I alone, I on my own initiative, I by virtue of my own divine authority say to you!", but rather, "I as God's unique Messenger, with God's authority and power, say this to you!" Can it be otherwise when Jesus is himself quoted as saying, almost in the words of Micaiah, "My teaching is not mine, but his who sent me" (John 7:16), and again, "The words that I speak to you, I do not speak on my own authority [or on my own initiative]" (John 14:10)? Without doubt Jesus' "Amen, I say to you" exceeded anything spoken by the Old Testament prophets, if for no other reason than that he, unlike them, had been given the Spirit without measure (John 3:34b). And yet with this formula he was in essence saying the same thing that they had said before him, but in a sharper, more insistent key: "You must listen to what I have to say, because the words I speak are not mine; they are the very words of God" (cf. John 3:34a).[54]

Furthermore, that Jesus, like the Old Testament prophets before him, was directed and inspired by the Holy Spirit in his teaching, may be inferred from an interesting passage in the Acts of the Apostles. There Luke writes to Theophilus these words: "In the first book . . . I have dealt with all that Jesus began to do and teach, until the day when he was taken up, after he had given commandment through the Holy Spirit to the apostles whom he had chosen" (Acts 1:1–2). Here, in a statement made awkward by all the material packed into it, is, nevertheless, the clear implication that Jesus was filled with the Holy Spirit *after* his resurrection, and from this measureless fulness of wisdom and power he gave new commands to his apostles (cf. Matt. 28:19–20; Luke 24:47; John 20:21–23).[55]

Now if this was characteristic of Jesus' postresurrection ministry, how much more must it have been characteristic of his preresurrection ministry, of his teachings and commands given prior to his passion? So from this passage in Acts it is possible to deduce that Jesus, during the days of his mission on earth, like the prophets, looked to the Holy Spirit to provide him with the message he was to speak and provide the power in which to speak it. The Spirit of God communicated the words of God to the incarnate Son of God so that he might speak them to those who would hear him in words that were understandable and effective.

Hence, it is recorded that he spoke as no other person had spoken (John 7:46), so that his words confounded the experts of religion (Luke 20:40), so that his answers stunned those trained in the intricacies of the Mosaic Law and as a result they became afraid to ask him any further questions (Matt. 22:46), so that the masses were awed at the graciousness of his words which conveyed to them God's favor (Luke 4:22), so that crowds of people thronged to hear him (Mark 2:1–2), and so on. But the captivating power of Jesus' teaching "lay not so much in the substance of what he taught as in the spiritual force with which his message was delivered."[56] And the source of that spiritual force was the Spirit of God within him.

The words of G. T. Stokes, commenting on Acts 1:2, although written nearly a century ago, are most apt:

> In the opening verses of this book [Luke] recognizes [Jesus'] complete and perfect humanity—"After that He had given commandment through the Holy Ghost unto the apostles." There was an ancient heresy about the perfection of our Lord's humanity, teaching that His divinity took the place of the human spirit in Christ. Such teaching deprives us of much comfort and instruction which the Christian can draw from a meditation upon the true doctrine as taught there by St. Luke. Jesus Christ was God as well as man, but it was through the manhood He revealed the life and nature of God. He was perfect Man in all repects, with body, soul and spirit complete; and in the actions of His manhood in the exercise of all its various activities, he required the assistance and support of the Holy Ghost just as really as we ourselves do. He taught, gave commandments, worked miracles through the Holy Ghost. The humanity of the Eternal Son required the assistance of the Divine Spirit. Christ sought that Divine aid in prolonged communion with His Father and His God, and then went forth to work His miracles and give His commands. Prayer and the gift of the Spirit and the works and marvels of Christ were closely connected together, even before the open descent of the Spirit and the wonders of Pentecost. There [is] a covenant blessing and a covenant outpouring of the Spirit peculiar to Christianity which was not

> vouchsafed till Christ had ascended. But the Divine Spirit had been given in a measure long before Christ came. It was through the Spirit that every blessing and every gift came to the patriarchs, prophets, warriors, teachers and workers of every kind under the Jewish dispensation. . . . And just as really the Holy Ghost rested upon the human nature of Jesus Christ, guiding Him in the utterance of those commandments, the outcome and development of which we trace in the book of the Acts of the Apostles.[57]

It would be incorrect or at least inadequate, however, simply to conclude that Jesus viewed himself as a prophet and no more than a prophet. The Gospel writers are themselves careful not to allow anyone to come to such a conclusion. For example, they record that when certain people came to Jesus and asked for a sign, he would only give them the sign of Jonah saying, "As Jonah was three days and three nights in the belly of the great fish, so the Son of Man will be three days and three nights in the heart of the earth. The people of Nineveh will rise up against this generation at the judgment and condemn it, for when Jonah preached they repented, and here is one greater than Jonah" (Matt. 12:40–41; cf. Luke 11:29–32). In effect the evangelists claim that Jesus was saying that the Ninevites, these strangers to Israel, had been able and willing to admit that the authority and presence of the true God was with the prophet Jonah. But here in himself was one greater than Jonah, "and yet his own people, the people of Israel, failed to recognize him and give him that respect and credence which should have been offered to him."[58] Thus, although it is true that Jesus did understand himself as a prophet, a Spirit-inspired and Spirit-empowered person, and his ministry as a prophetic ministry, yet it is also clear that Jesus would certainly have at least said of himself what he said about John the Baptist, "A prophet . . . and more than a prophet" (Matt. 11:9; Luke 7:26).

In any case, it is important to understand that according to the Gospel writers, Jesus himself, as well as they, recognized that the Spirit was *the* source of power for his ministry, that the Spirit was present within him, strengthening him in the great moments of his life: "The Spirit of the Lord is upon me precisely because the Lord has given me such an important commission, such a weighty task to carry out, that of bringing salvation to the poor, the prisoners, the blind, the hopeless and the down-trodden of this world" (cf. Luke 4:18–19).

2. The clearest statement that Jesus attributed his miraculous powers to the Holy Spirit at work within him and through him is found in that story where his critics accuse him of collusion with Satan (Matt. 12:22–30; Mark 3:22–27; Luke 11:14–23; cf. Matt. 9:32–34). Matthew and Luke introduce this narrative by saying that a demon-possessed man, who as a result was blind (Matt.) and unable to speak (Matt./Luke), was brought to Jesus. Jesus healed him (Matt.) by driving out the demon (Luke). As a result the man could both speak (Matt./Luke) and see (Matt.). The crowd of bystanders marvelled, or as Matthew puts it, were beside themselves with astonishment, when they saw what had happened. As a consequence they asked (only Matthew records their question), "Can this fellow be the Son of David" (i.e., the Messiah[59])?

This hope-filled response of the people to the healing triggered a negative reaction on the part of the scribes from Jerusalem (Mark) or the Pharisees (Matt.).[60] According to the story these scribes or Pharisees were (1) on the one hand, forced to admit that Jesus did have the ability to heal, but (2) on the other hand, determined to attribute it to his being in league with, or under the control of Beelzeboul,[61] the Prince of Demons.

It is Jesus' reply to this negative estimation of his person and work that is of great significance for the discussion at hand. First Jesus points out the fallacy of their thinking: (1) it is inconceivable to suppose that Satan would fight against his own demons and thus consent to the dismemberment and collapse of his kingdom, and (2) it is irrational for the Jews to say he exorcised demons by the demon-prince without also admitting the possibility that their own people exorcised demons[62] by the same evil agent. Then he discloses unequivocably the real source of his power to perform the miraculous: "If I cast out demons by the Spirit [Finger] of God, then the kingdom of God has come upon you" (Matt. 12:28; cf. Luke 11:20). The Spirit of God, thus, was the energizing force within him.

According to these Gospel writers, Jesus himself understood that his ability to heal, to make people whole, to restore sight to the blind and speech to the dumb, and to overthrow the destructive forces of evil lay not in himself, lay not in the strength of his own person, but in God and in the power of God mediated to him through the Spirit. In his action God acted. In his speech God spoke. His authority was the authority of God.

The fact that Jesus' words here are put in the form of a conditional sentence—"If I cast out demons by the Spirit of God"—does not at all weaken this conclusion. In Greek the particular kind of conditional sentence that Jesus used assumes the *if* clause to be a fact, to be real.[63] Hence, he did not mean, "If I cast out demons by the Spirit of God, and I may or may not be doing this," but rather, "If I cast out demons by the Spirit of God, *and I most certainly am doing so*, then the Kingdom of God has come upon you."

Nor does the fact that Luke's account has "finger of God"—"If I cast out demons by the finger of God"—in place of Matthew's "Spirit of God" in any way undermine the conclusion about the source of Jesus' power. Even if the expression, "finger of God," is actually what Jesus said, and "Spirit of God" is a Matthean interpretive modification of that saying,[64] the meaning is identical in both instances. For both, in differing ways, refer to the same thing—to the breaking forth of God's power into the world, to "God's direct and concrete intervention"[65] in history to accomplish the humanly impossible (Exod. 8:19; Deut. 9:10; Ps. 8:3). The "finger of God," like the "hand of God" (Exod. 7:4–5; 9:3, 15), is but an anthropomorphism, a figure of speech by which the writer or speaker wished to stress the immediate and effectual presence of the God who acts. And besides, in the Old Testament the "hand of God" ("the finger of God") and the "Spirit of God" were similar in meaning and performed similar functions (cf. 1 Kings 18:12 with 2 Kings 2:16; 1 Chron. 28:12 [Hebrew, see NIV] with 28:19; Ps. 8:3 with 33:6; Ezek. 3:14; 8:1–3; 37:1).[66]

> The equation, finger of God = power of God = Spirit of God, is one which arises directly out of the Hebrew understanding of God's action . . . , and one which was obvious to either Matthew or Luke when [one of the other altered the original]. Thus, whatever the precise language of [the original] at this point, its meaning is quite clear: Jesus claimed that his exorcisms were performed . . . by the power of God.[67]

Thus Jesus, aware of this power within himself, this power of the Spirit, this power that the ancient prophets had said would uniquely mark the new age, the Messianic Age (Isa. 42:1–4; 61:1–3), concluded that that promised age had already come.[68] He understood, therefore, that the kingdom of God, the eschatological kingly rule and saving power of God by which Satan and the forces of evil would be hurled back and overthrown, was no longer wholly future but was in some sense present in himself. It had arrived suddenly, even unexpectedly, at the grasp of those who saw and heard what he said and did, because the Holy Spirit was at work within him giving him the authority and the ability to exorcise demons and set their captives free.[69]

This conclusion is confirmed immediately. For precisely here in their Gospels both Matthew and Luke position the parable that Jesus told about the strong man. The strong man, Jesus said, is able to keep firm control over his household and his belongings unless someone stronger that he comes along to subdue him and spoil his goods. If this happens and if the strong is tied up by the stronger, then his possessions can be plundered (Matt. 12:29; Luke 11:21–22; cf. Mark 3:27).

The implication of this parable, placed in this special position in the narrative, cannot be missed. The strong man is Satan who has taken hapless people captive, subjecting them to sin, disease, and death. The One who binds the strong man, the One stronger than he, is Jesus who plunders Satan's stronghold and releases his captives. By placing the parable here, the Gospel writers say in effect that Jesus now had a clear understanding of who he was and what his mission was to be: He was the stronger One, made the stronger One by the power of the Holy Spirit, and his mission was that of confronting and dethroning Satan.[70] In his Spirit-empowered exorcisms, in his freeing of people from demonic oppression, he recognized that special binding of Satan and that special curbing of evil which was looked for at the end of the age (cf. Isa. 24:21–22; 49:24–25; 53:12; 61:2; cf. 1 En. 10:4–6; 54:4–5; Test. Levi 18:12; Test. Zeb, 9:8; 1QS 4:18). Hence his words, "Since I cast out demons by the Spirit of God, the Kingdom of God has come upon you" (see Matt. 12:28).

Once again it becomes very clear what it was that prompted Jesus to make this claim that the Kingdom of God had come. For him, the Kingdom of God was no longer something totally future, hoped for, longed for, but something present as well, something in a sense already realized. And for Jesus this was a fact because the power of the Spirit of God in its fulness was upon him, within him. The Kingdom of God that was to come had come in himself only because the Spirit of God was present in and working through him in his fulness. Hence, "it was not so much a case of 'Where [*Jesus* is] there is the kingdom,' as 'Where the *Spirit* is there is the Kingdom.' It was the manifestation of the power of God which was the sign of the Kingdom of God."[71]

This bold statement is supported, nevertheless, by what follows next in Matthew's Gospel. Matthew now records Jesus as saying, "For this reason I tell you that every sin and blasphemy will be forgiven, but blasphemy against the Spirit will not be forgiven. And whoever says a word against the Son of Man will be forgiven; but whoever speaks against the Holy Spirit will not be forgiven" (Matt. 12:31–32, cf. Mark 3:28–30; Luke 12:10).

Suddenly an otherwise enigmatic saying of Jesus becomes clear. The so-called "unpardonable sin," often misunderstood and the cause of needless painful anxiety to many people with sensitive but uninformed consciences, is no longer mysterious or mystifying. It is simply that some religious leaders who were hostile to Jesus had deliberately attributed the good he did *through the power of the Holy Spirit* to the power of the Evil One. Like the people denounced by the prophet Isaiah who deliberately called evil good and good evil (Isa. 5:20), so these are denounced by Jesus for the same kind of perversity. While admitting that he was a person possessed with a mighty spiritual power, they were unwilling to say, as Jesus himself had said, that this power was of God, that this power was the Holy Spirit of God. Instead they explained it away as being the power of Satan, the power of the evil Prince of Demons.

Thus this concluding section of the entire pericope that deals with Jesus' alleged collusion with Satan simply underscores the idea that has continued to emerge, namely that the source of Jesus' power was the Holy Spirit and that Jesus was keenly aware of this fact. It was as the Bearer of the Spirit that he consciously stood as the champion of God in the battle with Satan.[72]

NOTES

1. Isaiah 42:1–4, as Matthew quotes it, agrees in places with the Masoretic Text (MT) against the Septuagint (LXX), in other places with the LXX against the MT, and in still other places with neither the MT nor the LXX. Hence, it has been suggested that Matthew used an Aramaic collection of *testimonia* translated from a Hebrew text that differed both from that used by the Masoretes and the translators of the LXX (A. H. McNeile, *The Gospel According to St. Matthew* [London, 1915], 172). K. Stendahl remarks that "the unique interweaving of traditions of interpretation supported on different sides, and the completely original readings, render it difficult to understand the quotation in 12:18–21 as a 'free citation' or to be satisfied that it shows dependence on the M.T. It can only have a satisfactory explanation as a targumized text which is the fruit of reflexion and acquaintance with the interpretation of Scripture" (*The School of St. Matthew and Its Use of the Old Testament* [Uppsala, 1954], 115). On the possibility of a Hebrew background for this quotation, see J. Grundel, "Matthew xii 18–21," CBQ 29 (1967), 110–15.

2. But cf. Isa. 44:1.

3. Cf. McNeile, *Matthew*, 172–73.

4. It is even possible that the genitive *tou pneumatos* in Luke's phrase, *en tē dynamei tou pneumatos* ("in/with/by the power of the Spirit," 4:14), may be taken as a genitive of apposition and be translated, "[armed] with power, that is with the Spirit."

5. See G. H. P. Thompson, *The Gospel According to Luke*, NCBC (Oxford, 1972), 90.

6. There is a textual problem here that needs to be resolved. At least four variant readings are found in the mss: (1) *en tō pneumati tō hagiō* ("in/by the Holy Spirit," ℵ, D, L, Ξ, 33, 1241, *al.*, Nestle-Aland, 26th edition); (2) *en tō pneumati* ("in/by the spirit/Spirit," very likely P45, a few other Greek mss); (3) *tō pneumati tō hagiō* ("by the Holy Spirit," P75, B, C, K, Θ, *al.*, vg); (4) *tō pneumati* ("by the spirit/Spirit," A, W, and the Majority Text). The last in this list, which has poor ms support, is a simplification to avoid the strange expression, "rejoiced in the Holy Spirit." The second of these, though also weakly supported by the ms tradition, is nevertheless quite Lucan in style (cf. 2:27; 4:1), and even without the adjective *hagiō* always refers to the Holy Spirit. The strongest ms evidence, however, is for either variant 1 or 3, although it is not possible to decide whether *en* should be included or not (see Marshall, *Luke*, 433).

7. Jesus, who himself is "full of the Spirit" (Luke 4:1), and hence, who has authority (*exousia*, see pages 156–60) over unclean spirits and all forces of evil and darkness (cf. Matt. 12:28–29), is able to share this same authority with his disciples. Since he is full of the Spirit, the bearer of the Spirit par excellence (*der Geistträger*), he is able to perform "a kind of outpouring of the Spirit which equips his disciples to overcome the instruments of Satan and to destroy Satan's kingdom" (Jeremias, *New Testament Theology*, 1.237).

8. See G. Kittel, *TDNT* 4.130 and note 220.

9. Cf. Isa. 14:12; Rev. 12:7–12. This idea is also found in late Jewish tradition: *As. Mos.* 10:1; *Jub.* 23:29; *Test. Sim.* 6:6; *Test. Jud.* 25:3; Targum Jerus 1 Gen. 6:4; Pirqe R. El 22.11c.

10. Marshall, *Luke*, 428–29; K. H. Rengstorf, *Das Evangelium nach Lukas*, (1952), 138; A. Schlatter, *Das Evangelium des Lukas* (1931), 279.

11. Manson, *Luke*, 126; Creed, *Luke*, 155; W. G. Kümmel, *Promise and Fulfilment* (London, 1957), 113–14.

12. BAGD; LSJ; G. W. H. Lampe, *A Patristic Greek Lexicon* (Oxford, 1961).

13. BDF, 101.

14. K. G. Kuhn, *TDNT*, 5.345–46.

15. Kümmel, *Promise*, 114.

16. Manson, *Luke*, 127. The verb here is not *chairein*, "to rejoice," or any of its cognates. It is a much stronger verb—*agalliasthai*, "to exult"—which is "used most frequently in the New Testament of the joys of messianic redemption" (Ellis, *Luke*, 157; cf. Luke 1:14, 47; Acts 2:26; John 8:56; 1 Pet. 4:13). "This holy joy is a divine inspiration" (Plummer, *Luke*, 281).

17. V. Taylor, *The Person of Christ in New Testament Teaching* (London, 1958), 179.

18. See S. Kim's most enlightening article that deals with this very idea of Jesus' self-understanding growing out of his thoughtful reflection on just such Old Testament passages as these, in *Tradition and Interpretation in the New Testament: Essays in Honor of E. Earle Ellis*, ed. G. F. Hawthorne (Grand Rapids, 1987), 134–48.

19. Taylor, *The Person of Christ*, 181.

20. See Origen, *In Joh.* Frag. 48; Cyril of Alexandria; Brown, *The Gospel According to John*; Lagrange, *Évangile selon Saint Jean* (Paris, 1948); W. Thüsing, *Die Erhöhung und Verherrlichung Jesu im Johannesevangelium* (Münster, 1960).

21. This surely was the understanding of the early scribes who read and copied the Greek text of John 3:34, for the majority of these scribes added a subject for the sake of clarity. They added either "God" (*ho theos*), or "God the Father" (*theos ho patēr*), or "the Father" (*ho patēr*). The majority of modern interpreters also understand the text in this way: C. K. Barrett, *The Gospel According to John* (London, 1955); R. Bultmann, *The Gospel of John* (Philadelphia, 1971); E. Haenchen, *John* (Philadelphia, 1984); J. N. Sanders and B. A. Martin, *The Gospel According to St. John*, BNTC (London, 1968); R. Schnackenburg, *The Gospel According to John* (New York, 1980).

22. Cf. the saying of Rabbi Aha in Midrash Rabbah on Lev. 15:2: "Even the Holy Spirit resting on the prophets does so by weight [i.e. appointed measure], one prophet speaking one book of prophecy and another speaking two books"; see StrB 2.431.

23. Bultmann, *The Gospel of John*, 164; Schnackenburg, *The Gospel According to John*, 1.386.

24. Swete, *The Holy Spirit*, 57.

25. But see Barrett, *Holy Spirit and Gospel Tradition*, 18; M. Hengel, *The Charismatic Leader and His Followers* (Edinburgh, 1981), 63; E. Best, *The Gospel as Story* (Edinburgh, 1983), 77.

26. Creed, *Luke*, 19, 20; Fitzmyer, *Luke I–IX*, 350; W. Grundmann, *TDNT*, 2.301; H. von Baer, *Der Heilige Geist in Lukasschriften* (Stuttgart, 1926). This same equating of *power* with *the Holy Spirit/the Spirit of* God is also to be found in Paul, e.g. 1 Cor. 5:4; 6:14.

27. Cf. Deut. 3:24; Ps. 17:33, 40 (18:32, 39).

28. Grundmann, *TDNT*, 2.302.

29. Büchsel, *Der Geist Gottes*, 123–25.

30. StrB 1.470; Windisch, "Jesus und der Geist," 225. Justin Martyr contrasting Jesus with the Greek sophists wrote: "His words were brief and to the point, for he was not a sophist and his message (*logos*) was the power of God" (*Apol.* 1.14). See also W. Foerster, *TDNT*, 2.567–69.

31. Fitzmyer, *Luke I–IX*, 547.

32. Lane, *Mark*, 76. In Mark's account, the evil spirit is said to have addressed Jesus as the "Holy One of God." By using such an unusual title, not a known messianic designation or a common Christian way of referring to Jesus (Taylor, *Mark*, 174), Mark directs attention back to the baptism of Jesus when the Holy Spirit came into him, and thus he underscores, in a not too subtle way, the source of Jesus' authority, both to teach and to overcome demonic powers (see W. Manson, *Jesus and the Christian* [London, 1967], 42–43; Mansfield, *Spirit and Gospel in Mark*, 51.)

33. H. W. Beyer, *TDNT*, 1.621–625.

34. The plural "people" (*anthrōpois*) that appears here need not be interpreted to mean that Matthew understood this as an authority given to all human beings indiscriminately, or as referring to an authority given only to Jesus and his disciples, or only to the ministers of the church of Matthew's own day. Rather, as is clear from Matt. 2:20, in a generalization like this, the plural can stand for *one* person (BDF, 141). Here that one person is Jesus and only Jesus, the supreme *Geistträger*, the supreme bearer of the Spirit.

35. M. Hooker, *The Son of Man in Mark*, 90.

36. Mansfield, *Spirit and Gospel in Mark*, 56–57.

37. Lane, *Mark*, 413; J. Kremer, "Jesu Antwort auf die Frage nach seiner Vollmacht. Eine Auslegung von Mk 11:23–33," *Bibel und Leben* 9 (1968), 128–36.

38. See Jeremias, *Theology*, 1.78, who also remarks, "As a false prophet, according to Deut. 18.20, . . . he had to die, and the execution had to take place during the feast (see Deut. 17.13) in order to deter others from this crime."

39. See G. Friedrich, *TDNT*, 6.843–45.

40. Josephus, *Ant.* 16.2.3.

41. Cf. C. H. Cave, "The Sermon at Nazareth and the Beatitudes in Light of the Synagogue Lectionary," Studia Evangelica II/2 (TU 88, Berlin, 1964), 231–35; A. Guilding, *The Fourth Gospel and Jewish Worship* (Oxford, 1960), 125–26; C. Perrot, "Luc 4, 16–30 et la lecture biblique de l'ancienne synagogue," *RevScRel* 47 (1973), 324–40.

42. It was customary for the Scripture to be read while the reader stood (Luke 4:16), and for its exposition to be given with the teacher seated.

43. Ellis, *The Gospel of Luke*, 97.

44. Leaney, *The Gospel According to Luke*, 118; W. H. Brownlee, "Messianic Motifs of Qumran and the New Testament," *NTS* 3 (1956–1957), 205–206.

45. F. Delitzsch, *Biblical Commentary on the Prophecies of Isaiah* (reprinted ed., Grand Rapids, 1949), 2.424, although Delitzsch does not himself accept this interpretation of Isa. 61.

46. Fitzmyer, *Luke I–IX*, 530. See further Y. Yadin, *Israel Exploration Journal* 15 (1965), 152–54; M. de Jonge and A. S. van der Woude, "11QMelchizedek and the New Testament," *NTS* 12 (1965–1966), 301–302; J. A. Fitzmyer, *Essays on the Semitic Background of the New Testament* (London, 1971), 250, 265–66.

47. Mark 6:4/Matt. 13:57 records essentially the same proverb but the wording differs slightly: "A prophet is not without honor, except in his own country (and among his own relatives [Mark]), and in his own house."

48. In this connection Luke 13:33 should also be noted. Some Pharisees were said to have come to Jesus urging him to leave the area because Herod intended to kill him (13:31). Jesus replied, in effect, "I shall continue my work for the present; nevertheless I shall shortly go on my way—not because Herod threatens but because a prophet must not perish outside Jerusalem" (See Creed, *Luke*, 187). Although once again Jesus was citing a popularly held idea and was not thereby *primarily* describing his own vocation, yet it is certain, nonetheless, that in doing this he did in fact count himself among the prophets. He did so not only by applying this popular saying to himself, but more particularly by preparing to exemplify its meaning in his own death in Jerusalem (see Friedrich, *TDNT*, 6.841).

49. Fitzmyer, *Luke I–IX*, 530.

50. Ibid., 536.

51. Thirty-one times in Matt.; thirteen times in Mark; six times in Luke and twenty-five times in John (always in the doubled form, "amen, amen").

52. T. W. Manson, *The Teaching of Jesus* (Cambridge, 1951), 107.

53. See StrB 2.127–38.

54. Cf. Manson, *The Teaching of Jesus*, 107: "The descent of the Holy Spirit . . . signifies something permanent. It is not that Jesus receives an inspired messge, but that the spiritual source of all inspiration takes possession of him, so that when he speaks it is not that he repeats words given to him but that the Spirit of his Father speaks in him."

55. Because of the amphibolous position in the Greek text of the phrase, "through the Holy Spirit," doubt has arisen as to (1) whether it should be taken with "after he had given commandment," or (2) with "whom he had chosen." The majority of commentators and translators prefer option 1: "after he had given commandment through the Holy Spirit to the apostles whom he had chosen" (cf. RSV, NIV, NASB, NEB, TEV, NKJV, etc.). But I. H. Marshall prefers option 2: "he gave his instructions to the apostles he had chosen through the Holy Spirit" (cf. JB). Marshall is of the conviction that the awkwardness of the Greek is due to a desire for emphasis on Luke's part and concludes by saying, "The Holy Spirit [was] the source of guidance for Jesus choosing the apostles" (*The Acts of the Apostles*, TNTC [Grand Rapids, 1980], 57 and 57 n.1).

56. Swete, *The Holy Spirit in the New Testament*, 57.

57. G. T. Stokes, *The Acts of the Apostles*, Expositor's Bible (New York, 1893), 21–22. See also J. V. Bartlett, *The Acts*, Century Bible (Edinburgh, n.d.); R. C. H. Lenski, *The Interpretation of the Acts of the Apostles* (Columbus, Ohio, 1944), 22; T. M. Lindsay, *The Acts of the Apostles* (Edinburgh, 1884), 38; T. Walker, *The Acts of the Apostles* (reprint ed., Chicago, 1965).

58. T. H. Robinson, *The Gospel of Matthew* (London, 1928), 115.

59. G. H. Dalman, *The Words of Jesus* (Edinburgh, 1902), 319–21.

60. Luke says that "some of them," i.e., some of the crowd of bystanders, reacted in this negative way. They may have been scribes and/or Pharisees, but one could not learn this from the Lucan account.

61. There are different spellings for this name in the mss (Beelzeboul, Beezeboul, Beelzebub), and its derivation is uncertain—derived from the name of the god of Ekron (2 Kings 1:2) meaning, "Lord of Flies," or a derisive corruption of that name meaning, "Lord of Dung," or a derivation of an Aramaic word meaning, "Lord of the Dwelling" (cf. Matt. 12:29).

62. For the exorcising of demons by Jews see Tob. 8:1–3; Josephus, *Ant.* 8.2.5; StrB 4.1, 527–35; cf. Acts 19:13–16.

63. BDF 371.1; 372.

64. There is some debate about which of these is to be recognized as original and which as the modification. A majority of scholars argue that *finger* stood in the source, Luke retained it, and Matthew, to avoid any anthropomorphisms, changed it to *Spirit.* (See S. Schultz, Q-Die Spruchquelle der Evangelisten [Zurich, 1972], 205, n. 218; but also C. S. Rodd, "Spirit or Finger," *ExpT* 72 [1960–61], 157–58; Dunn, *Jesus and the Spirit*, 45–46.

65. H. Schlier, *TDNT*, 2.20.

66. See R. G. Hammerton-Kelly, "A Note on Matthew XII.28 par. Luke XI.20," *NTS* 11 (1964–65), 165–67; Barrett, *Holy Spirit*, 63; Beasley-Murray, "Jesus and the Spirit," 469–70.

67. Dunn, *Jesus and the Spirit*, 46.

68. The verb translated, "had already come," is *ephthasen* (the aorist indicative of *phthanō*, "to come before, to precede." For an important discussion of the meaning given here, see C. H. Dodd, *The Parables of the Kingdom* (1961), 44; idem, "The Kingdom of God has Come," *ExpT* 48 (1936–37), 138–42; G. Fitzer, *TDNT* 9.88–92; Kümmel, *Promise and Fulfilment*, 105–109; K. W. Clark, "'Realized Eschatology,'" *JBL* 59 (1940), 367–83.

69. But then it has been asked, "If [Jesus'] exoricsms are worked 'by the Spirit of God,' and this is an indication that the Kingdom of God has already arrived in power, why should not the successful exorcisms of other Jewish exorcists [Matt. 12:27/Luke 11:19] be equally good evidence of the arrival of the Kingdom?" (Beare, *Matthew*, 279). McNeile answers the question by suggesting that Matt. 12:28 did not originally follow 12:27 and that the sayings contained in these verses must have been spoken on different occasions and from different points of view (McNeile, *Matthew*, 176; see also Creed, *Luke*, 161; Bultmann,14; Kümmel, *Promise and Fulfilment*, 105–106). Marshall suggests that Jesus may be claiming that the kingly rule of God is present wherever and whenever the power of God is demonstrated. So if Jesus' exorcisms were carried out by the power of God (as had those of the Jewish exorcists), then they, too, constitute evidence that the Kingdom of God has arrived. "The logical connection [between Matt. 12:27–28/Luke 11:19–20] is sound enough, and does not justify the conclusion that we necessarily have two

independent sayings here" (Marshall, *Luke*, 475). Dunn is much more on target. He assumes that the two sentences belong together (see E. Percy, *Die Botschaft Jesus* [Lund, 1953], 179–80), but says that Jesus was simply using an *ad hominem* argument. He was *not* implying that Jewish exorcisms demonstrated that the Kingdom of God was present. On the contrary, he distinguished himself from them, as the adversative conjunction *but* (*de*, Matt. 12:28/Luke 19:20) implies. Furthermore, Jesus stressed the point that *his* exorcisms—without making any judgment about other exorcisms—were performed by the Spirit of God by giving to the expression "Spirit/Finger of God" the position of emphasis in the sentence (Dunn, *Jesus and the Spirit*, 48, 374). It should be noted, too, that the rabbis did not mention the Spirit of God as one of the many means by which their exorcists drove out demons (StrB 4.532–535).

70. W. Grundmann, *TDNT* 3.400–401.

71. Dunn, *Jesus and the Spirit*, 48–49; cf. R. Otto, *The Kingdom of God and the Son of Man* (London, 1938), 104. "Of course," as Dunn says, "later Christological deduction emphasized that it was not the unique empowering of the Spirit that made the difference, but the unique empowering of *the unique* man Jesus" (*Jesus and the Spirit*, 49; idem, "Spirit and Kingdom," *ExpT* 82 (1970–1971), 36–40.

72. Lane, *Mark*, 143.

6. The Spirit in the Death and Resurrection of Jesus

The evidence collected in the preceding chapters presses one to the conclusion that for the Gospel writers the Holy Spirit was at work in every phase of Jesus' life—creating his body from the substance of Mary, giving him gifts and graces that protected him and provided for him in the years of his youth, enlightening his mind so that he might understand his unique relationship with the Father and his mission in life, filling him at his baptism, leading him into the arena of conflict with the devil and assisting him in overcoming that adversary, guiding him throughout his life, enabling him to preach and teach with authority, and infusing him with the power to do his mighty works (*dynameis*). The evangelists go on record as saying that from the conception to the cross the Holy Spirit played an extraordinarily significant role in the life of Jesus. In a word, they agree that Jesus was dependent upon the Spirit for the successful completion of the work God had given him to do in this world throughout the whole of his life (cf. John 17:4).

Now the questions arise, did this activity of the Holy Spirit, so prominent in the life of Jesus, carry over into the death of Jesus by which sins are forgiven and eternal redemption is provided? Was Jesus aided by the Spirit when he offered himself as an atoning sacrifice, or did he accomplish this saving work solely by himself? And further, did the activity of the Spirit reach into the tomb of Jesus? Was the Holy Spirit *the* power by which Jesus was raised from the dead, or did he himself break loose from death by means of his own intrinsic divine power?

The four Gospels are silent here, having nothing to say about the role of the Holy Spirit in the passion of Jesus or in his resurrection. They provide no answers to these questions. But there are places in the New Testament outside the Gospel accounts that promise help. It is to these texts that one must look for solutions.

The classic passage—in fact the only New Testament passage—that could possibly link the Spirit with the death of Jesus is Hebrews 9:13–14: "For if the sprinkling of defiled persons with the blood of goats and bulls and with the ashes of a heifer sanctifies for the purification of the flesh, how much more shall the blood of Christ, who through the eternal Spirit offered himself without blemish to God, purify your conscience from dead works to serve the living God."[1]

At first glance, according to the RSV, this text appears to be conclusive proof that the Holy Spirit was present at the passion of Jesus, that the Spirit was the agent through whom Jesus, in dying, accomplished eternal redemption for all. But unfortunately the key phrase, "through the eternal Spirit," is most difficult to interpret. As a consequence, commentators and translators are divided both as to how the phrase shoud be translated and as to what it means.

In Greek the problematic phrase is *dia pneumatos aiōniou* (literally, "through eternal spirit") with no help whatsoever coming from the Greek as to whether the noun, *pneumatos*, should be written *spirit* or *Spirit.* Hence, it is not surprising to discover that some interpreters of Hebrews understand this phrase to be *spirit*, meaning that which is spiritual as opposed to *flesh*, meaning that which is physical, outward, transitory. These interpreters understand *pneumatos aiōniou*, therefore, to be a reference to Jesus' own eternal spiritual nature by virtue of which he offered himself to God and thus was able to make a sacrifice of infinite worth and of eternal value.[2] "It was because Jesus was what he was by nature that his sacrifice had such final value; its atoning significance lay in his vital connexion with the realm of absolute realities; it embodied all that his divine personality meant for men in relation to God."[3] Or in the words of Hugh Montefiore, "[Jesus], who in self-sacrifice offered to God his full and perfect humanity, was himself eternal by nature; and because of this, the salvation that he procured is everlasting."[4]

Other interpreters take a middle-of-the-road position. These note that the noun *pneumatos* ("spirit"), in the phrase *dia pneumatos aiōniou* ("through eternal spirit"), has no definite article, and they conclude that to translate it as most English translations do—"through the eternal Spirit"—is too bold a translation that goes beyond grammatical bounds. They are of the opinion that it is more correct to interpret the term "eternal spirit," not as referring to Jesus' own spirit (i.e. to his own divine, eternal, spiritual nature), nor as referring to the Holy Spirit, but to *spirit* in a general sense. That is to say, *spirit* here as used by the writer of Hebrews refers to an outlook on life, an attitude toward existence on Jesus' part. The "spirit" Jesus had was not the spirit of the world, that spirit or vision of existence that limits one's vision to what the physical eye can take in. Rather, it was a spirit that enabled him to see all of existence from the standpoint of the invisible and eternal. For this reason, therefore, Jesus was able to endure the cross and scorn the shame; he possessed the long look, a look that allowed him to penetrate beyond the physical fact of the cross to its ultimate spiritual outcome. "He was upheld by a sense of the great issues of life, and in view of them could offer himself to God."[5]

Now it is a fact that the Greek word *pneuma* ("spirit") may on occasion refer to an attitude, a disposition, an outlook on existence, a philosophy of life (cf. 1 John 4:1–3). But such a meaning for *pneuma* here is totally foreign to the way the writer of Hebrews uses this word elsewhere in his epistle,[6] and it certainly does not do justice to the context in which it appears (Heb. 9:11–22).

It is also true that *pneuma* ("spirit") can mean the spirit or soul of a person, the innermost part of an individual's personality. But to infer from this that the writer had in mind the divine nature of Jesus when he wrote, "through eternal spirit he offered himself blamelessly to God," seems both awkward and redundant. Had this author intended to say "through *his* eternal spirit," he could have said so quite simply.[7] And if he had wanted by this phrase to contrast the involuntary sacrifices of beasts with the voluntary sacrifice of Jesus,[8] then he was simply adding unnecessary words, since he had made clear the voluntary nature of Jesus' sacrifice when he wrote that Jesus offered himself (*heauton*). Having said he "offered *himself*," the writer said all that he needed to say about Jesus' nature, for bound up in that one word, *heauton* ("himself") was all that he was—human/divine, physical/spiritual, temporal/eternal (cf. Heb. 1:2, 8; 2:14, 17–18; 4:15; 5:8).

Thus the most satisfactory interpretation is the interpretation that understands *eternal spirit* to be the Holy Spirit. Calvin says that the writer of Hebrews "now shows clearly how the death of Christ is to be regarded; not from its external act but from the power of the Spirit. Christ suffered as a man, but in order that His death might effect our salvation it came forth from the power of the Spirit."[9] This is to say, that although Jesus' self-sacrifice can be described as "a spiritual and eternal sacrifice" (NEB), yet more than this is intended by the writer's words. Behind his thinking

> lies the portrayal of the Isaianic Servant of the Lord, who yields up his life to God as a guilt offering for many, bearing their sin and procuring their justification. When this Servant is introduced for the first time, God says: "I have put my Spirit upon him" (Isa. 42:1). It is in the power of the Divine Spirit, accordingly, that the Servant accomplishes every phase of his ministry, including the crowning phase in which he accepts death for the transgression of his people, fulfilling the two-fold role of priest and victim, as Christ does in this epistle.[10]

Thus the difficult phrase, "through the eternal Spirit," interpreted in this way, is but "the logical deduction from the gospel portrait of Jesus."[11]

If, as the Gospel writers affirm, the Spirit was extraordinarily important to Jesus throughout his life, enabling him to carry out his earthly ministry in a highly satisfactory way, how much more was the presence and power of the same Holy Spirit necessary at this the high water mark, the culmination, of his ministry.

But why would the writer of Hebrews be saying in this text (Heb. 9:14) that the Spirit was of such significance to Jesus at this final moment? Did he not begin his epistle with a most exalted view of Jesus, describing him as Son, Divine, God even (Heb. 1:2–12)? Yes, to be sure. And yet paradoxically his emphasis throughout this document is upon the genuineness of Jesus' humanity. He certainly affirms the preexistence of Jesus, but he equally affirms the realness of Jesus as a human being. He does not try to reconcile these two characteristics in the same individual, or to explain how the divine related to the human in Jesus. But it is fundamental to his entire argument that Jesus faced life *and death* as a person of flesh and blood (Heb. 2:14), not as a person who by virtue of his divine nature had a distinct and unparalleled advantage over all other persons.[12] The writer of Hebrews believed that Jesus "had to be made like [other people] in every way" (2:17 NEB), that he was "tempted in every way, just as we are—yet was without sin" (4:15 NIV), and that "he himself suffered when he was tempted" (2:18 NIV). He believed that Jesus, in facing his own death, was in desperate straits and that as a consequence he prayed with loud cries and tears to God who could save him from death (5:7). This writer believed, perhaps, that in Gethsemane Jesus faced his greatest of all temptations—the intense temptation to live, the temptation to flee death, to draw back from the cross, to say "NO!" to the Father's will for whatever reasons might have been coursing through his mind. But just as Jesus had overcome all previous temptations, even temptations to go his own way and do his own will, aided in these victories by the Holy Spirit, so now as well: "Through the eternal Spirit [Jesus] offered himself without blemish to God" (Heb. 9:14). Just as Jesus was strengthened throughout his life by the Holy Spirit, upon whom he had depended to help him make the right moral choices, so now at this ultimately crucial moment he was strengthened by the Spirit so that he was able to choose for God and against himself and to say, "Not my will but yours! Here I am! I have come to do your will, O God" (Heb. 10:7; cf. Mark 14:34–36 and parallels).

Understood in this way the phrase, "through the eternal Spirit," means that it was by the aid of, through the morally strengthening support of, by the power of the Spirit that Jesus offered himself as the perfect sacrifice to God. It is thus possible to conclude that the Holy Spirit even now at the end of Jesus' life, as throughout the whole of it, was playing a tremendously vital part in his ministry. For the Spirit was the instrument, the agent, the enabler by whose power Jesus achieved his greatest work on earth, that of providing eternal redemption for all (Heb. 9:12). Therefore, it is here in the passion of Jesus that one is struck full force with the overwhelming significance of the Holy Spirit in the life of Jesus.

The Spirit in the Resurrection of Jesus

That Jesus Christ died for our sins, that he was buried, and that he was raised to life again from among the dead, is the essence of the Gospel (1 Cor. 15:3–8). According to the New Testament, the death of Jesus was no accident. Rather, from the very beginning the death of Jesus was in the redemptive plan of God (Acts 2:22–23). To be more precise, it was *the* plan of God (1 Cor. 1:23–24), and as such, Jesus, who was sent from the Father to do the will of the Father (cf. John 4:34; 5:30; 6:38), voluntarily accepted death as his mission—a mission to carry out to completion (Mark 14:36). Therefore, like a priest (Heb. 5:5) Jesus gladly and freely offered up to God as the ultimate atoning sacrifice not the death of an irrational animal but the death of himself, aided in doing this by the Holy Spirit (Heb. 9:14).

The death of Jesus, however, is consistently linked together with the resurrection of Jesus (Mark 8:31; 9:31; 10:32–34; Acts 3:15; 4:10; 5:30; 10:39–40; 13:29–30). To the New Testament writers the one is inconceivable without the other, for the resurrection validated the death of Jesus, established the universal worth of his atonement, and guaranteed forgiveness of sin (Rom. 1:3–4; 1 Cor. 15:16–19). Now the question comes, "What power raised Jesus from the dead? Did he rise from the grave by virtue of his own inherent power, or was it the power of another that released him from death and raised him to life again?"

There are some passages in the New Testament that give the distinct impression that Jesus indeed raised himself from among the dead by his own power. John 2:19–21 (cf. Mark 14:58) is one of these. Here it is recorded that Jesus said, "Destroy this temple, and I will in three days raise it up." His words are accompanied by John's explanatory note, "The temple he had spoken of was his body" (v. 21 NIV).

Another passage is John 10:17–18 where Jesus is recorded as saying, "The Father loves me, because I lay down my life, that I may take it again. No one takes it from me, but I lay it down of my own accord. I have power to lay it down, and I have power to take it again." Two things need to be noted in considering the impression left by these texts:

1. Both of them are found only in the Gospel of John, a Gospel that is admittedly Christological/theological (John 20:30–31). Like the Epistle to the Hebrews, the Gospel of John sees in Jesus one who is both divine and human, God and man. But whereas the writer of Hebrews found it fundamental to his argument to emphasize the humanity of Jesus (see above pp.182–83), the writer of the Gospel of John found it fundamental to his argument to stress the divinity of Jesus. This is not to say that John had no interest in history but only in theology or that he had cut his Gospel loose from the common tradition about Jesus.[13] Rather it is to say that while quite aware of the tradition about Jesus and in full sympathy with it, he nevertheless set himself the task of drawing out to the fullest extent possible the implications of this tradition. "In this way John is adding a new but legitimate dimension to the story of Jesus; he is not 'filling in' but 'filling out.'"[14] Thus, although it is striking to learn that seemingly John insists that Jesus rose by his own power, it should not come as a surprise, given the nature of his Gospel.

2. This insistence that Jesus rose by his own power is, however, on each occasion qualified, tempered, brought more into line with the teaching of the rest of the New Testament by the context in which each of these statements about the resurrection appears. In John 2:19 Jesus says, "Destroy this temple [his body], and in three days I will raise it up." But then John immediately goes on to say about Jesus that "when he *had been raised* from the dead, his disciples recalled what he had said" (John 2:22). His use of the passive voice here, "had been raised," indicates that in the final analysis a power other than Jesus' own power brought about his resurrection.[15]

In John 10:18a Jesus' claim that he can lay down his life and take it again is immediately tempered by what he says next: "This command I received from my Father" (10:18b NIV). Now this *command* of the Father is the same as the *will* of the Father and involved the mission of Jesus that culminated in his obedient death. It included both the death of Jesus and his resurrection. For "the resurrection is not a circumstance that follows the death of Jesus, but the essential completion of the death of Jesus." Especially in John's Gospel Jesus' suffering, death, resurrection, and ascension make up one single indissoluble saving action that is the will of the Father for the Son.[16] Thus one can say, even about this passage, that for John the resurrection was "the completion of the works given by the Father to the Son to do; [and] like the rest of those works it is ultimately the work of the Father through him" (John 14:10; cf. John 5:36; 10:25).[17]

What may only be implicit in the Gospel of John is made explicit in the rest of the New Testament, namely, that Jesus *was raised* to life again, that *God raised* Jesus from the dead. This is the triumphant theme of every sermon recorded in the Acts; each comes to its climax in words similar to these: "You put Jesus to death by having him crucified; but God raised him from the dead."[18]

That God raised Jesus from the dead is the essential component in the Gospel that Paul preached and is found in almost every letter that bears his name.[19] According to Paul there could be no "good news" had not God acted to raise Jesus to life again:

> If Christ had not been raised, then our gospel is null and void and so is your faith; and we turn out to be lying witnesses against God, because we testified that he raised Christ to life, whereas, if the dead are not raised, he did not raise him. For if the dead are not raised, then Christ was not raised; and if Christ was not raised, your faith is without meaning and you are still in your sins. Furthermore, those who have died in Christ are utterly lost.
>
> *1 Cor. 15:14–18*

"Basic to Paul's view of things . . . Christ did not rise from the dead, but . . . God raised him. Therefore, the inevitable chain of events set in motion by Christ's resurrection has ultimately to do with God's own absolute authority over all things, especially death."[20]

Peter takes up this same theme and writes with similar forcefulness: "You have come to trust in God who raised him [Jesus] from the dead and gave him glory, and so your faith and hope are fixed on God" (1 Pet. 1:21 NEB). Seventeen times in the Acts and the Epistles it is expressly stated that God raised Jesus from the dead.[21] It follows from the numerous times the aorist (or perfect) passive form of the verb *egeirein* ("to raise, to rise") is used, often with the agent named, to refer to the resurrection of Jesus,[22] that this form must be understood as a real passive ("had been/has been raised") rather than simply intransitive ("had/has risen"). The overwhelming testimony of the New Testament is *not* that Jesus raised himself from the dead by his own inner divine power, but rather that God raised him and in so doing set his stamp of approval on the saving quality of his life and death.

God raised Jesus from the dead! But how did he do this. What was the means or agent by which God accomplished this great work? In light of the discussion contained in the previous chapters concerning the Holy Spirit, who was everywhere and at all times present and at work in the life and even in the death of Jesus, it is possible to infer that the Holy Spirit was that power by which God the Father raised up Jesus from the dead and gave him life again. But is there evidence to confirm or support such an inference? The answer is "Yes," although one could wish that the evidence were more abundant and more clear.

1. All that was said about the Spirit in chapter 1—God manifest in action, God exercising his power in the world, and so on—should be kept in mind here. One should especially note such passages as Ezekiel 37:13–14: "Then you, my people, will know that I am the Lord, when I open your graves and bring you up from them. I will put my Spirit in you and you will live" (NIV). And note, too, the rabbinic teaching derived from such passages. For example, "In this world my Spirit has given wisdom within you, but in the future my Spirit will make you alive again" (*Exod R* 48 [102d]).[23] In reflecting on texts like these one is drawn to the conviction that the Spirit of God is life (*to pneuma zōē*) and that the Spirit is the one who gives life, the one who makes people live (*to zōopoiein*).

2. Furthermore, it is important to keep in mind that the Spirit of God played an important role both in creation (Gen. 1:2) and in recreation and renewal (Job 33:4; Ps. 104:30), and to understand from this that "the analogy between creation and resurrection is an obvious one."[24] It is clear, then, that the Holy Spirit was from the

beginning and still is God's agent in bringing that which does not exist into existence, the dead to life again.[25]

3. But what is most significant for this study is the fact that several New Testament texts implicitly, if not explicitly, ascribe to the Spirit an active role in the resurrection of Jesus from among the dead.

Romans 1:1–4 is one of these: "... the gospel of God ... concerning his Son, who was descended from David according to the flesh and designated Son of God in power according to [spirit/Spirit] of holiness by his resurrection from the dead, Jesus Christ our Lord." "According to spirit/Spirit of holiness" (*kata pneuma hagiosynēs*) is the crucial expression for this discussion, and it is problematic. As a result numerous explanations of what Paul intended to say by it have been suggested.[26] This expression is problematic because the Greek preposition (*kata*) that introduces it, followed as it is by the accusative case, has a wide range of meaning—"in accordance with, corresponding to" (Rom. 2:16); "with respect to, in relation to" (Rom. 7:22); "because of, as a result of" (Matt. 19:13); "by, by means of" (1 Cor. 12:8), and so on. Its meaning here is difficult to narrow down precisely (see the translations). Perhaps Paul's intent in using it was to be purposely vague. Or perhaps Paul chose it strictly for rhetorical reasons, so as to balance *kata sarka* ("according to flesh") formally with *kata pneuma* ("according to spirit/Spirit") without necessarily meaning the same thing by each use of *kata*.[27] But whatever the reason for choosing it, or whatever its precise meaning may be, at least this much can be said: this prepositional phrase links together in some fashion the ideas of Son, spirit/Spirit, and resurrection.

It is also problematic because of the unusual nature of the expression, "spirit of holiness." Paul frequently speaks of the Holy Spirit, but nowhere else in his letters does he refer to the Holy Spirit as the "Spirit *of holiness*." As a consequence some interpreters have understood that with this phrase Paul was referring either to the human spirit of Jesus as "distinguished ... from that of ordinary humanity by an exceptional and transcendent holiness,"[28] or to his divinity (his own divine nature),[29] not, however, to the Holy Spirit. But the term, "spirit of holiness," as Professor Dunn has shown, "is clearly Semitic in character, modeled on the Hebraic form (not the LXX) of Ps. 51:11 and Isa. 63:10–11 (see also Test. Levi 18:11; 1QS 4:21; 8:16; 9:3;

1QH 7:7–17; 9:32; 12:12, etc.)," and would therefore, "almost certainly be understood by Paul and the first Christians as denoting the Holy Spirit, the Spirit which is characterized by holiness, partaker of God's holiness."[30]

It is possible, then, to include this text among those New Testament texts that lead one to the conclusion that the Holy Spirit was the agent by which God raised Jesus from the dead. J. B. Phillips, in his *New Testament in Modern English* clearly expresses this understanding when he translates: "[Jesus Christ our Lord], a descendant of David by human genealogy and patently marked out as the Son of God by the power of that Spirit of holiness which raised him to life again from the dead."

Romans 8:11 is another text: "If the Spirit of him who raised Jesus from the dead is living in you, he who raised Christ from the dead will also give life to your mortal bodies through his Spirit, who lives in you" (NIV). Paul has much to say about the Holy Spirit in Romans 8, especially in verses 1–11. He uses such expressions as "the Spirit of life," "The Spirit," "The things/affairs of the Spirit," "The Spirit of God," "The Spirit of Christ," "The Spirit who dwells in you," and so on. In verse 11 he says without equivocation that God is going to raise up and give life to the mortal bodies of Christians, and he is going to do this *by the Spirit (dia tou pneumatos)*![31] This resurrection of Christians, however, which will break the terrifying grip of sin and death that has held them captive (Rom. 8:2), is but part of a prior resurrection, the resurrection of Jesus, and is the direct result of that resurrection, "Him who raised Jesus from the dead . . . will also give life to your mortal bodies through his Spirit" (Rom. 8:11).

The resurrection of Jesus, therefore, was an eschatological event. That is to say, it inaugurated the Last Days, the age to come, a period marked out by the resurrection of the dead and by fulness of life. This present age is running to its close, and at its end death will be completely done away with (1 Cor. 15:26). That first event, the resurrection of Jesus, was the pledge and guarantee of the last event, the resurrection of Christians. But it is important now to observe that these two events are "connected by the presence and activity of the Holy Spirit . . . who brought the life-giving activity of God to bear on every stage of the intervening period."[32]

To be sure, verse 11 does not state explicitly that God raised Jesus from the dead by the Spirit. But one may safely infer that if, as *is* stated clearly, God is going to finish the process of resurrection *by the Spirit*, he must surely have begun that process in the same way, *by the Spirit*. Indeed, the final phrase of verse 11 as it is constructed in Greek seems to confirm this inference, for it is quite possible to translate it not, "through *his* Spirit who lives in you," but "through *the same* Spirit who lives in you."[33] If this new translation is the correct one, then it makes clear that the *same* Spirit by which God will yet give life to the mortal bodies of Christians was the very Spirit by which He already raised Christ from the dead. Romans 8:11, amplified to bring out this meaning, would read as follows: ". . . he who raised Christ from the dead by the Holy Spirit will also give life to your mortal bodies through that same Spirit. . . . " This verse, then, becomes another text supporting the suggestion that God raised Jesus from among the dead by the power of the Holy Spirit.

1 Corinthians 6:14 is still another of these texts: "God both raised our Lord and will raise us up [out of death] *by his power*." This striking statement comes in a context where Paul argues against those Corinthians who apparently were claiming that all things were lawful for them, that nothing was off limits to them as enlightened, spiritual Christians. Their argument seems to have gone something like this: "Just as food is for the stomach and the stomach for food, so sex is for the body and the body is for sex. Both are equally matters of indifference, since God is going to destroy both the body and all those things that go towards satisfying the cravings of the body in the end" (cf. 6:12–13). If this was the direction in which their thinking was going, then, according to Paul, it was decidedly wrongheaded. They had failed to understand one of the most fundamental tenents of the Bible and of Paul's teaching—the body is *not* a matter of indifference to God, as food or drink to the stomach, nor will God allow the body, like food, to be destroyed, to be forever done away with as waste that disintegrates into nothingness. The body is not for destruction, but for resurrection. "The body is . . . *for* the Lord," and what is even more astonishing, "the Lord is *for* the body" (1 Cor. 6:13). Hence, even should the body succumb to death and go down into the grave, God is going to raise it up again from the dead and give it life as surely as he raised up the Lord Jesus from the dead and gave him life (1 Cor. 6:14). Such is the importance of the body to God!

But that which is of the greatest significance in this particular text for the discussion at hand is the prepositional phrase, "through/ by his power" (*dia tēs dynameōs autou*)—"God both raised the Lord and will raise us *by his power.*" What did the apostle mean by this phrase? What was in his mind when he spoke of God's power? And what was it that this power effected? In answering these questions it is important to keep several things in mind:

1. Paul took for granted that *God* raised Jesus from the dead and that Jesus did not raise himself.

2. In this particular section (1 Cor. 6:12–14) the apostle is intent on claiming that the body of the Christian is not destined for destruction but for resurrection, and he substantiates his claim by tying the resurrection of the Christian to the resurrection of Jesus—"God both raised the Lord and [therefore] he will raise us."

3. The prepositional phrase, "by his power," although placed last in the sentence perhaps for emphasis, nevertheless modifies both verbs ("raised . . . will raise"). It is the power of God that will effect the resurrection of the Christian in the future, as it already did effect the resurrection of the Lord in the past.[34]

4. The intermediary agent by which God raised Jesus from the dead was his *power*.

5. Elsewhere in his letters Paul often links *power* together with the Holy Spirit; perhaps he even identifies them as one and the same. Note, for example, these statements of his (italics mine): Jesus Christ was "designated Son of God in *power* according to the *Spirit* of holiness" (Rom. 1:4); "may the God of hope fill you with all joy . . . so that by the *power* of the *Holy Spirit* you may abound in hope" (Rom. 15:13); "my speech and my message were . . . in demonstration of the *Spirit* and of *power*, that your faith might not rest in the wisdom of men but in the *power* of God" (1 Cor. 2:4–5); "for our gospel came to you not only in word, but also in *power* and in the *Holy Spirit* . . . " (1 Thess. 1:5).

Therefore, here is yet another text (1 Cor. 6:14) to be added to those that support the claim that the Holy Spirit was the divine agent that effected the resurrection of Jesus Christ from the dead. For from these words of Paul—"God raised the Lord *by his power*"—one may correctly infer that the apostle meant to say that God raised Jesus *by the power of the Holy Spirit*, or, to put it in a slightly different way, that God raised Jesus from the dead and gave him life by his power, which is the Holy Spirit.[35]

1 Timothy 3:16 is yet one more text, but it is the most problematic of them all. The RSV translates:

> He was manifested in the flesh,
> vindicated in the Spirit,
> seen by angels,
> preached among the nations,
> believed on in the world,
> taken up in glory.

Research in recent years has done much to uncover a number of very early Christian hymns or hymn fragments that long lay unnoticed within the pages of the New Testament. 1 Timothy 3:16 is one of these,[36] whose lyrical beauty is often obscured in translation but is stunningly obvious in Greek. Although this hymn begins simply with a relative pronoun (*hos*, "who"), which the RSV translates, "he," it is clear that the *who/he* is Jesus. It is, then, another Christ-hymn of the New Testament, each line of which was Christologically important to the early church. Only the initial two lines, however, are of significance for the present discussion.

The hymn begins with a statement filled with deep thankfulness as the church at worship celebrated the incarnation—"He [Christ] was manifested [*ephanerōthē*] in the flesh [*en sarki*]." Here is a powerful statement filled with meaning that early Christians would have readily understood but that needs to be unpacked so that its same meaning may be as readily understood by Christians today:

1. Note first of all the force of the passive verb used in this first line—"was manifested" (*ephanerōthē*). There is in the choice and use of this particular form of the verb a reference to the preexistence of Christ[37] as well as to his incarnation.[38]

2. Note further that the modifying phrase, "in the flesh" (*en sarki*) states clearly that this divine person showed up on earth and lived

out his days in this world as a genuine human being (cf. John 1:14; Rom. 1:3; 8:3; 9:5; Eph. 2:14; Col. 1:22; Heb. 5:7; 1 Pet. 3:18).

3. Note finally that this simple phrase "in the flesh" (*en sarki*) embraces the whole of "the days of his flesh" (Heb. 5:7), the entirety of his human existence from birth to death, as it does elsewhere in the New Testament of other human beings (cf. Gal. 2:20; Phil. 1:22, 24).

It is in light of these observations that the second, more problematic line, is to be understood—"vindicated in the Spirit" (*edikaiōthē en pneumati*). What precisely was the hymn writer referring to when he wrote these words? Once again it is necessary to examine this extraordinary statement in detail.

1. The verb of this line is *edikaiōthē*, a word frequently used by Paul to describe God's act of acquitting sinners, of pronouncing and treating them as just or putting them right with himself.[39] But this can hardly be its meaning here, for this is a hymn about Christ. It is inconceivable that those earliest Christians, who first sang it, thought of Jesus as one who like themselves, and in the same way as themselves, needed to be justified by God.

This verb, however, can also mean "to vindicate," that is, "to prove someone to be right or innocent or good" when, for whatever reasons, that person might otherwise have been thought to be guilty or wrong or evil. It is in this sense that *edikaiōthē* must be understood here—"he was vindicated."[40] For recall that Jesus had been arrested, tried before both religious and civil tribunals, pronounced guilty of wrongdoing, sentenced to death by crucifixion—a mode of punishment reserved for the worst offenders—and crucified outside the city of Jerusalem. In the eyes of the majority of onlookers, he died as a criminal. What was there to indicate that he was anything other than this? Hence, if the judgment of the human courts was to be overturned and the understanding of the masses reversed, something or someone had to proclaim his innocence to the world in a powerful and effective way; something or someone had to vindicate him.

2. Note that this verb is also passive in form meaning that some outside agent did the vindicating. Someone other than Jesus himself proved him innocent and demonstrated that he was right and that all he said and did was right and good. Who/what was this agent, and by what means did this agent vindicate Jesus? Almost without a

second thought, impelled by the momentum of this study thus far, one is inclined to say that the agent who demonstrated to the world the innocence of Jesus was the Holy Spirit, and the way in which he did this was by raising him from the dead (cf. Rom. 1:3–4).

3. Hence it comes as no surprise to learn that the verb *edikaiōthē* ("he was vindicated") is immediately modified by the prepositional phrase, *en pneumati*, which the RSV translates, "in the Spirit," but which can as correctly be translated "*by* the Spirit" (i.e. "*by* the Holy Spirit.)"[41] The meaning then is this: Jesus was put to death as a criminal, crucified for his supposed crimes, but vindicated in the end, declared to be innocent, proclaimed far and wide to be righteous by the Holy Spirit who raised him from the dead (cf. Rom. 8:11).[42]

These, then, are the principal texts that indicate the means, the power by which God raised Jesus from the dead. One might wish for an explicit statement such as, "God raised Jesus from the dead by the Holy Spirit," but it does not exist in the New Testament. Nevertheless, lacking such, the wording of the texts just now examined is sufficiently clear so as to leave no doubt that God's agent effecting the resurrection of Jesus was God's Spirit, the Power of God. This Power from the very beginning of creation has been at work in the world, creating, vivifying, energizing, and from the very conception of Jesus and throughout his life, death, and resurrection has played a similar and equally important and significant role in that life. The Holy Spirit, then, was that divine agent by which God the Father raised Jesus from the dead.

NOTES

1. So also ASV, TEV, JB, KJV, NASB, NIV, Goodspeed.

2. T. Hewitt, *The Epistle to the Hebrews*, TNTC (Grand Rapids, 1960), 148. See also G. L. Archer, Jr., *The Epistle to the Hebrews, a Study Manual*, (Grand Rapids, 1961), 54; A. B. Davidson, *The Epistle to the Hebrews*, (reprint ed., Edinburgh, 1950), 177–78; R. C. H. Lenski, *The Interpretation of the Epistle to the Hebrews* (Columbus, Ohio, 1937), 300; J. Moffatt, *Epistle to the Hebrews*, ICC (Edinburgh, 1924); H. Montefiore, A *Commentary on the Epistle to the Hebrews*, HNTC (New York, 1964); A. Nairne, *The Epistle to the Hebrews* (Cambridge, 1917), 90; C. Spicq, *L'Épître aux*

Hebreux (Paris, 1953) 2.258–59; B. F. Westcott, *The Epistle to the Hebrews* (1892; reprint ed., Grand Rapids, n.d.), 261–62.

3. Moffatt, *Epistle to the Hebrews*, 124–25.

4. Montefiore, *A Commentary on the Epistle to the Hebrews*, 155; See Spicq, who comments that the expression "eternal spirit" is "non une disposition d'espirit . . . ni son ame, ni l'Espirit Saint . . . mais: en vertu de sa personnalité même ou de sa puissance propre, d'une valeur transcendante, qui lui assurait une vie et un sacerdote éternel à même a travers la mort . . ." (*L'Épître aux Hebreux*, 258–59).

5. Swete, *The Holy Spirit in the New Testament*, 252–53.

6. Heb. 1:14; 2:4; 3:7; 4:12; 6:4; 9:8, 14; 10:15, 29; 12:9, 23.

7. F. F. Bruce, *The Epistle to the Hebrews*, NICNT (Grand Rapids, 1964), 205.

8. Archer, *Hebrews*, 54.

9. J. Calvin, *The Epistle of Paul the Apostle to the Hebrews*, trans. W. B. Johnson (reprint ed., Grand Rapids, 1963), 121.

10. Bruce, *The Epistle to the Hebrews*, 205; see also Guthrie, *New Testament Theology*, 568; P. E. Hughes, *A Commentary on the Epistle to the Hebrews*, (Grand Rapids, 1977), 359; Hagner, *Hebrews*, 117; S. J. Kistemaker, *Exposition of the Epistle to the Hebrews*, NTC (Grand Rapids, 1984), 251–52; R. McL. Wilson, *Hebrews*, NCBC (Grand Rapids, 1987); F. D. V. Narborough, *The Epistle to the Hebrews*, CB (Oxford, 1930), 117.

11. Guthrie, *New Testament Theology*, 568.

12. See Wilson, *Hebrews*, 154–57.

13. See the introduction to the Gospel of John in S. S. Smalley, *John: Evangelist and Interpreter* (Nashville, 1983), for an excellent discussion of the relation between history and theology in the fourth Gospel.

14. Smalley, *John: Evangelist and Interpreter*, 244; see also J. A. T. Robinson, "The Place of the Fourth Gospel," in *The Roads Converge*, ed. P. G. Smith (London, 1963), 74 (see also 57–74).

15. The verb *ēgerthē* is passive in form. But it is only fair to point out that for this particular verb the passive form may be either passive in meaning or simply intransitive—"was raised" or "rose" (Moule, *Idiom Book*, 26). Those places, however, within the New Testament where the passive of this verb, *egeirein*, is intransitive are obvious (cf. Matt. 1:24: "Rising [*egertheis*] from sleep Joseph did as the angel had said," not, "When he was raised from sleep . . . "; cf. also Matt. 2:13; 8:15; Mark 2:12; 13:8; Luke 11:8). But here in John 2:22 it is not so obvious whether it is a true passive or simply intransitive. Yet in light of the overwhelming testimony of the rest of the New Testament that Jesus *was raised* from the dead, and the nineteen times that the New Testament explicitly says that God the Father raised him from the dead, it is best to assume that John intended it to be passive here. Most translations understand it in this way and so translate it (ASV, KJV, TEV, NASB, NIV, RSV; but contrast JB). Perhaps, however, it is useless to try to make a distinction between "was raised" and "rose" here in John 2:22 for in the Gospel of John it becomes clear that the Father's power is also Jesus' power, so what one does the other does also (John 10:30)—but it is always a delegated power, a power given him by the Father (5:19,

22, 30; 8:28). Even that power of possessing and giving life was a power given him by the Father (5:25–26).

16. Brown, *John I–XII*, 399.

17. Smalley, *John: Evangelist and Interpreter*, 172. See again John 5:19, 22, 26, 30; 6:37; 8:28, and note Brown's remark: "Since in Johannine thought the Father and Son possess the same power (x.28–30), it really makes little difference whether the resurrection is attributed to the action of the Father or of the Son" (Brown, *John I–XII*, 399).

18. Acts 3:15; 4:10; 5:30; 10:40; 13:30, 37.

19. Cf. Rom. 1:4; 4:24; 6:4, 9; 8:11 (bis), 34; 10:9; Gal. 1:1; Eph. 1:20; Col. 1:18; 2:12; 1 Thess. 1:10; 2 Tim. 2:8.

20. G. D. Fee, *The First Epistle to the Corinthians*, NICNT (Grand Rapids, 1987), 746–47; this emphasis on God's sovereignty can be seen in the repetition of *pas/pantes* ("all," ten times) in 1 Cor. 15:24–28.

21. Acts 3:15; 4:10; 5:30; 10:40; 13:30, 37; Rom. 4:24; 8:11 (bis); 10:9; 1 Cor. 6:14; 15:15; 2 Cor. 4:14; Gal. 1:1; Eph. 1:20; Col. 2:12; 1 Thess. 1:10.

22. Matt. 16:21; 17:9, 23; 20:19; 27:64; 28:6, 7; Mark 14:28; 16:6; Luke 9:22; 24:7, 34; John 2:22; 21:14; Rom. 4:25; 6:4, 9; 7:4; 8:34; 1 Cor. 15:4, 12, 13, 14, 15, 16, 17, 20; 2 Cor. 5:15; 2 Tim. 2:8.

23. Quoted by Cranfield, *Romans*, 1.392, n. 2.

24. Cranfield, *Romans*, 1.392, n. 2.

25. E. Schweizer, *TDNT*, 6.422.

26. See W. Sanday and A. C. Headlam, *The Epistle to the Romans*, ICC (Edinburgh, 1895), 9; Lagrange, *Épître aux Romains*, 7; J. Huby, *Saint Paul: Épître aux Romains* (Verbun Salutis), ed. S. Lyonnet (Paris, 1957), 45; O. Michel, *Der Brief an die Römer* (Göttingen, 1966), 38–39; C. K. Barrett, A *Commentary on the Epistle to the Romans* (London, 1957), 18–19; Cranfield, *Romans*, 1.64.

27. Cf. the NIV: "Who *as to his human nature* [*kata sarka*] was a descendent of David, and who *through the Spirit* [*kata pneuma*] of holiness was declared . . . the Son of God" (Rom. 1:3–4, italics mine).

28. Sanday and Headlam, *The Epistle to the Romans*, 9, as quoted by Cranfield, *Romans*, 1.63.

29. Lagrange, *Épître aux Romains*, 8.

30. J. D. G. Dunn, *Romans 1–8*, WBC (Dallas, 1988), 15.

31. There is an important variant reading here with good support: *dia to enoikoun autou pneuma en hymin* ("because of/on account of his Spirit which lives in you"), instead of *dia tou enoikountos autou pneumatos en hymin* ("through/by his Spirit who lives in you"). If the former reading is chosen, then the Spirit which indwells Christians cannot be thought of as the means by which God will raise them to life again, but rather the reason why he will do so (cf. Rom. 8:23; 2 Cor. 1:22; 5:5; Eph. 1:13–14). But the latter variant is to be preferred for the reasons given by Cranfield, *Romans*, 1.391–92 and Metzger, *Textual Commentary*, 517. It is the reading adopted by most of the recent translations.

32. Barrett, *Romans*, 159–60.

33. The Greek of this phrase is *dia tou enoikountos autou pneumatos*. Most translators take the *autou* as a personal pronoun in the genitive case to show possession—"his Spirit." But as in classical Greek, the New Testament writers are in the habit of placing the possessive genitive of personal pronouns "either after an anarthrous substantive without repetition of the article or before the article," although, of course, there are exceptions to this rule (BDF, 284.1). Here in Rom. 8:11 *autou* is placed after the article and before the noun—*within* the article-noun group. It is in the customary position for what is referred to as the identifying adjective meaning "same." J. B. Phillips catches this understanding of the text when he translates it, "Nevertheless once the Spirit of him who raised Christ Jesus from the dead lives within you he will, *by that same Spirit*, bring to your whole being new strength and vitality" (italics mine).

34. See Fee, *First Epistle to the Corinthians*, 254, 256, and note the NIV: "By his power God raised the Lord from the dead, and he will raise us also" (1 Cor. 6:14). This translation captures the intention of the apostle.

35. Such an inference is in full harmony with what Paul has written elsewhere about the Spirit—"The Spirit makes alive" (*to pneuma zōopoiei*, 2 Cor. 3:6). A text similar to 1 Cor. 6:14 and with similar implications is Col. 2:12: "You were buried with him, in baptism in which also you were raised to life with him through your faith in the *active power* [*tēs energeias*] of God who raised him from the dead."

36. See M. Dibelius and H. Conzelmann, *The Pastoral Epistles*, trans. P. Buttolph and A. Yarbro (Philadelphia, 1972), 61.

37. J. H. Bernard, *The Pastoral Epistles* (Cambridge, 1922), 63, says that the verb *phaneroun*, ("to manifest, show, reveal"), "when used in the passive [here] . . . implies the pre-existence of the Person Who is the subject of the sentence." See also N. Brox, *Die Pastoralbrief*, Regensburger NT (Regensburg, 1969). J. N. D. Kelly, A *Commentary on the Pastorals* (New York, 1963), 90, is more cautious. He writes: "His [Christ's] pre-existence is probably, though not necessarily implied [by this word]." So also P. Dornier, *Les Épîtres Pastorales*, Sources Bibliques (Paris, 1969). Dunn, on the other hand, *Christology in the Making*, 237, rejects the thought that preexistence is indicated in this text at all: "[The verb *phanerousthai*, 'to manifest'] may well be used here simply in the sense of 'appear', without any particular intention of implying a previous (pre-existent) hiddenness."

38. The verb *phaneroun* is elsewhere used of the incarnation of Jesus and of his ministry as a human being (John 1:31; Heb. 9:26; 1 Pet. 1:20; 1 John 1:2; 3:5, 8).

39. Cf. the KJV: "justified in the Spirit" (1 Tim. 3:16).

40. And so the majority of translations of 1 Tim. 3:16: e.g., NIV, NEB, RSV, TEV ("was shown to be right").

41. *En* with the dative in the NT may denote personal agent (Matt. 9:34; 12:24; Acts 17:31; 1 Cor. 6:2; Col. 1:16). See BDF, 219, and NIV, Goodspeed (1 Tim. 3:16).

42. By no means are all commentators and translators agreed on this interpretation. The parallel structure of the first two lines, *ephanerōthē en sarki/edikaiōthē en pneumati*, one ending in *en sarki* and the other in *en pneumati*, causes many to understand *sarki* as referring to Christ's humanity in general and *pneumati* to Christ's spiritual nature in particular—not to the Holy Spirit. Bernard, *Pastoral Epistles*, 63;

Dibelius and Conzelmann, *Pastoral Epistles*, 62; D. Guthrie, *The Pastoral Epistles*, (reprint ed., Grand Rapids, 1984), 89–90; G. D. Fee, *1 and 2 Timothy and Titus* (New York, 1984), 55–56; A. T. Hanson, *The Pastoral Epistles*, NCBC (Grand Rapids, Mich.1982), 85–86; Kelly, *Pastoral Epistles*, 90–91; Spicq, *Les Épîtres Pastorales*, 107–108. The bibliography on the interpretation of this hymn is vast, but for an extremely useful discussion of the hymn itself, see R. H. Gundry, "The Form, Meaning and Background of the Hymn Quoted in 1 Timothy 3:16," in *Apostolic History and the Gospel*, ed. W. W. Gasque and R. P. Martin (Grand Rapids, 1970), 201–222. Gundry makes a good case for understanding *en pneumati* to mean "by the Spirit," but himself rejects such an interpretation (211–12).

7. The Spirit as the Key to the Kenosis

The direction of this study now takes a new and important and yet intimidating turn. Up until this point, the discussion has focused on those biblical texts that concern themselves with the Spirit and Jesus, and on an exegesis of those texts. This chapter, on the other hand, will be much more tentative, much more speculative, and for that reason much more open to criticism. It arises out of the fact that I believe that the preexistent Son of God became a human being in space and time in the person of Jesus of Nazareth (see chapter 1), and only in Jesus of Nazareth—this Jesus and only this Jesus is the "human face of God," to borrow an expression from the late Bishop Robinson. "But how can you believe this?" you ask. "How is it possible for one person to be both God and a man simultaneously—and *fully* God and *fully* human at that?" That is the question I wish to try to address in this chapter, for it is a question that has been with me for a very long time.

The fact of the matter is (and perhaps it is a fact that should be a warning to me), apparently this question posed no problem to the writers of the New Testament. For while they talk about Jesus both in human terms and also in superhuman terms, they make no attempt to explain how one person could be both human and superhuman, God and man, the God-man. They simply take it for granted.

They accept it as fact, holding both in tension, and base all that they have to say about how God acted in history to save the fallen race of people to which I belong, on this fact.

But at least from the earliest post-New Testament stages of the church's history, it has troubled the church. It is a question that has been and is still being asked with all seriousness by theologians and nontheologians alike. And as a consequence, many different attempts to reconcile this seemingly irreconcilable paradox have been made.

For example, Docetism, which probably should not be called a doctrine in that it was hardly a unified formulation of Christian teaching, was nevertheless one of the very first attempts at explanation. Possessing a high Christology that was rooted more in Greek philosophy than in the New Testament, Docetists answered the question of how it was that the same person could be both God and human by essentially denying the existence of the human in Jesus. According to the writings of those who were their critics, the Docetists (such as Cerinthus and Serapion, Bishop of Antioch, A.D. 190–203) considered the humanity and sufferings of Jesus as only apparent rather than real—his humanness only seemed to be; it never was authentic. Very likely it was this unorthodox Christology that already was being encountered *and countered* in the New Testament (cf. Col. 2:8–9; 1 John 4:1–3; 2 John). If so, it shows how early it was that "solutions" to this question began to appear and how early it was that the church began to test such solutions.

The Ebionites, a Jewish Christian group that also flourished in the early centuries of Christianity, attempted to resolve the problem of the person of Christ in quite an opposite manner to that of the Docetists. For them Jesus was the Messiah, but he was not God. He was really human, the son of Joseph and Mary, but not divine. To be sure, the Holy Spirit came upon him in such power that one might say it raised him to the status of a superhuman being, but at best he could only be thought of as a second-grade divinity, not as himself fully God.[1]

Arius[2] (ca. 250–336), possibly a presbyter and a deacon of Alexandria, was nevertheless a thinker who struggled with this same question. The answer he gave was to say that Jesus was the Son of God but not eternal. Rather, he was a being created out of nothing by the Father as the instrument by which the Father would bring the world into existence. Jesus was for Arius neither true God nor true man; he possessed neither the substance and nature of the Father, nor the soul of a human being. He was given the title Son of God only because the Father foresaw his unswerving loyalty and abiding righteousness. Arius exercised considerable influence, drew a large following, and caused bitter controversy within the early church. Eventually he was branded as a heretic for his views and was excommunicated.

And there were the Monarchian Modalists who in their teaching on the Trinity in effect denied that Jesus was the eternal Son of God, for they rejected any idea of the permanence of the three persons within the Godhead—God simply manifested himself to the world in three modes of being. They claimed that the Father, the Son, and the Holy Spirit were only different names for the same person. Thus, in Jesus Christ the only one God appeared on earth physically and redeemed human beings by his death on the cross and his resurrection. This naive form was refined under the influence of philosophical speculations about the Logos, so that somehow or other in their teaching (called Sabellianism, after a little known person named Sabellius) the Logos, which had become incarnate in Jesus Christ, had to be confessed as the Son of God. But he differed in some significant way from the Father—as different as a boat is from the boat-builder, as someone who came into being by a creative act of the Father.

Apollinarius (ca. 310–390), bishop of Laodicea, also attempted to solve the problem of the divine and human in Jesus. He asserted the Godhood and the manhood in Jesus and stressed the full deity of Jesus, but he denied that there could be any moral or ethical development in Jesus' life, for Jesus in this sense was always perfect.[3] His argument ran something like this: In human beings there coexist body, soul, and spirit. But in Jesus Christ there were only the human body and human soul, but no spirit. The spirit of Jesus was replaced by the divine Logos.

The consequence of this kind of thinking was that the highest part of humanity, the mind or rational soul, was thereby made superfluous; the humanity of Jesus was strictly impersonal, confined totally to the realm of the physical. Thus Apollinarianism solved the problem of how Jesus could be both God and human again at the expense of his full humanity. God-in-a-body, as one might describe the Jesus of

Apollinarianism, could never be called a human being in the true sense of the word.

Nestorius (ca. 451) entered a monastery at Antioch and was thereby greatly influenced by the Antiochene theological method. He gained a great reputation as a preacher and was a self-proclaimed upholder of orthodoxy. He, too, engaged in the debate over the person of Christ, and all that was characteristic of the thinking of the theologians of Antioch came to culmination in his teachings. He taught the full deity of the divine Logos and also the full humanity of the man Jesus, but seemingly he was never able to teach convincingly of Jesus as just one person. Always it appeared that there were not only two different natures in the incarnate Christ but two separate persons, the one divine and the other human, without any adequate explanation of how the two persons related to each other. Nestorius did take the humanity of Jesus seriously, however. There was nothing in his teaching of an impersonal humanity, and he seemed to see the divine Logos as uniting with the whole man, not just with Jesus' human body. But at the deepest level Jesus remained in essence two separate persons within a single body with no logical way of explaining him otherwise.

Eutyches (ca. 378–454), the superior of a large monastery in Constantinople and a person with great influence at court, was keenly opposed to Nestorianism. As a consequence, his opposition forced him into a theological stance that failed to discern the difference between the two natures of Christ, blurring them so that Jesus was neither truly God nor truly human but a sort of third entity arising from a blending of the divine and human together. He has been called the father of Monophysitism (Jesus had only one nature). Eutyches also denied that the humanity of Jesus was of the same substance with that of other human beings.

Adoptionism was a Christology that claimed that Jesus was not the Son of God ontologically (i.e., in the essence of his being) but was only a man, a particularly good man, no doubt, a human person whom God decided to adopt as his Son at some point of time in his life because of his loyal obedience to the Father, perhaps at the time of his baptism or his resurrection. As a well thought-out Christological system, it did not come into its own until the eighth century. Yet it was a way of thinking about Jesus that was already in the air, so to speak, and that had already placed its stamp on many of the earlier Christologies discussed above.

There were many other early attempts at solving this question which cannot be discussed here. Usually, however, these attempts at probing into the mystery of the person of Jesus proved futile. Whatever answer was forthcoming seemed destined either to impair the reality of the divinity of Jesus or the reality of the humanity of Jesus, or hopelessly to confuse the two.

Then came the Council of Chalcedon (A.D. 451), a council of 500–600 bishops, most of whom were from the East, which produced the so-called Chalcedonian Definition, a definition that was crucial for the church and became the touchstone for orthodoxy for centuries. It asserted the full divinity of Christ against Arianism, the full humanity of Christ against Apollinarius, the unity of Christ's person against Nestorius, and the permanence of Christ's two natures without confusion against Eutyches. It was stated in these words:

> Following therefore the holy Fathers, we confess one and the same our Lord Jesus Christ, and we all teach harmoniously [that he is] the same perfect in Godhead, the same perfect in manhood, truly God and truly man, the same of a [rational] soul and body; consubstantial with the Father in Godhead, and the same consubstantial with us in manhood, like us in all things except sin; begotten before ages of the Father in Godhead, the same in the last days for us; and for our salvation [born] of Mary the virgin *theotokos* in manhood, one and the same Christ, Son, Lord, unique; acknowledged in two natures without confusion, without change, without division, without separation—the difference of the natures being by no means taken away because of the union, but rather the distinctive character of each nature being preserved, and [each] combining in one person and *hypostasis*—not divided or separated into two persons, but one and the same Son and only-begotten God, Word, Lord Jesus Christ, as the prophets of old and the Lord Jesus Christ himself taught us about him. . . .[4]

The Chalcedon Definition was a brilliant effort to tie all the loose ends together and to present to the church a perfect explanation of the person of Jesus Christ. But in reality it never answered all the questions that had been raised then, and it does not now answer the questions that are being raised today. The language that the bishops of the council used was Greek. The terms they used to forge their concept of Christ were steeped in ancient Greek philosophy, terms such as *hypostasis*, *substance*, *nature*, *person*.

And furthermore, the wording was sufficiently obscure so that, on the one hand, what the bishops intended was not always correctly understood with a distortion of some truth about Christ as the result, or, on the other hand, part of what they intended and what was correctly understood was overstressed, with equally unfortunate results. Good people, honest people, orthodox people for whatever reason—because of correct understanding or because of misunderstanding—were sometimes aided by the Chalcedon Definition to arrive at unbiblical conclusions about the person of Jesus Christ.

For instance, cast in the vocabulary of Greek thought as it was, the Chalcedon Definition was interpreted in such a way by some of the church fathers as to strengthen their own presuppositions about the immutability, the unchanging static nature of God including his impassibility (his inability to suffer). This in turn made it difficult for them in reality to see how the unchangeable God, who by nature is incapable of suffering, could ever become human and suffer for the sins of the world. And thus for them the historical Jesus, whom they proclaimed as both God and man, took on a sort of dual existence.

This meant that they spoke about Jesus in language similar to the following: "Thou art compassionate in terms of our experience and not compassionate in terms of thy being."[5] Or they held such views as that the Logos while incarnate on earth was still seated at the right hand of the Father upholding the universe. Or the influential words of Cyril: "While visible as a babe in swaddling clothes and yet in the bosom of the Virgin who bare Him, [the Son of God] was filling all creation as God, and was enthroned with Him who begat Him." And Cyril again, "So then, the Son of God enters upon this lower world, descending from His heavenly seat without retiring from the Father's glory."[6] Or the words of Athanasius: "He spat in human fashion, yet his spittle was charged with deity, for therewith he caused the eyes of the man born blind to recover their sight."[7] Or the statement of Leo the Great, Bishop of Rome from A.D. 440, until his death in 461:

> Each nature performs what is proper to itself in communion with the other; the Word, that is, performing what is proper to the Word, and the flesh carrying out what is proper to the flesh. The one of these is brilliant with miracles, the other succumbs to injuries. . . . To feel hunger, thirst and weariness and to sleep is evidently human; but to satisfy thousands with five loaves, and to bestow living water on the Samaritan woman . . . is without doubt divine.[8]

The ideas expressed in statements such as these by such notable and prominent fathers of the church have had a powerful influence on the church for centuries, from their day even until today. In a legitimate concern to preserve at all costs the deity of Jesus Christ, many contemporary teachers of the church have followed the lead of the ancient fathers and have become *de facto* Docetists, failing to estimate fully the humanity in which divinity made itself visible. Seldom belittling, but often neglecting the clear New Testament teaching of the full humanity of Jesus, many of these have not adequately stressed that Jesus was made like us "in every respect" (Heb. 2:17), except in the matter of sin (Heb. 4:15), have refused to accept the fact that there were things that Jesus did not know (Matt. 24:36), have rejected out of hand the idea that there were things he could not do (Mark 6:5), and have overlooked that he performed his miracles by the Spirit of God (cf. Matt. 12:28). They have preferred rather to side with the fathers who taught that Jesus as man may have been limited, but that the very same person at the same instant was unlimited as God—that he was weak as a man, but that he knew all things as God.[9] Such teaching, however, while claiming in theory to hold fast to the humanity of Jesus, in reality lets it slip away.

If one should ask why it is that the church has repeatedly neglected Christ's true humanity, some would venture to reply that it is because its teachers are either ignorant of the Chalcedonian Definition, or have failed to appropriate what it was saying, or have (unintentionally) misrepresented its fundamental intent. But the neglect of Christ's true humanity is *not* because of Chalcedon itself.

Thus, there are those who call for a reaffirmation of the Chalcedonian Definition, but ask that it be restated, translated, explained, and intelligently defended.[10] Others, for better or worse, have attempted to break new ground, to reexamine the crucial texts of the New Testament, to rethink how the humanness and the divineness come together meaningfully in the person of Jesus Christ. Thus Christological thinking goes on with each new generation making its own contribution to the discussion,[11] trying a number of different answers each without total success.

That doctrine of the person of Jesus Christ to which my study has driven me, and which in my judgment best complies with the teaching of the New Testament as I have attempted to describe it in the preceding chapters is that which often goes by the name of "Kenotic Christology."[12] Its biblical basis is the "Christ Hymn" found in Philippians 2:6–11,[13] and 2 Corinthians 8:9.

But I do not at all have in mind, nor do I want to be identified with, the more radical kenotic Christologies of the very early proponents of this theory, those put forth by the nineteenth-century theologians, G. Thomasius,[14] W. F. Gess[15] and F. Godet.[16] These scholars, starting with the Greek verb, *kenoun* ("to empty"), of Philippians 2:7, argued in one of two ways: (1) The eternal Logos emptied himself of the "relative [relational] attributes" that belong to deity—omniscience, omnipotence, and omnipresence—the attributes that are expressions of God's relation to the world, but did not relinquish the "essential [immanent] attributes" of holiness, love, and justice, [17] attributes that express the essence of the divine life, God's own inner-relatedness as a Trinity, and are in no way dependent on God's relation to the world (Thomasius' position).[18] Or (2) the Logos became incarnate by emptying himself of every attribute of deity, so that for all intents and purposes during the period of the incarnation he ceased to be God, since the presence of any of the divine attributes would destroy the reality of Jesus' humanness (Gess and Godet's position).[19]

These views of Thomasius, Gess, and Godet were vigorously opposed, and rightly so. But as a consequence not only did the doctrine of the kenosis earn for itself an unfavorable reputation, but any chance for fruitful discussion along these lines was prematurely broken off without being effectively renewed. Nevertheless, as Vincent Taylor consolingly remarks,

> fashions in theological thinking are not altogether without profit. They provide an opportunity for new suggestions which often by contrast reveal the value of older methods. In the present case no good alternative [to the kenosis theory] has been advanced, and it is significant that when the opponents of kenoticism state their own theories, they are driven to put forward hypotheses which, because they must account for the human limitations involved in the incarnation, prove to be a considerable extent kenotic.[20]

Thus, at this point, while I am still willing to be tagged with a kenotic label, I wish, however, to be identified more closely with such thinkers as Austin Farrer,[21] P. T. Forsyth,[22] H. R. Mackintosh,[23] O. C. Quick,[24] Vincent Taylor,[25] and more recently Brian Hebblethwaite.[26] With them I refuse to say that in the incarnation the eternal Son of God gave up, surrendered, laid aside a single attribute belonging to deity, as if attributes of God were like garments that could be taken off and hung up somewhere until needed again. With Chalcedon, I affirm that Jesus was *truly* God, *fully* God, God undiminished by emptying himself of even a single attribute! When Philippians 2:7 is looked at through this lens, one discovers that the expression, "emptied himself," does not say that he emptied himself of anything. Hence, one should not think that the phrase means that Christ discarded divine substances, essences, or attributes. Quite the contrary. The series of participial phrases immediately following the description of this event—"he emptied himself *by taking* the form of a slave, *by becoming* in the likeness of human beings, *by being found* in human form"—indicates quite emphatically, although paradoxically, that Christ's self-giving was accomplished by taking, that his self-emptying was achieved by becoming what he was not before, that his kenosis came about not by subtraction but by addition, that his *kenōsis* (an emptying) was in reality a *plerōsis* (a filling). Thus, there is nothing in this crucial text that could possibly lend credence to any theory that claims that the eternal Son gave up any of his attributes in the incarnation,[27] or that humanity is a realm which by definition excludes God. It seems, rather, to imply that there is an innate suitability of humanness for God and God for humanness, God having made human beings originally in his "own image and likeness" (Gen. 1:27).

Thus, this key text goes on to stress equally the reality, the genuineness of Jesus' humanity. In a concatenation of nouns similar in meaning to each other yet with shades of difference—"form (*morphē*) of a slave," "likeness (*homoiōma*) of human beings," "shape (*schēma*) of a man"—the author intends not to stress the difference in their meaning , but rather to pile up similar ideas in a hymnlike fashion to produce a threefold emphatic reiteration of one fundamentally important idea, namely, that he who was equal with God in every respect completely identified himself with humanity, that in the act of the incarnation the eternal Son became truly human, not merely in outward appearances but in thought and feeling.[28]

But how does one go about holding together these two inalienable tenents of the Christian faith (neither of which I am prepared to surrender) without portraying a being who appears to be two distinct persons, one divine and one human, both existing side by side in one body, alternating in thinking and acting between the two—a being unlike any other being in the world that we are familiar with, certainly one that would not at all be like a truly human being as we know human beings to be?

The particular view of the person of Christ which seems to me most able to do this and which seems most in harmony with the whole of the teaching of the New Testament is the view that, in becoming a human being, the Son of God willed to renounce the exercise of his divine powers, attributes, prerogatives, so that he might live fully within those limitations which inhere in being truly human.

Divine attributes, including those of omniscience, omnipotence, and omnipresence, are not to be thought of as being laid aside when the eternal Son became human but rather thought of as becoming potential or latent within this incarnate One—present in Jesus in all their fulness, but no longer in exercise.[29] Knowledge of who he was and of what his mission in life was to be were given to him as he developed[30] by revelation and intuition, especially at times of crisis in his life, and during times of prayer and communion with his

Heavenly Father. Such experiences as these were remembered, brought frequently to mind, and "formed the undertone of His life and ministry."[31] But they were not always so central in his thinking, so uppermost in his understanding, so firmly fixed in his mind, so overwhelmingly convincing to him that this eliminated any possibility of his really experiencing those temptations, testings, frustrations, and disappointments that belong to a truly human life. There were times, to be sure, when the splendor of his glory pierced through the weakness and concealment of the flesh.[32] But on the ordinary levels of his human existence, the consciousness that he was the divine Son seems not always to have burned with equal intensity. There were levels of ecstasy (see the discussion of this in the preceding chapters), when he had increasingly clear understanding of his relationship to the Father. And no doubt there were levels when such understanding seemed almost to be in eclipse.

This view of the person of Christ gives meaning and reality, for example, to the temptations he faced. For if indeed it was not possible for him to sin,[33] there is nevertheless the possibility that he was not aware of it. The limitation of Christ's knowledge cannot be questioned. He himself is quoted as saying that he did not know about the day nor the hour when the Son of Man was to come. He seemed even not to be sure of the Father's will regarding the cross until the very last, or at least he was hoping for another course of action. His prayer was, "My Father, if it be possible,[34] let this cup pass from me" (Matt. 26:39). And thus may we not say that such lack of knowledge on Jesus' part extended even

> to the area of His own moral nature, and so provide for sin the temptable conditions which put Him in line with our dark conflict, and which truly moralize and humanize his victory when *potuit non peccare*? He knew he came sinless out of each crisis; did He know He never could be anything else? How could He? Would it have been moral conflict if He had known this?[35]

But to put all this together in still clearer fashion, so that one might get a better grasp of what is being said about how it is possible for Jesus to be in reality truly God and truly human, I turn now to a summary outline of the basic elements which have been provided by Vincent Taylor, to whom I am indebted for helping to focus my own thinking:

1. First, it is necessary to address the question of the Ego, the *I* of the divine/human Son of God. Is it human or divine? One's natural inclination might be toward describing it as a completely human *I* with its own will and consciousness. But this would mean, then, that Jesus would be a mere man, a prophet, a teacher, but not the Son of God. Certainly his contemporaries, even his own disciples saw him as a man, thought of him as a man, called him a prophet, rabbi, and so on but this does not necessarily imply that the Ego of Jesus was human and nothing more. "All the relevant facts compel us to affirm that the subject of the human life of Christ is the Logos, the Eternal Son, but in the form and under the conditions of human existence."[36] It is not that the Eternal Son added humanity to his divinity, for such a claim smacks of that teaching which viewed the human form as a guise that he put on, or of that teaching which viewed the humanity of Christ as impersonal. Rather, "the Word *became* flesh" (John 1:14, italics mine); hence, "it is as a man, and within the limitations of manhood, that the Son of God is incarnate."[37] This is to say that the Logos, the Son, God the Son, "set the divine life in human neighborhood"[38] and for our sake put himself at our level, so that he actually thought and acted, viewed the world, and experienced time and space events strictly within the confines of a normally developing human person. Under these conditions of humanness it is possible to dare to say that God—God the Son—learned as we learn, felt as we feel, laughed as we laugh, was surprised as we are surprised, suffered to the full our sorrows and disappointments, hurt as we hurt, died as we die. "He wove up his life, as each of us must, out of the materials that were to hand."[39] The Word became flesh. The Son of God became human!

2. In the second place, to make this self-limitation possible, it is necessary to assume that before time began, certainly before the incarnation took place, the Son, in obedience to the Father, made a conscious decision to set aside everything that would be incompatible with his ministry of humiliation and redemption. The words of Philippians 2:6–8 and 2 Corinthians 8:9 (cf. John 1:14 with 17:5; 3:13; 16:28; Rom. 15:3) at least allow such a premundane act of surrender

to be envisioned. Thus, this act is not only that of the Son; it is also one shared in by the Father (cf. John 3:16). "The renunciation of divine glory, by which the Son of God enters into the world, is the supreme act of love which engages the activity of all the Persons of the Trinity, Father, Son, and Holy Spirit."[40]

3. Such an understanding of the person of Christ presupposes that the divine attributes of omniscience, omnipotence, and omnipresence are potential and latent during the Son's earthly life—present but not operative. This claim is supported both by the Gospel record of his life and by theological arguments.

By the Gospel record of his life: Certainly the man, Jesus of Nazareth, was confined to time and space, and thus he was not omnipresent—no opponent of any form of the kenotic theory would say that he was omnipresent. And as has been pointed out throughout the entire discussion carried on in this book, there is ample indication in these same Gospel accounts that there were things that Jesus did not know and things that he could not do. The miracles that he performed and the prescience he displayed can be accounted for by the power and illumination of the Spirit that was in him. Thus it can also be claimed that "in the normal course of His life the Jesus of history was not omniscient and was not omnipotent."[41]

By theological arguments: Thomasius was justly criticized for his views that the Son of God surrendered the attributes of omniscience, omnipotence, and omnipresence. For none of the attributes of God are accidental qualities that can be put off or put on as one would put on or off a garment of some kind. They belong to the very nature of deity, so that divested of them one can justly say that God is not God. "Equally, without these attributes, as well as those of justice, holiness, and love, the Son is no longer the Son."[42] He is only a human being. In this those critics of a kenotic Christology are quite right. But, as Taylor points out, no sufficiently good reason has been put forth to say that

> within the limitations necessary to the Incarnation, the attributes of omniscience, omnipotence, and omnipresence should not have remained latent or potential, existent, but no longer at the centre of the Son's consciousness and in conscious exercise, but undestroyed and capable of manifestation in appropriate circumstances.[43]

Only if one assumes that the divine attributes were potential rather than active does it seem possible to talk about a real incarnation. If the Logos enters time and space omniscient, omnipotent, omnipresent, his entrance is a theophany. He certainly is not a human being like us. But on the other hand, if he abandons these attributes—attributes that belong to the essence of deity—he is reduced to the level of a mere human being. In the one case the humanity is not humanity at all; in the other case divinity is not divinity. The dilemma is resolved, however, if it is assumed that all the attributes of deity are present but latent, conditoned "by the circumstances of a truly human existence."[44]

4. In the fourth place, this kind of kenotic Christology does full justice to the unity of Christ's person as both human and divine. There is no iron curtain between the earthly life of Jesus and his heavenly mode of existence. There is a curtain, but through it shines "a celestial glow, and there are breaks in the fabric through which the light shines." Such a Christology presupposes one Christ. He is not cut off from the life of God. Yet he consents to live on earth within the bounds of human limitations.

> His human nature is the life He leads as a man, subject to the conditions of time and space; His divine nature is the existence which He shares with the Father and the Holy Spirit. The uniting bond between these two modes of existence is His divine will, which in His human life is limited and confined by the conditions appropriate to that life, but is unlimited and unconfined within the triune life of God. . . . [This view does not mean that the Son has no human will.] The human will is the divine will restrained by conditions which are accepted fully and completely. His will is the subject of His divine life, and by self-limitation is also the subject of His human existence.[45]

Taylor contends that this hypothesis of a single will transcends the unreal distinctions faced in the Monothelite[46] controversy, which ended in the affirmation of two wills and two consciousnesses, one human and one divine. This decision was the logical result of the tendency to hypostasize (i.e., "to give essential reality to," "to think of as 'person'") the two natures of Christ. Without a human will, so the argument ran, Jesus' human nature was not perfect, and without a divine will he could not be divine. But as Archbishop Temple remarks, "We are thus brought very near Nestorianism; for if there is a divine Will side by side with a human will, how is this to be distinguished from a divine Person side by side with a human person?"[47]

This can be overcome by affirming not a human will in contrast to a divine will,

> but a divine will which can function in both realms, unconfined in its trinitarian relationships, limited in its expression by human conditions. . . . It is the mark of a kenotic Christology that, along with other advantages, it can give whole-hearted assent to the unity of Christ's Person by taking seriously that self-limitation which is the sign of the grace of God.[48]

This conclusion of Dr. Taylor's, namely, that to do "full justice to the unity of Christ's person, as both human and divine"[49] we must accept the hypothesis of a single will, may be the most controversial part of his attempt at resolving the question of how Jesus could be both God and man.[50] And yet, because I am not adequate to the task of penetrating more deeply into this awesome, reverence-creating mystery, it seems to me that Taylor's view, or at least his way of articulating his view, is superior to that view which is very old and widely held and which has been articulated by so able a scholar and theologian and spokes-person as B. B. Warfield.

> It will be well to bear in mind that Jesus was definitely conceived by the Evangelists as a two-natured person, and that they made no difficulties with his duplex consciousness. In almost the same breath they represent him as declaring that he knows the Father through and through and, of course, also all that is in man, and the world which is the theatre of his activities,[51] and that he is ignorant of the time of the occurrence of a simple earthly event which concerns his own work very closely; that he is meek and lowly in heart and yet at the same time the Lord of men by their relations to whom their destinies are determined. . . . In the case

> of a Being whose subjective life is depicted as focussing *in two centers of consciousness* [italics mine], we may properly maintain some reserve in ascribing distinctively to one or the other of them mental activities which, so far as their nature is concerned, might properly belong to either.[52]

Or yet again:

> The Christ of history was not unconscious, *but continually conscious* [italics mine], of His deity, and of all that belongs to His deity. He knew Himself to be the Son of God in a unique sense—as such, superior to the very angels and gazing unbrokenly into the depths of the Divine Being, knowing the Father even as He was known of the Father. He felt within Him the power to make the stones that lay in His pathway bread for His strengthening, and the power . . . rather to bruise his feet on them.[53]

This view makes it extremely difficult, if not impossible, for one to think in terms of the unity of the person of Jesus Christ, but rather it portrays two separate persons with two minds or two consciousnesses—one human, the other divine—in one person with alternating thoughts, emotions, and actions. And if this is a fair assessment of the position Warfield advocated (and many others with him), then it is difficult, if not impossible, for one to think of Jesus as being in reality a genuinely human being. Such a person as Warfield so described, having two separate organs of thought and action and using both alternately, in my judgment could not be human at all.

Thus, I choose to side with Taylor, who advocates his own modified version of the unfashionable kenotic theory. His view of the person of Christ, including his explanation about the need for positing a single will in Jesus, may be the nearest that it is possible to get to a solution of this the greatest of all mysteries, the mystery of Jesus.

5. Finally, I echo Dr. Taylor in saying that while a kenotic Christology can make a contribution to speculative questions, "no just demand can be made upon it, or indeed upon any Christology, that it should be able to solve ultimate problems."[54] The problem of the person of Christ is not solved by any process of reasoned argument.

Rather, worship as well as reflection must be, and have indeed been, behind the greatest Christian affirmations. "We do not first discover who Christ is and then believe in Him; we believe in Him and then discover who He is."[55]

I have admitted to the fact that I have leaned heavily upon such thinkers as Forsyth, Macintosh, Hebblethwaite, and others, especially Vincent Taylor, but only secondarily have I done so. That is to say, I have relied upon them only as lenses for bringing my own growing understanding of the person of Jesus Christ into sharper focus. That understanding has been developing over many years (1) out of a personal commitment of myself to this wonderfully mysterious, captivating Person in faith, and (2) out of long hours of study—both of the Scriptures, especially the New Testament, that speak prominently and so eloquently of him, and of the teachings of the church. I do not wish, however, by giving such a testimony to claim that the view I espouse is the only one, but it is the view to which I have come by faith and by reflection. And if it is in line with the thinking of such distinguished people as those I have mentioned above, it is because they and I have travelled somewhat the same paths of faith and intellectual pursuit. Hence, at this stage of the discussion, I am not saying anything different from them; I am not claiming that I have added anything significantly new to their ideas up to this point.

What may be new, however, and that which I offer as possibly a small contribution to the undertanding of what Oscar Cullmann calls the New Testament paradox,[56] is this: The Spirit who was present and active even in the conception of Jesus, in his boyhood and youth, throughout all of his adult ministry, in his death and resurrection, was what might be called—dare I say it?—the "Holy Synapse" by which the truly human Jesus was made aware, made conscious, of the fact that he *was* indeed the Unique Son of God. Taylor in his analysis writes that "the knowledge of [Jesus'] heavenly origin and divine nature was given to Him by revelation . . . at His Baptism, Temptation, and Transfiguration. . . . "[57] If this is so, and I do believe that it is, the force of the argument set forth in the preceding chapters of this book drives me to the conclusion that such a revelation was given to Jesus by the Spirit. Note that the Spirit is described by the evangelists as being prominently present both at the baptism of

Jesus and during the course of his temptation. Is it not reasonable to assume that he was present and active at the transfiguration? And not only was the Spirit present with/within Jesus in these events, but in every other high point of ecstasy, in every other momentous event of his life when it became increasingly clear to him who he was in relation to his Heavenly Father, and what he was to do in obedience to the Father's will. These insights regarding his person and mission came to him through the quiet influence of the Spirit who filled him, "the spirit of wisdom and understanding, the spirit of counsel and might, the spirit of knowledge and the fear of the Lord" (Isa. 11:2) that was upon him and in him so that his delight was always in the fear of the LORD.

Again, Taylor wrote that no iron curtain hung between the earthly life of Jesus and His heavenly mode of existence, but that there was indeed a curtain through which could shine a celestial glow, and that there were breaks in the fabric through which the light shined.[58] If this is a proper metaphor, may I suggest that that by which the breaks in the fabric were made was the Holy Spirit, allowing the light of the divine to break through the curtain and dawn upon the consciousness of Jesus.

Reflection upon certain aspects of the life of Jesus as described in the Gospels, e.g., "Jesus was full of the Holy Spirit . . . and was led by the Spirit . . . " (Luke 4:1; cf. Mark 1:12; Matt. 4:1), and also upon certain texts in Paul such as Romans 8:14–16: "For all who are led by the Spirit of God are sons of God. For you did not receive the spirit of slavery to fall back into fear, but you have received the spirit of sonship. When we cry, 'Abba! Father!' it is the Spirit himself bearing witness with our spirit that we are children of God" (cf. Gal. 4:6), allows one to at least think analogously. That is to say, just as the Christian, who through the process called the "new birth" is made a child of God, a partaker of the divine nature (cf. 2 Pet. 1:3–4), and yet only becomes aware of this fact at the existential level or at the level of consciousness by the Spirit of God, so may it not also have been true in the experience of Jesus? Although I wish to affirm that Jesus was uniquely the Son of God and that he differs from all others of us in kind, yet is it not possible to imagine that in the process of becoming human, in that great act called the incarnation, he placed himself so fully alongside us that, like us, he too relied upon the Spirit to inform him of who he really was by nature, of what his true relationship was to the Father? In whatever way the mystery of the incarnation is finally to be explained, in whatever way one is finally to understand and explain how the divine and human relate to each other in the person of Jesus, one must ultimately take into account the role of the Holy Spirit in resolving this riddle.

There is one more matter that I wish to address at this point. If it is true that the Holy Spirit played such a significant part in the life and ministry of Jesus, even bringing to the level of his consciousness who he was and what he was to do in this world, how did he differ from other human beings with whom he had bound himself, who also are dependent upon the Holy Spirit for the extraordinary in their lives? Jesus' consciousness of his relationship with the Father has already been discussed (see above), and it was extraordinary! His knowledge about people was also extraordinary. He saw and could describe precisely the kind of person Nathaniel was even before Philip invited him to become a follower. He could tell what was in the hearts and minds of people without them ever saying a word. He could command the wind and calm the sea that was being whipped to frenzy. He is said to have healed the sick and raised the dead and to have prophesied about his own death and resurrection.

How did all this differ from those extraordinary things recorded as having been done by prophets and apostles who lived before and after Jesus? Did not Moses raise his hand over the Red Sea and the waters parted so that the people of Israel could cross over on dry land (cf. Exod. 14:21, 26)? Was not Elijah able to raise the widow's son to life again, and stretch her handful of meal and little jar of oil so as amply to feed both her and her son and himself throughout the length of the three-year famine (1 Kings 17:1–16)? Did not Elisha have the power to heal a man of leprosy and cause another to become leprous (2 Kings 5:1–27)? Did he not have the power to tell the King of Israel the secret plans of the Syrian army, apparently without the aid of any informant (2 Kings 6:12)? Did he not have power over the elements of nature so as to cause an axe head which had fallen into the water to float (2 Kings 6:5–7)? Did not Peter have the power to bring Dorcas back to life (Acts 9:40–41), to see into Ananias' mind to detect his lie and to judge him accordingly (Acts 5:1–11)?

And what of the miracles done by Paul (Acts 13:9–11; 19:11–12; 28:3–6, 8)? Did not Jesus say to his disciples that they would do even greater things than those things which he had done (John 14:12)? In what sense, then, did Jesus differ from other people who did spectacular things, extraordinary things, impossible things?

Did he differ, as some have suggested, in that he taught and acted as the Spirit directed and permitted (cf. Matt. 12:28; John 3:34; Acts 1:2; 10:38), "but when thus permitted, He knew, taught, and performed, not, like the prophets, by power communicated from without, but by virtue of his own inner divine energy (Matt. 17:2; Mark 5:41; Luke 5:20–21; 6:19; John 2:11, 24–25; 3:13; 20:19)"?[59] I rather think that this was not the way things were. For although the glory that was seen in Jesus when he was transfigured was indeed that inner glory that he had with the Father before the world began, and although the words of Jesus to the little girl, "I say to you arise!" appear quite different from those of Peter, "in the name of Jesus Christ of Nazareth, walk!" yet it seems to me that the Spirit played a more significant role in the life of Jesus than that of being merely a sort of divine traffic officer to direct the flow of Christ's power. There are many other passages (discussed in the preceding chapters) that indicate clearly that Jesus was truly dependent upon the Holy Spirit, not for permission to use his own power, but for the very power itself with which he did his mighty works. I do not wish to say that Jesus as the God-man did not have power to do all these things recorded of him in the Gospels and even more, but I do wish to emphasize that that power was latent within him, that he did not use his own power. John Walvoord's words are most fitting at this point: "It would seem that Christ *chose* to perform miracles in the power of the Spirit rather than that he had no alternative."[60]

Jesus possessed the power himself, but (as has been argued above) by a preincarnate deliberate decision the eternal Son of God chose that all his intrinsic powers, all his attributes, would remain latent within him during the days of his flesh and that he would become truly human and limit himself to the abilities and powers common to all other human beings. Therefore he depended upon the Holy Spirit for wisdom and knowledge and for power to perform the signs and wonders that marked the days of his years.

Thus, in answer to the question of how Jesus differed from other people who depended upon the Spirit for the *extra* in their lives, it is possible to answer that in terms of his humanness it differed in essentially no way. By this I mean that God the Son, who became flesh in Jesus, became a real human being, and as such he *needed* the Spirit's power to lift him out of his human restrictions, to carry him beyond his human limitations, and to enable him to do the seeming impossible. To be sure, only of Jesus was it said that the Father gave to him the Spirit "without measure." To be sure, the Spirit met with no natural resistance in Jesus as in those of us whose lives have been hardened and scarred by sin. To be sure the Spirit—his influence and guidance—was always central and perfect in Jesus, while this is never so in all others of us. But apart from these differences, which certainly are considerable, Jesus was nevertheless a human being commissioned to do the will of God in this world, and filled with and empowered by the Holy Spirit to bring it all to a successful completion. Thus, Jesus Christ becomes an object lesson, the source of tremendous encouragement and hope for every believer who studies his life and aspires to emulate him.

NOTES

1. See J. Daniélou, *The Theology of Jewish Christianity*, trans. J. A. Baker (London, 1964), 56, who quotes Epiphanius' *Panarion*, 30.16, the primary and most precise source of information about the Ebionites: ". . . They say that God has established two beings, Christ and the Devil. To the former has been committed the power of the world to come, and to the other the power of this world. They say that Jesus was begotten of human seed, and chosen, and thus called by election Son of God, Christ having come upon him from on high in the form of a dove. They say that he was not begotten by God the Father, but that he was created, like the archangels, but greater than they. He came into the world and he taught. . . . "

2. For this discussion of Arianism and of the other Christological viewpoints surveyed in the following sections, see F. L. Cross and E. A. Livingstone, *The Oxford Dictionary of the Christian Church*, 2nd ed. (Oxford, 1974); A. N. S. Lane, "Christology Beyond Chalcedon," in *Christ is Lord*, ed. H. H. Rowdon (Leicester, 1982), 257–81; H. Lietzmann, *A History of the Early Church*, trans. B. L. Woolf (New York, 1953); L. P. Qualben (New York, 1942); J. A. Ziesler, *The Jesus Question* (London, 1980), 99–132.

3. In this connection see Hagner, *Hebrews*, 26: "The perfection [spoken of in Heb. 2:10] is not a moral or ethical perfection, for Jesus in this sense was always perfect."

4. This translation is found in *Christology of the Later Fathers*, ed. E. R. Hardy, Library of Christian Classics (Philadelphia, 1954), 373.

5. Anselm, *Proslogion*, 8, quoted by Lane, *Christology*, 266.

6. *The Oecumenical Documents of Faith*, ed. T. H. Bindley (London, 1899), 214, 227, as quoted by Lane, *Christology*, 268.

7. *Epist. ad Serap*. 4.14, quoted by Robinson, *The Human Face of God*, 111.

8. Bindley, *Oecumenical Documents*, 227; quoted by Lane, *Christology*, 268.

9. Cf. these recently published remarks taken from *The Omniscience of Christ, Four Authors Speak Out* (Everyday Publications Inc., Scarborough, Ontario, Canada, 1984), 8, 9, 25: "Some writers, supposedly evangelical, are sponsoring the notion that Jesus as a youth thought of Himself as the son of a carpenter but **gradually** . . . or **suddenly** . . . He learned that He was the Messiah of Israel. If the Lord Jesus was only a great prophet we could believe that He was not aware of it at first . . ." And again, "The Growing Messianic Awareness theory is therefore a crude and very thinly disguised attack on the Deity of Christ. Some who go along with this theory may not be aware of its implications, but they must face this: If Christ was God manifest in the flesh, there is no way to believe He did not know who He was." And yet again, "Conservative Bible scholars have long held that Christ is eternally omniscient, and that there has never been a time, not even during Christ's early years on earth, that He was not *fully aware of all things* [italics mine], including His own death and Messianic mission." Remarks like this make it difficult for one who is in fact a conservative to differ from such authors. They place that differing person automatically among those who wish to undermine the faith and cut away at the important doctrine of the deity of Jesus Christ. All hope of weighing and considering alternative views is gone. And that is a pity.

10. See E. L. Mascall, *Words and Images* (London, 1957); idem, *Theology and Images* (London, 1963); idem, *Theology and the Future* (London, 1968); idem, *Theology and the Gospel of Christ* (London, 1978).

11. For those Christologies that put the stress on event not nature/person, see D. M. Baillie, *God was in Christ* (London, 1948); O. Cullmann, *The Christology of the New Testament* (London, 1959); A. T. Hanson, *Grace and Truth* (London, 1975); J. Knox, *The Humanity and Divinity of Christ* (Cambridge, 1967); N. Pittenger, *Christology Reconsidered* (London, 1970); M. Wiles, *The Remaking of Christian Doctrine* (London, 1974); those Christologies that see divinity in humanity, W. Pannenberg, *Jesus: God and Man* (London, 1968); those that see divinity as complementary to humanity—God was in Christ as in everyone, but in a paramount fashion, God's total presence permeating Christ's whole person without resistance—see P. Schoonenberg, *The Christ* (London, 1972); those Christologies that wish not to talk of a Logos Christology but a Spirit Christology, G. W. H. Lampe, "The Person of Christ," in *Christian Faith and History*, eds. S. W. Sykes and J. P. Clayton (Cambridge, 1972), 111–30. See Ziesler, *The Jesus Question*, 123–32 for a summary

of several of these recent Christologies. See also T. F. Torrance, *Space, Time and Resurrection* (Grand Rapids, 1976); idem, *Space, Time and Incarnation* (Oxford, 1969).

12. Kenotic or kenosis are really Greek words that have been used so frequently in recent discussions of the person of Christ that they have become part of the English language jargon. They are simply transliterations—not translations—of the Greek adjective, *kenotikos*, or the noun, *kenosis*, both related to the verb *kenoun*, "to empty," that is used in Phil. 2:7.

13. See G. F. Hawthorne, *Philippians*, WBC 43 (Waco, Tex. 1983), 75–97 for a detailed exegesis and explanation of this passage.

14. G. Thomasius, *Christi Person und Werk*, 2 vols. (Erlangen, 1886[3]).

15. W. F. Gess, *Das Dogma von Christi Person und Werk*, 3 vols. (Basel, 1887).

16. F. Godet, *Commentary on the Gospel According to St. John*, trans. T. Dwight (New York, 1886).

17. Cf. the famous, well-loved, often-sung hymn of Charles Wesley (1707–1788), who might be called a precursor of some of the later kenoticists: "He left His Father's throne above/So free, so infinite His grace/*Emptied himself of all but Love*/And bled for Adam's helpless race . . ." The fact of the matter is that although kenotic Christology found little place in the thinking of the church until the nineteenth century, and quickly fell into disfavor, it was widely found in sermons, hymns, prayers, and liturgies. Wesley's hymn is but one indication of this.

18. See D. G. Dawe, "A Fresh Look at the Kenotic Christologies," *SJT* (1962), 343–44.

19. For the classic description of the kenosis theories of Thomasius and Gess, see A. B. Bruce, *The Humiliation of Christ* (Edinburgh, 1881[2]), 138–52.

20. Taylor, *The Person of Christ*, 60.

21. A. Farrer, "Very God and Very Man," in *Interpretation and Belief*, ed. C. Conti (London, 1976).

22. P. T. Forsyth, *The Person and Place of Jesus Christ* (London, 1909).

23. H. R. Mackintosh, *The Doctrine of the Person of Jesus Christ* (Edinburgh, 1912).

24. O. C. Quick, *Christian Beliefs and Modern Questions* (London, 1923), 53–74; idem, *Doctrines of the Creed* (London, 1938), 146–83.

25. Taylor, *The Person of Christ*.

26. B. Hebblethwaite, *The Incarnation* (Cambridge, 1987), especially 1–10 and 21–26.

27. Hawthorne, *Philippians*, 86.

28. Ibid., 87–88. Cf. also Quick, *Christian Beliefs*, 64: "Wherever Christian doctrine has lost its gospel and been found spiritually unsatisfying, its failure has been a failure to preserve together both natures of our Lord's person, divine and human, and to preserve them in their full unity. Whenever the manood is neglected or explained away, the Christian's pattern and example is lost, and orthodoxy of faith or worship is substituted for the imitation of Christ. Whenever the Godhead is neglected or explained away, we must write the word Ichabod even over the human example of Jesus' life, because the mysterious glory of God's saving condescension has departed from it. So-called orthodoxy has often taught men to

worship Christ instead of following Him. Unitarianism, on the other hand, loses all the inspiration of the faith that God became as one of us to serve and suffer with us out of the love He bore us."

29. Perhaps white light provides a possible analogy to what is being said here. White light contains the infinite variety of colors in the spectrum—they are all there. But these colors, in a sense are latent, potential, for they can only be seen when white light is refracted by a prism.

30. Cf. the words of F. Weston, *The One Christ* (London, 1907), 190: "[Jesus'] self-consciousness as divine Son is at every moment to be measured by the capacity of His human soul to mediate it."

31. Taylor, *The Person of Christ*, 288.

32. Cf. G. C. Berkouwer, *Studies in Dogmatics: The Person of Christ* (Grand Rapids, 1954), 354.

33. Note the words of Hebblethwaite: "If the life of Jesus was a 'perfect and unbroken response' to his heavenly Father, this could only have been because his human life was lived out of a centre in God. (There is no reason to suppose that this protected him from profound experience of temptation, but it is sheer romanticism to suppose that 'peccability' is of the essence of human nature, and that the whole God-man relation was really put at risk in the Incarnation. The freedom of Jesus, we must suppose, was always exercised in conformity with the Father's will, just because the human freedom was the vehicle of the divine freedom.)" (*The Incarnation*, 72).

34. The construction of this Greek conditional sentence is one that puts the emphasis "on the reality of the assumption," closely bordering on causal, "since" (BDF, 371, 372), and implies that in his thinking there may be an alternative—"If it is possible, and it is . . . " or "Since it is possible. . . . " But was it possible? Was there an alternative?

35. Forsyth, *The Person and Place of Jesus Christ*, 301.

36. Taylor, *The Person of Christ*, 289.

37. Ibid., 290.

38. A. Farrer, *Saving Belief* (London, 1964), 99.

39. A. Farrer, *A Celebration of Faith* (London, 1970), 89.

40. Taylor, *Person and Work*, 291.

41. Ibid., 292; Cf. Brunner, *The Mediator*, 363–64.

42. Taylor, *The Person of Christ*, 292.

43. Ibid., 293; see also Forsyth, *Person and Place of Jesus Christ*, 308–309; Mackintosh, *The Person of Jesus Christ*, 477–79. In my judgment not even B. B. Warfield's incisive criticism is sufficient reason to deny this: "God to be God must be all he can be actually. . . . When he ceases to be actually what God is, he ceases of course to be God," quoted by R. Swanton, *Reformed Theological Review*, 17 [1958], 88–89. Warfield certainly was a giant Christian intellect, and I do not pretend to pit mine against his. Nevertheless, a remark like this one, though it sounds powerfully correct and convincing, seems to me in reality to be false. For were Warfield's statement true, then how could one even begin to imagine an incarnation (which by definition implies a limitation or curtailment of power of some kind on the part

of God), or how would creation be thought of as a possibility, for creation in itself involves divine self-limitation. It has been said that "self-limitation is an essential form of the divine manifestation. God is God when He stoops no less than when He reigns." (W. Neil, *ExpT* 74 [1962], 42). See also Moule, *Manhood of Jesus*, 96–98, who, while he does not agree that Phil 2:6–7 has anything to do with kenotic theories, yet after study of this passage concludes that "the limitations of Jesus are seen as a positive expression of his divinity rather than as a curtailment of it."

44. Taylor, *The Person of Christ*, 294.

45. Ibid., 295. Cf. also A. Farrer, *The Glass Vision* (London, 1948), 39: "The Person of Christ . . . is . . . the height of supernaturality; for in it the first and second causes are personally united, the finite and infinite centres in some manner coincide; manhood is so taken into God, that the human life of Jesus is exercised from the centre of deity." And again Farrer writes ("Very God and Very Man," 128): We must think of "human existence so rooted and grounded in God's will and action as to be the personal life of God himself, under the self-imposed conditions of a particular human destiny" (both quoted by Hebblethwaite, *Incarnation*, 115).

Perhaps Quick's homely illustration may help: "Suppose a learned professor of some science wishes to teach a child the elements of the subject in which he is an expert. If his teaching is to be ideally good, the first essential must be that he put himself at the child's point of view, so that he sees things with the child's eyes and feels the child's perplexities. In other words, he must in some degree take on himself the nature of the child. And this will involve a very real self-limitation. He must put out of his mind the problems with which he has been grappling for his forthcoming book; he must forget the language of his classic article in the latest technical encyclopaedia. He must put himself back at the beginning of the subject, that he may guide another beginner along the first stages of his journey. And yet the one thing he must not forget is the way to go. His own more recondite knowledge will not occupy his attention; yet it will reveal itself surely and clearly in the certainty with which he surmounts the initial obstacles and avoids the easy-looking by-paths which lead to nothing. The expositon of a teacher less expert could not be at once so simple and so true to the deepest principles of the science.

"May we not in all reverence imagine to ourselves that what the human professor may do in a very small and imperfect degree, the Son of God did perfectly, completely and once for all? He descended infinitely far to take man's nature wholly upon Him and literally to become man. In His flesh, then, He was not conscious of anything of which human faculties, so placed and so conditioned at that particular point of time and space, could not have made him conscious . . . Yet by means of developing human faculties He trod man's path to God, taught about God, knew God, knew Himself as God's appointed man, all with an undeviating sureness such as no mere man could have shown" (*Christian Beliefs*, 70–72).

46. Monothelitism, a seventh-century heresy confessing only one will (*mono* + *thelein*) in the God-man. "The heresy was of political rather than of religious origin, being designed to rally the Monophysites [those who believed that Jesus had only one nature—*mono* + *physis*] to their orthodox (Chalcedonian) fellow-Christians

when division endangered the Empire, faced with Persian and later with Mohammedan invasions," in *Oxford Dictionary of the Christian Church*, 932.

47. W. Temple, *Christus Veritas* (London, 1926), 135–36. Cf. the remarks of H. C. Thiessen, *Introductory Lectures in Systematic Theology* (Grand Rapids, 1956), 305: "Christ had an infinite intelligence and will and a finite intelligence and will; . . . He had a divine consciousness and a human consciousness. His divine intelligence was infinite; his human intelligence increased. His divine will was omnipotent; his human will had only the power of unfallen humanity." This view of Jesus is most troubling to me and makes it extremely difficult for me to believe in the realness of the humanity of the Jesus so described.

48. Taylor, *The Person of Christ*, 296.

49. Ibid., 295.

50. See also Hebblethwaite: "We have to suppose that while the man Jesus in his earthly life was presumably unaware of his divinity, the Blessed Trinity was perfectly well aware of what was being done, experienced and suffered. This is not to attribute two consciousnesses to *Jesus*. But it is to assert that the consciousness of the man Jesus was the limited human expression of the omniscient divine consciousness. God, *qua* God, knew what he was doing; *qua* man he learned obedience like any other Jewish child. Similarly we do not predicate two wills of the man Jesus. But his human will, perfectly dedicated to do his heavenly Father's will, was nevertheless the earthly expression of the divine will. . . . It is at this point that we must remember that we are struggling to speak of the infinite, internally differentiated, being of God, whose own eternal love, given and received within the Trinity, is mirrored in the love of Jesus for the Father, that human love being expressed in categories of thought and action provided by the faith of Israel in which he grew up." And again, "If we are to subscribe positively to the doctrine of 'enhypostasia' [the doctrine that in the incarnate Christ the personal humanity of Christ was not lost, but included within the hypostasis of the Godhead, and that thereby He included within Himself all the attibutes of perfect humanity, *ODCC*, 458] and hold that the human life of Jesus was lived out from a centre in deity, and negatively to the doctrine of 'anhypostasia' and hold that Jesus was not independently a merely human subject, these doctrines must not be taken to imply that Jesus lacked a human mind, will, consciousness or personality. But they do imply that the metaphyical subject of the human life of Jesus was the eternal Son of God, and that we cannot think of the man Jesus apart from his being God incarnate . . . We are to construe the personal relation between the man Jesus and his heavenly Father as the incarnate expression of the eternal relation subsisting between the Son and the Father. By contrast the relation between the divinity and the humanity of Christ is not itself a personal relation or even a relation at all. It is a matter of identity. Jesus is the incarnate Son" (*Incarnation*, 68–70).

51. See my explanation of Jesus' knowledge of the Father and of his prescience in the earlier chapters and how this can be thought of as possible without positing two natures, which comes very close to meaning two distinct personalities within the confines of one man.

52. Warfield, *Person and Work*, 95.

53. Ibid., 261–62.

54. Taylor, *The Person of Christ*, 297. Taylor then addresses himself to a consideration of the objections to which his own particular Christology is exposed: (1) that it is not new and has been rejected by a considerable body of opinion, (2) that it is mythological, and (3) that, on its presuppositions, the divine consciousness of the Son is not always at the same pitch of intensity, and at times may even be in eclipse—the sense of Sonship is intermittent so that successively Christ is God and man. To each objection he provides answers. See pages 299–304.

55. Ibid., 305.

56. O. Cullmann, *Christology of the New Testament* (London, 1959).

57. Taylor, *The Person of Christ*, 288.

58. Ibid., 294.

59. A. H. Strong, *Systematic Theology* (Philadelphia, 1947), 696.

60. J. F. Walvoord, *The Doctrine of the Holy Spirit* (Dallas, 1943), 107.

8. The Spirit in the Life of the Follower of Jesus

In the preceding chapters an attempt has been made to show that the Holy Spirit, the Spirit of God, was significantly at work in every phase of Jesus' life—his conception and birth, his boyhood and youth, his mission and ministry, his suffering and death, his resurrection and vindication.

Each of the Gospel writers describes Jesus with an emphasis peculiar to the interests and purposes of that writer. But all agree on at least two fundamental matters: (1) Jesus was indeed a human being, a genuine human person, owning all the limitations that pertain to humanity, and (2) that Jesus depended upon the Holy Spirit throughout his entire life to enable him to burst the boundaries of his human limitations. The Holy Spirit, who descended upon him at his baptism, entered into him, and filled him, was the Spirit of God who infused him with the power to overcome temptations, teach with authority, challenge established religious structures in the name of God, see people not in the mass but as individuals, sense the inner joy of each person or their pain and hurt, reach out and touch people, lift them up, help them, heal them, find them, redeem them, save them, restore them to wholeness, and turn them back to God—in a word to effectually carry to completion the mission his Father had given him to do and which only he could do in this fallen, broken world.

It is not only the Gospel writers who stress the realness of Jesus' humanity. It is the consistent witness of all the writers of the New Testament, some going so far as to say that anyone who fails to openly acknowledge that Jesus Christ has come in the flesh (*en sarki*), that he has become a human being, not only does not belong to God but belongs instead to the thinking and attitude of the antichrist (1 John 4:3).

But the writers of the New Testament never seem content to leave the story of Jesus by saying that he was only a man, merely a bonafide member of the human race and nothing more, however important such an affirmation may be. They seem equally concerned to say that Jesus was more than an individual whose personal existence can be defined solely in terms of natural descent from human parents. They insist that he was more than a person whose link with humanity can be traced in precisely and only the same way that other persons can trace their linkage with the human race—biologically, historically, sociologically. These writers seem intent on saying that Jesus was not simply a man whom God adopted as his Son, nor was he God masquerading as a man, but he was indeed eternity invading history, the divine genuinely entering the stream of human existence, God becoming a man. Their insistent testimony appears to be that the preexistent Son became incarnate in Jesus of Nazareth, and that this singular event was absolutely necessary if the whole of the fallen human race was to experience conversion, salvation, recreation. Thus the centrally important theme that these writers shared, their fundamentally integrating message, seems to be that preexistence and incarnation—the eternal Son of God becoming a human person in time and space—are essential for the restoration of this broken world, that only the remaking of the world from within by God incarnate is sufficient to rescue it from its self-centeredness and to save human society from its warped condition.[1]

Both of these ideas, therefore, the realness of Jesus' humanity and the realness of Jesus' divinity, together constitute the warp and woof of the message of the New Testament. To deny one or the other would be to tear at the very fabric of the Gospel, God's Good News of hope. To stress one to the exclusion of the other would be equally destructive.

Both appear to be emphatically affirmed by the writers of the New Testament, and both are affirmed with equal emphasis by this writer as well. The writers of the New Testament make no attempt to answer the question of how this could be—how the same person could be divine and human, God and man, and both at the same time—holding these seemingly paradoxical statements about Jesus together without apology or any sense that they need explanation. This writer, on the other hand, has chosen to pry into this mystery, to attempt to understand something of its inscrutable nature, and to offer some explanation of how it was possible for Jesus to be wholly divine and wholly human, God and man, the God-man.[2]

The key to this mystery lies, it seems, in the Holy Spirit and the work of the Holy Spirit in the experience of Jesus.

The grand salvific plan of God as described in the language of the New Testament is twofold: (1) God acted to save the very people who had turned their backs upon God, who had become disobedient to God, who had become hostile to God, who having lost their capacity to respond to God and their will to respond, had turned away from life to death. (2) Since the whole human race had been started on this downward spiral to destruction by one man, Adam, God acted to reverse this ruinous course, to undo all the damage that had been done, to set people free to choose to leave the tragedy of their warped humanity and to live as new persons by one other man, Jesus Christ, the God-man. "God was in Christ reconciling the world to Himself" (2 Cor. 5:19 NASB; see also Rom. 5:6, 8, 12, 18; 1 Cor. 15:21–22, 45).

Now the one thing that is most necessary to single out and reiterate simply because it is often lost sight of is this: according to the New Testament the unalterable, deliberate plan of God purposed that human beings, caught in the web of fallen humanity from which they could not extricate themselves, should nevertheless be saved by a human being—Jesus! Whatever else can be said about Jesus (i.e., that he is also divine, the eternal Son, God become human, and so on), it is certainly necessary to say that he was indeed a human being in the fullest sense of this term lacking none of those things that go into making a person human, with the exception of sin (cf. Heb. 2:17; 4:15). Thus, on the one hand, without either surrendering a single characteristic of true humanity or, on the other hand, without giving up any attribute of divinity, the eternal Son, in the mystery of the incarnation, nevertheless so chose to "encapsulate" his divinity within the confines of humanity, so chose to make his attributes latent, potential within him (however one is to say it) that he faced life *precisely* like any other human being faces life—not as some colossus striding unfeelingly over the earth, but as a person limited physically and mentally, exposed to all kinds of diseases, subject to all sorts of temptations, susceptible to misunderstandings or hated, unshielded from weakness and weariness, unprotected from frustrations and vexations, vulnerable to death, and on and on. He learned as other people learn—by the difficult road of diligence and discipline of mind. He grew strong in body through the hard work of rigorous living. He spoke for the poor and disenfranchised by knowing firsthand what it was himself to be poor and outside the structures of social and political power. He gained compassion by purposely living among the sick and diseased, the ostracized and the sinners, the weak and the oppressed, the helpless and the dying, and by choosing not to shield himself from the hurts, pains, and suffering of the marginalized people of his time and place. He faced his impending death with trepidation, accepted his own mortality, and died, really died.

But, and here now is the significant thesis of this book, Jesus was aided in all phases of his living (and dying) by the wonderful gift of the Father to him, a gift which he gratefully accepted and acknowledged, and whose promptings he always obeyed—the powerful presence of the Holy Spirit which filled him, certainly from his baptism onward, and no doubt before as well.

Was Jesus a person who from earliest times was by nature a devout person basically oriented toward God the Father? Probably he was. Nevertheless he did experience severe times of testing when he found himself being challenged to pit his own will against the will of the Father. In these periods of temptation, however, the Spirit was present with him to enlighten his mind, to clarify the issues, to urge him toward the right choice, but not to make that choice for him.

Was Jesus naturally, even from childhood, drawn to the Torah, the Law of God? Was he a person captivated by its message, its record of origins, and its guide for living properly and well in society? Was he a person who read it, memorized it, filled his mind with it, sought to understand it, searched for its inner meaning? Luke's Gospel indicates that he was just such a person. But knowledge of and a natural gift and love for the Law of God are not sufficient in themselves. That which gave authority to Jesus' words when he taught the Law and preached the Good News of the Kingdom of God, that which made his proclamations creatively alive, that which made his message life-transforming, was the Holy Spirit. The Spirit illumined his mind, gave him insight into the truth of God, and enabled him to speak with an authoritatively convicting power never experienced by the scribes, the learned teachers of the Jewish law, or by the Pharisees, the guardians of the Law. The maxim of Paul, "The letter kills, but the Spirit gives life," became a reality in the person and work of Jesus.

Was Jesus a physically strong person capable of travelling great distances on foot, going without food for long periods of time, working for days with little or no rest, doing still other Herculean tasks? There are hints within the New Testament that he may not have been such a person, that is, a person of immense physical strength. Paul, for instance, is unafraid to speak of the "weakness" of Jesus (2 Cor. 13:4). Further, the incident of pressing Simon from Cyrene into carrying Jesus' cross (Mark 15:21) may indicate that he was physically incapable of shouldering it himself. John writes in his Gospel an account that seems to indicate that Jesus was exhausted from travel and sat by a well while his disciples went into the city for food (John 4:6). Whatever may have been the case, whether Jesus was physically strong or slight of build with limited energies, there were certainly limitations to his human capacities. And yet it is clear from the Gospel records that there were times when Jesus exceeded his physical limitations, burst the bounds of his natural strengths, and accomplished the humanly impossible. How? The accumulated evidence of the preceding chapters points to the conclusion that it was the Spirit of God who was the source of this power, that it was the Holy Spirit who infused him with a power sufficient to extend his human abilities beyond that which his mother, his disciples, or perhaps even he himself imagined possible.

Was Jesus by birth and environment a naturally sensitive person who easily felt the hurts of people around him and was pained by their pain? The evangelists say that he was, and so they show him most frequently among the sick, those who were shut out of the normal circles of society (e.g. lepers, tax collectors, prostitutes), the poor, the downtrodden, and the grieving—always for the purpose of restoring, lifting, enriching, accepting, and leading the lost person back to the Father's house. But if Jesus was this kind of person by nature, it is also true that these natural tendencies were heightened by the Spirit of God who filled him and who anointed him to preach the Gospel to the poor, to proclaim release to the captives, to set free those who are oppressed, and to proclaim the favorable year of the Lord.

Was Jesus born with natural psychic and healing powers so that he was able to stretch out his hand and cure the sick with a touch or see into the hearts and minds of people and know what they were thinking before they had a chance to speak? It is not possible to say for certain. But it is possible to say that the writers of the Gospels fill their accounts with stories of Jesus healing people who were ill with all sorts of diseases and exorcising destructive demons of various kinds. A very large part of Jesus' ministry is described in terms of restoring broken people to wholeness again, wholeness of body and soul. But by Jesus' own admission, the reason he was able to do these mighty acts of healing and restoring was because of the Spirit within him, the Spirit of the Lord who had anointed him to bring freedom to the bound and healing to the ill, release to the captives and recovery of sight to the blind.

Was Jesus born with an innate sense of justice, so that from his earliest actions he himself treated people fairly and was concerned that others do the same? Was it only this that made him champion the cause of the weak and unmask with such vehemence the domination of these weak ones by the leaders of a religious structure used to hold them in subjection: "Woe to you teachers of the law, you scribes! For you weigh people down with burdens too hard to bear, while you yourselves will not even touch the burdens with one of your fingers" (Luke 11:46)? Was it simply some inborn sense of justice that brought him into conflict with the political structures of his day by unyieldingly proclaiming as his central message the reign of God, a kingdom of righteousness, a kingdom of justice, a kingdom different from and over against the kingdoms of this world (cf. Matt. 4:17; Mark 1:14; John 19:12)?[3] Perhaps so. But the Gospel writers hint at the possibility that more was involved than merely that Jesus was a man who by nature was inclined toward justice. Rather, they seem to say that he championed justice and stood for righteousness because here in him was the fulfillment of ancient prophecies not only concerning the Servant of the Lord but also concerning the Spirit of God: "Behold my Servant," says the Lord, "whom I uphold; my chosen in whom my soul delights! I have put my Spirit upon him, he will bring forth justice . . . " (Isa. 42:1). Once again, "The Spirit of the Lord will rest on him . . . he shall not judge by what his eyes see, nor decide by what his ears hear; but with righteousness he will judge the poor, and decide with equity for the meek of the earth" (Isa. 11:2–4). Seemingly, then, it was the Spirit within Jesus that gave birth to or at least strengthened his stand for justice, that infused him with the courage necessary to challenge any who practiced injustice, and that fortified him against yielding up the truth he proclaimed even though by refusing to do so meant that he must lose his life.

Was Jesus exempt from human suffering? Was he a person of such strength that he was unaffected by pains that affect the mind and body of ordinary people? Was he immune to dying and death? The answer, of course, is "No!" Just look into the accounts of Jesus in Gethsemane where, faced with his immediate future, he was "appalled and profoundly troubled" (cf. Mark 14:33). There is no indication whatsoever in the canonical Gospels that Jesus was above feeling the pain of the lashing he received or of the nails that were driven through his hands (wrists) and feet.[4] And certainly he was mortal, for one of the basic tenents of the gospel is that Jesus *died* (1 Cor. 15:1–3). But present with him in his suffering and death, strengthening him to accept suffering and death, to endure them, and to win out over them, was the Holy Spirit. And it was by the Holy Spirit, the mighty power of God, that he was raised from the dead, released from suffering, resurrected into a totally new phase of life, a totally new kind of existence.

The Spirit of God, the Holy Spirit, played a most significant and extremely important role in the life of Jesus, in every part and at every phase of his life.

If all of this is so, if indeed Jesus was God having become *truly* human, if indeed Jesus really experienced the same kinds of things that all other human beings experience, suffered the same kinds of pains they suffer, felt the same emotions they feel, knew the same lure of temptation they know, and so on, and if indeed Jesus stood strong against all the kaleidoscopic adversities of human existence and resisted all the many pressures to cave in, quit, give up the cause, and go his own way, and if indeed Jesus finally brought his God-given mission to a triumphant completion—and all of this because he was a person filled with the Spirit—then the followers of Jesus are faced with a stupendous fact: Not only is Jesus their Savior because of who he was and because of his own complete obedience to the Father's will (cf. Heb. 10:5–7), but he is the supreme example for them of what is possible in a human life because of his own total dependence upon the Spirit of God. Jesus is living proof of how those who are his followers may exceed the limitations of their humanness in order that they, like him, might carry to completion against all odds their God-given mission in life—by the Holy Spirit. Jesus demonstrated clearly that God's intended way for human beings to live, the ideal way to live, the supremely successful way to live, is in conjunction with God, in harmony with God, in touch with the power of God, and not apart from God, not independent of God, not without God. The Spirit was the presence and power of God in Jesus, and fully so. Thus the life of Jesus was the realization on earth, perhaps for the first time, of God's ideal for human beings, the fulfillment of the divine intention for them when God said, "Let us make man in our image, and after our likeness" (Gen. 1:26). But Jesus' life was not only the realization of the ideal, it is the pattern to follow, the source of hope for every succeeding generation of Jesus' followers. The words of a teacher/scholar of a different generation may serve to express what is intended here:

> [Jesus] was truly the eternal God, very God, of very God. But when He came down from yonder heights of glory He suspended the direct operation of His own independent power and became voluntarily dependent upon the power of God through the Holy Ghost. . . . He purposely took His place side by side with us, heeding equally with the humblest disciple the constant power of God to sustain Him in all His work. . . . And so He went through life in the position of dependence, that He might be our public

> example and teach us that we too have the same secret of strength and power that He possessed, and that as surely as He overcame through the Holy Ghost, so may we.[5]

Yes, Jesus was a genuine human being in the fullest sense of this term, hemmed in by the limits of his humanity. But he was a human being filled with the Spirit, the Spirit who on more than one occasion enabled Jesus to break through those human limits that bound him, so that the otherwise impossible became possible.

Now what is of extraordinary importance to women and men today, people of all ages and from every country and social strata, is this: The very first thing Jesus did immediately after he was resurrected from among the dead and reunited with his followers was to pass on to them, as a gift from his Father (cf. Acts 2:23), that same power by which he lived, triumphed, and broke the bands of his own human limitations. On the very day of his resurrection, he came to them locked in by their fears, "breathed" (*enephysēse*) on them and said, "Receive the Holy Spirit" (John 20:22).

Now there are several things of importance about this action of Jesus and about his word to those who were in that room, the nucleus of the church, that must be noticed:

1. The first thing to note is that the verb describing Jesus' action (*empysaō*, "breathe on," or more literally, "breathe into") is wonderfully significant. It appears nowhere else in the New Testament, but it is the verb used in the Genesis description of the beginning of the human race. There it says that God "breathed" (*enephysēse*) into Adam's nostrils the breath of life and he became a living person (Gen. 2:7). It is found also in that famous section of the Old Testament that contains the vision of the valley of very dry bones. Here the prophet is asked, "Can these bones live again?" And when he skeptically replies, "O Lord God, you know," the word of the Lord comes to him with a firm answer and a command: "Thus says the Lord God to these bones, 'Behold, I will cause breath to enter you that you may come to life. . . . ' [And to the prophet], 'Prophesy to the breath [wind/spirit/Spirit], prophesy, son of man, and say to the breath, Thus says the Lord God, Come from the four winds, O breath, and breathe (*emphysēson*) on these slain that they may live.'" When

Ezekiel obeyed and prophesied as commanded, the breath (i.e., the Spirit) was breathed over those dry bones, and they came to life! (Ezek. 37:2–4, 9).[6] It seems obvious, then, that the choice of this rare verb to tell of Jesus' first postresurrection act was intentional. It seems that the writer of the Gospel of John intended to make it obvious to everybody that just as a lump of clay fashioned from the earth or a pile of bones bleaching in a valley were caused to spring to life by the breath of God then, so now the followers of Jesus are being given the opportunity to spring to life with a new spiritual vitality by that same breath of God. This, then, heralded the beginning of the new creation for human beings (2 Cor. 5:17), the fulfillment of Jesus' own words, "I have come that you may have life and have it in abundance" (John 10:10).

2. The second thing to note is the word of Jesus: "Receive (*labete*) the Holy Spirit" (John 20:22). Since Jesus breathed upon all those in that upper room, none being excluded, it is clear from this act that the gift of the Spirit was being freely offered by him to all. But the fact that it is to be received (*labete*, an imperative mood with its intrinsic appeal of will to will) "demands a responsive effort on the part of [the one] to whom it is offered."[7] This is to say, because the Spirit is the promised gift of the Father to the resurrected Jesus for him to pour out on others—the same Holy Spirit which had been abundantly poured out on him (cf. Luke 4:1; Acts 2:32–33)—Jesus has, in his act of breathing on his followers, done precisely that. Yet just as the Spirit never infringed upon the personal nature of Jesus' inward life and did not force him to do what he might choose not to do, so Jesus does not impose the Holy Spirit on his followers; he does not infringe upon their freedom nor does he overpower their wills. He simply gives the gift to all. All, however, must *receive* the Holy Spirit on their own, by their own choice. It follows that just as Jesus remained master of his will and consciousness yet nevertheless deliberately chose to subject himself to the guiding influence of the Spirit throughout his life and thus lived powerfully and triumphantly, so his followers must do as he did if they would experience the same power and triumph in their own personal experiences. The choice is theirs—to receive the Spirit or not; to subject themselves to the Spirit's leading or not.

This truth of the gift of the Holy Spirit of God given freely for all the followers of Jesus to receive has some astounding implications:

1. Jesus was a real human being, but he was anointed by God with the Holy Spirit. Thus he became *the* Christ par excellence (cf. 1 Sam. 10:1, 6; 16:13 with Luke 3:21–22; 4:1), enabled by the Spirit to know the mind of God and authorized to carry out the work of God.

In a similar way the followers of Jesus, who have received this gift of the Spirit, are thus anointed by God with that same Holy Spirit and so become God's contemporary "christs," so that they might know the mind of God and be authorized to carry out his will in this day and age (cf. 1 John 2:20, 27).

It is no accident, therefore, that Paul in writing to the Corinthian Christians places two key words side by side (unfortunately they go unnoticed in translation): "Now He who establishes us with you in Christ (*Christon*) and anointed (*chrisas*) us is God" (2 Cor. 1:21 NASB), i.e., "the one who establishes us in the *Anointed One* and *anointed* (*christon kai chrisas*) us is God." Thus just as it is recorded of Jesus that he said of himself, "The Spirit of the Lord is upon me, because he has anointed me . . ." (Luke 4:18), and as Peter is reported as having said to Cornelius, "God anointed Jesus of Nazareth with the Holy Spirit and with power . . ." (Acts 10:38), just so in this same way Christians are now spoken of as anointed ones because they, too, have received the Holy Spirit and are thus set apart to serve God, authorized to act in his behalf.

2. Jesus was a genuine human person. But he was filled[8] with the Holy Spirit (Luke 4:1), and it was this filling that made all the difference between an ordinary human being and one who was extraordinary. Luke calls attention to this filling at the threshold of Jesus' ministry (Luke 4:1), without necessarily meaning to say that Jesus had not been filled with the Spirit before that time (cf. Luke 1:35). But by calling special attention to this action at this point in Jesus' life, the evangelist is saying that Jesus now, precisely because of this filling, was enabled to see through the most subtle of temptations and resist yielding to any of them. He was enabled to do his mighty works of healing the sick, opening the eyes of the blind, putting strength into the limbs of the lame, and exorcising demons.

He was enabled to teach with authority, preach with power, stand for what was right, champion the cause of the oppressed, and proclaim Good News to the poor. He was enabled to free people from all kinds of bondage—self-inflicted or otherwise. The evangelist was saying that Jesus was endowed with supernatural power and that the Spirit was the giver of this power, even that the Spirit was this power (cf. Luke 7:22 with Isa. 61:1).

And as it was true of Jesus, so it is true of his followers: "As the Father has sent me, even so I send you" (John 20:21b). As Jesus was filled and equipped by the Spirit, so those who belong to Jesus are filled and equipped by the Spirit (Acts 2:4), or at least potentially so (Eph. 5:18). Just as it was true that this filling of Jesus enabled him to be and do the extraordinary, so it is true of those who believe in him. The Acts of the Apostles (or "of the Holy Spirit"), to say the very least, was intended to show something of the nature of those things that God is able to do through people who yield themselves willingly to the influence of the Spirit. Through the Spirit those people of the very early church were enabled to preach boldly, convincingly, and authoritatively (Acts 2:14–41), to face crises and surmount obstacles with a courage and resoluteness and power they never dreamed they had (4:29–31), to cheerfully face persecution and suffering, and even to accept death with a prayer of forgiveness (5:40–41; 7:55–60), to heal the sick and raise the dead (9:36–41; 28:8), to arbitrate differences and bring about peace (15:1–35), to know where to go and where not to go, what to do and what not to do (16:6–10; 21:10–11), and so on. There is no reason whatsoever to believe that what was true of those earliest Christians is any less true of Christians in this century. Surely contemporary crises are no less great, the pains of the world are no less meliorated, the challenges to one's strength, wisdom, patience, and love are no less demanding of resources beyond human resources than they were in the first century, and followers of Jesus today are no more sufficient for all these in and of themselves than were his followers yesterday. Furthermore, God's program of enabling people to burst the bounds of their human limitations and achieve the impossible is still in place and still effective—that program that involves filling people with his Spirit, filling them with supernatural power.

> In the spiritual as in the natural world there is a law which teaches that the same cause will, under the same conditions, produce the same consequence. Hence, under the same conditions of surrender and dependence as in which our Lord lived His earthly life, the same cause—the Eternal Spirit—will produce the same consequence, and our lives can thus be like His life (in kind though not in degree), in the reality and beauty of holiness."[9]

Are you a minister of the Gospel or a teacher, intelligent, educated, learned in the Scriptures? The life of Jesus teaches that intelligence and learning are not in themselves sufficient when it comes to making God's message meaningful to those who hear it. It is the Spirit of God within the minister that makes the word a living word, sharper than any two-edged sword (Acts 2:4, 14–37, especially vv. 33 and 37). It is equally important, however, to say that God frowns on neither intelligence nor education, nor on people continuously pushing themselves to go beyond the supposed limits of their abilities. What he is concerned about is that spiritual work never be done solely in a natural way, only with natural endowments. Rather he wishes by the power of his Holy Spirit present and available, as in the life of Jesus, to make it possible for the followers of Jesus to exceed the *real* limits of their humanness and thus speak to the hearts of people with a life-creating, life-transforming power. Recall, "the letter kills, but the Spirit gives life" (2 Cor. 3:6 NASB).

Are you among the healers of this world, those who through years of study, discipline, and unreasonably hard work have trained themselves to learn the art of healing those who are sick in body and mind? The life of Jesus teaches you that as a Spirit-filled person, whatever powers you possess, whatever skills you have developed, whatever diagnostic abilities you own, whatever faculty you enjoy of penetrating to the root of a problem and resolving it—any or all of these can be strengthened and lifted beyond the limits of your natural abilities by the Spirit of God. For the Holy Spirit stands with you against every destructive force at work in your world and only waits for you to yield to him, as did Jesus, the control of your life.

And in this connection, what is to be said of those followers of Jesus who claim to have the gift of healing yet who have never been certified by the accredited schools of medicine? In spite of one's own personal experience, which may be devoid of ever having seen a miracle of healing and which thus may cause one too easily to stand among the skeptics, the testimony of the New Testament, nevertheless, is that certain people did have the ability to heal with a touch or with a word (Acts 9:34; 10:38; 28:8). And when Paul lists the gifts that were given by the resurrected Jesus to his church, the gift of healing is numbered among them (1 Cor. 12:9, 28). There are no grounds for saying, therefore, other than one's own biases, that such a gift has been withdrawn from among the ranks of the followers of Jesus or has ceased to be in existence. But what is of importance for this study is to realize that such a gift is a gift of the Spirit (1 Cor. 12:1, 7–9). The earthly life of Jesus, a life that was filled with the Spirit, underscores this statement and makes it clear that if and when one person heals another person directly, immediately, instantaneously, it is by the power of the Spirit that that person does so.

Are you a creative person, an artisan, an artist, a teacher, a writer, a musician, a performer, a designer? Are you a person whose divine calling in life is to beautify the world, to create something new, to do what has never been done before? Are you a person gifted to make other people think or laugh or cry? Then know with full assurance that it is God's plan and pleasure to enhance your talents by the power of his Holy Spirit (cf. Exod. 31:3–4), to thus increase your skills, enhance your abilities, enlarge your knowledge, and deepen your insights so that you might be a better artisan, artist, teacher, writer, musician, performer, designer, so that you might more effectively serve your God in your world and, like Jesus, fulfill your God-given mission in life.

Are you a person whose life seems humdrum, consumed by the endless round of unexciting daily chores, by work that is often judged by others (and perhaps by yourself) as unfulfilling but that is nevertheless necessary if, for example, there is to be a home provided and a family fed and held together in wholeness, health, and contentment? Recall, then, that if the thrust of this book is correct, the Holy Spirit was present with and in Jesus, who was as truly human as you, for the purpose of strengthening him, enthusing him, aiding him to live meaningfully during the majority of the years of his life when his days, too, were filled with very menial, humdrum, repetitive, perhaps even boring tasks. But Jesus teaches by example that the Holy Spirit is here and available in the midst of just such tasks, and that his power is a power to quicken, enliven, inspire so that one's life need never sink to the level of the inconsequential.

Are you one who truly wants to do the will of God, knowing that the will of God is good, pleasing, and perfect, and yet you are severely tempted at times to take things into your own hands, to go your own way, to do your own will? Are you a person whose lack of strength is amplified by important and worthwhile tasks you have accepted that seem vastly too big for you, and are you inclined to take the easy way out and quit? Are you overwhelmed with the problems of poverty and injustice for which there seem to be no solutions and you wish to give up the struggle? If any of this is so, reflect again on the life of Jesus and the powerful resource of the Spirit of God that was always present with him. The Spirit within him, filling him, aiding him both to recognize real temptation when it came and helping overcome it, is your resource too. The Spirit within him that infused him with power, strengthened his weakness, and fortified him to such a degree that he could do the humanly impossible, is the Spirit that is in you. The Spirit that was in Jesus, that drew him to the poor, the disenfranchized, the outcasts of society, that gave him the moral courage not to give up the task of being their spokesperson and their Savior—that same Spirit is also with you, in you, ready to infuse you with what it takes to finish the task to which God has called you.

Are you one of the many who faces death with dread, weeping in the face of your impending mortality? Jesus shares your grief and understands your anguish, for he, too, faced his own death with "horror and dismay" (Mark 14:33 NEB), and was heard to say to his disciples, "My heart is ready to break with grief" (Mark 14:34 NEB). But the Holy Spirit was present with Jesus in the hour of his death, strengthening him to accept death, to endure its pain, and by it to guarantee eternal salvation for all who wish to follow him. And it was the Holy Spirit, the power of God, that raised Jesus from the dead and gave him the victory over death and the grave. It is that same Holy Spirit who is present in you now even at the very moment of your dying. Hence, listen to the joyously exultant affirmation of the church: "If the Spirit of him who raised Jesus from the dead dwells within you, then the God who raised Christ Jesus from the dead will also give new life to your mortal bodies through his indwelling Spirit" (Rom. 8:11 NEB). And thus it is that Paul prays for you,"that your inward eyes may be illumined, so that you may know what is the hope to which [the Lord Jesus Christ] calls you," and that you may know how vast are the resources of his power to those who trust in him—resources measured by the strength and the might (i.e. the Spirit) of God "which he exerted in Christ when he raised him from the dead" (Eph. 1:18–20 NEB).

The significance of the Holy Spirit in the life of Jesus extends to his followers in all of the little and the big things of their existences. The Spirit that helped Jesus overcome temptations, that strengthened him in weakness, that aided him in the hard job of taking on himself the hurts of the hurting, that infused him with a power to accomplish the impossible, that enabled him to stay with and complete the task God had given him to do, that brought him through death and into resurrection, is the Spirit that the resurrected Jesus has freely and lavishly (note the force of the verb in Acts 2:33) given to those who would be his disciples today!

It is worth closing this section with a warning, however. The Holy Spirit of God must never be thought of as a genie whose presence and power is available for personal enrichment or aggrandizement. When Jesus had been led into the desert, the arena of testing, by the Spirit and was tempted to use the power of the Spirit that was available to him to change stones into bread to satisfy his own real hunger, he refused to do so. Why? Because he knew that the power that filled him was power to do the Father's will, not his own will. It was power to equip him to triumphantly complete the mission God had given him to do, even if that involved hunger, not to prove to anyone, especially the devil, that he could perform the spectacular. Much later when Simon the magician saw the signs and great miracles performed by Philip and the other apostles through the power of the Spirit, he came with money in his hands, saying, "Give me also this power, that any one on whom I lay my hands may receive the Holy Spirit." But he was sternly rebuffed by Peter for such an iniquitously selfish desire to manipulate the Spirit for his own gain (Acts 8:9–23).

The Holy Spirit is God present and active in the lives of Jesus' followers not to make life rich and comfortable for them, but to equip them to fulfill God's mission for them in the world. It is a mission of helping, serving, healing, restoring, giving, sharing, and loving, a mission of binding up the broken, of being just and striving for justice, of proclaiming the Good News that God is King, of taking the Gospel everywhere preaching the message that God has acted to save the world and transform people in and through the life, death, and resurrection of his Son Jesus Christ.

> O Holy Spirit of God, visit now this soul of mine, and tarry within it until [the] eventide [of life]. Inspire all my thoughts. Pervade all my imaginations. Suggest all my decisions. Lodge in my will's most inward citadel and order all my doings. Be with me in my silence and in my speech, in my haste and in my leisure, in company and in solitude, in the freshness of the morning and in the weariness of the evening, and give me grace at all times to rejoice in Thy mysterious companionship. Amen.[10]

NOTES

1. See Moule, *The Holy Spirit*, 59.
2. See chapter 7.
3. See the challenging book by Jon Sobrino, S. J., *Christology at the Crossroads*, trans. J. Drury (Maryknoll, N. Y., 1978).
4. Contrast the *Gospel of Peter*, 4: "And they brought two malefactors and crucified the Lord in between them. But he was silent, as if felt no pain."
5. A. B. Simpson, *The Holy Spirit* (New York, 1896), 2.25.
6. Cf. also Wis. 15:11 where it is said of the potter, who fashioned a false god from the same clay from which he came, that "... he did not recognize by whom he himself was moulded, or who it was that inspired [*empneusanta*] him with an active soul and breathed into [*emphysēsanta*] him the breath of life" (NEB).
7. J. H. Bernard, *A Critical and Exegetical Commentary on the Gospel According to St. John* (Edinburgh, 1928), 2.678. Hear the other possibility to receiving, taking, accepting the gift of the Spirit in Jesus' words in John 14:17, where he

speaks of "the Spirit of truth [i.e., the Holy Spirit] which the world is not able to receive."

8. This expression, "filled with the Spirit," is not to be taken literally as though the Spirit is some kind of liquid that may be poured into a person as into a container, but, metaphorically, meaning that the Holy Spirit to whom one must willingly accede is then totally present endowing that person with insights and powers beyond human limits.

9. J. S. Holden, *The Price of Power* (New York, 1908), 40.

10. J. Baillie, *A Diary of Private Prayer* (New York, 1949), 89.

Index of Authors

Index of Ancient Sources

The New Testament